BACK TO NORMAL

BACK TO NORMAL

Why Ordinary Childhood Behavior Is
Mistaken for ADHD, Bipolar Disorder,
and Autism Spectrum Disorder

ENRICO GNAULATI, PHD

Beacon Press
Boston

Beacon Press
25 Beacon Street
Boston, Massachusetts 02108-2892
www.beacon.org

Beacon Press books
are published under the auspices of
the Unitarian Universalist Association of Congregations.

16 15 14 13   8 7 6 5 4 3 2 1

This book is printed on acid-free paper that meets the uncoated paper
ANSI/NISO specifications for permanence as revised in 1992.

Text design and composition by Wilsted & Taylor Publishing Services

Portions of chapter 5 were previously published in *Life Learning Magazine*.

Library of Congress Cataloging-in-Publication Data
Gnaulati, Enrico.
Back to normal : why ordinary childhood behavior is mistaken for ADHD,
bipolar disorder, and autism spectrum disorder / Enrico Gnaulati.
    p. ; cm.
Includes bibliographical references and index.
ISBN 978-0-8070-7334-6 (alk. paper) — ISBN 978-0-8070-7335-3 (ebook)
    I. Title.
[DNLM: 1. Child Behavior—psychology. 2. Adolescent.
3. Behavioral Symptoms—diagnosis. 4. Child. 5. Diagnostic Errors.
6. Medicalization. 7. Mental Disorders—diagnosis. WS 105]
RJ506.B44
618.92'89—dc23   2013009182

For Janet and Marcello,

my source of real happiness

Contents

Introduction

This book is about the normalcy of children's seemingly abnormal behavior. Mostly, I wrote it to give parents of struggling children hope, perspective, and direction. However, I also wrote it to counteract the pervasive tendency in our society to medicalize children's behavior and to categorize an increasing array of normal childhood reactions to stressful life situations as proof positive of a psychiatric diagnosis. Critics of American society insist that we are a nation of people who overpsychologize. Yet nowadays, when it comes to understanding children's behavior, clearly we underpsychologize. We shy away from trusting our own ability to decipher the ordinary human meanings, motives, and developmental reasons for why children act the way they do. This book aims to correct this imbalance.

While working as a psychologist with children and families for the past twenty-five years, I've observed that parents are nothing short of desperate for answers that will help them to tease apart whether their kid has transitory problems or is showing signs of a diagnosable condition. The truth is, it's exceedingly difficult to distinguish between, on the one hand, things like a lag in social and emotional growth, a mismatch between where a kid is developmentally and what is expected of him or her at school, patterns of emotional reactivity in the parent-child relationship, a difficult personality trait, or a perfect storm of all of these and, on the other hand, evidence of a psychiatric condition like ADHD (attention deficit hyperactivity disorder), bipolar disorder, or autism spectrum disorder. Yet when we look at the number of kids with these disorders, we get the impression that it's exceedingly easy.

As we'll see, ADHD is thought to be as prevalent as the common cold, with 1 in 10 children meriting the diagnosis—about as many children as use cold remedies at any given time.[1] Figures out of the famed Centers for Disease Control and Prevention estimate that 1 in 54 boys and 1 in 252 girls have autism spectrum disorder,[2] while bipolar disorder among youth has undergone a fortyfold increase in the past decade.[3] What explains these sky-high numbers?

Part of the answer lies in how similar many of the symptoms associated with these disorders are to everyday childhood behaviors. This can make the diagnostic process overly subjective and thereby slant it in the direction of doctors and therapists yielding false positives. Take attention-deficit/hyperactivity disorder. We can see shades of all children in the core symptoms of ADHD: distractibility, forgetfulness, problems with follow-through, not listening, talking excessively, fidgetiness, and difficulty waiting one's turn. Sophisticated clinical language characterizing autism spectrum disorder, such as "deficits in social-emotional reciprocity, nonverbal communication, and developing and maintaining age-appropriate relationships," really boils down to run-of-the-mill behaviors like showing yourself to be happy when someone else is happy, keeping good eye contact, responding to your name, and finding other kids your age interesting—phenomena that toddlers, the youngsters most apt to be under the autism spectrum lens, often have difficulty mastering. Similarly, when a toddler repeats words and phrases, is entranced by stimulating objects, and has rigid food preferences, is he or she working through something developmentally or on the spectrum? The common criteria for bipolar disorder are hard to separate from evidence of a difficult adolescent passage: irritability, temper outbursts, moodiness, fluctuations in motivation, sleep irregularities, overconfidence, and a propensity to engage in risky behaviors. This is particularly true in our twenty-first-century media-saturated culture, where ready bedroom access to screens interferes with teenagers' sleep, causing teens to be groggy and irritable, and where participation in social-network sites like Facebook almost requires them to be self-promotional.

Another part of the answer for why these disorders are massively overdiagnosed lies in how casual we have become about incorporating mental health jargon into our everyday conversations. We pin diagnoses on ourselves as if they are faddish labels or give us outlaw celebrity status. "ADHD" happens to be the name of a song by the English alternative-rock band Blood Red Shoes, and the rapper Krizz Kaliko's hit "Bipolar" can be downloaded as a cell phone ringtone. It can seem cool to be bipolar when high-roller actors like Mel Gibson and Catherine Zeta-Jones, and legendary rock stars like Axl Rose, refer to themselves that way.

Yet there are good reasons to be cautious when it comes to these diagnoses. We may be remarkably casual about tossing around mental health labels, but unfortunately, studies show that the average American still harbors negative stereotypes about kids and teens with psychiatric disorders. Large swaths of the American public still believe that a depressed teenager is a would-be violent teenager. A mental health diagnosis can also follow a kid into adulthood and potentially disqualify him or her from careers in law enforcement, the military, and other professions; make it difficult to obtain a pilot's or trucker's license; and jack up life and disability insurance rates for him or her. And, of course, an easygoing attitude toward diagnosing can pave the way for uncritical consumption of medications, minimizing the undesirable side effects that often accompany their use.

The story of how pharmaceutical companies oversell the general public on mental illness and medications to boost their profits is a story that has been told many times. However, I will retell the relevant parts of this tale, taking the reader behind the scenes to look at how pharmaceutical reps often drive doctors' diagnostic habits, what recent research shows about the effectiveness of medications routinely used with children, and the latest ideas by leading scholars that call into question brain-based and chemical-imbalance theories of behavior.

I also will tell another story, one that most parents probably haven't heard before. This story is about how doctors' and therapists' education and training primes them to think in terms of disease and disorder and often blinds them to humanistic, developmental, and commonsense explanations for children's troubling and troublesome behavior. I am a psychologist, so telling this story has been disquieting—to say the least. When parents bring their child to me for help, I like to first consider the likelihood that the child is experiencing a stressful reaction to life events, but is otherwise normal. I am comfortable with the idea that there's great variation across children in the rate at which their social and emotional development unfolds. Sometimes a child's troubles simply mean that he or she is slow to mature in an area and will do just fine with some combination of adjustments to his or her daily environments, targeted parenting interventions, and garden-variety talk and play therapy. I like to think in terms of normal human variation, developmental glitches, and wellness. This is not to say that I don't go into high gear when, over time, after an assortment of interventions, there is unquestionable evidence that a child has a disabling psychiatric condition and needs medication and other, more rigorous interventions. Sadly, however, when it comes to children's mental health, this way of thinking is not widely shared by doctors and therapists. Often parents face overwhelming pressure to medicalize and medicate their kid's behavior from the get-go in doctors' and therapists' offices. I want parents to be aware of the larger forces influencing the field of children's mental health.

One issue I address is why boys are far more likely to be perceived as behaviorally disturbed than girls, and what parents of sons can do about it. As a father of a son, I'm particularly sensitive to this issue. I see my son and quite a few other males his age act squirrelly, roughhouse, shun reading, stuff homework into messy backpacks, clam up verbally unless they have a shared activity to pursue or technical topic to discuss, and be quick to react when their pride is injured. Such observations give me a firm grounding in what's normal. I'm thankful for that grounding. It has helped me to see more clearly how, as politically incorrect as it may sound, our understanding of "normal" behavior for children has become feminized. We tend to judge boys using standards of behavior applicable to the average girl, not the average boy.

Another theme that I explore is how mental health symptoms sometimes are actually ancient, innate personality traits and coping mechanisms that have helped us adapt and survive as humans for thousands of years. Despite all the pathological talk about depression and mania, children and teens are capable of experiencing "healthy depression" and "healthy mania." At manageable levels, depression and mania are time-honored human responses reflecting the brain's hardwired ways of helping us to cope with attachment and loss in relationships, as well as to energetically strive for success and greater social status. Symptoms such as anxiety, aggressiveness, and action-orientedness are personality traits that would have been highly adaptive during hunter-gatherer times, but which are a liability in today's "chalk and talk" classroom. I will share with the reader practical ways in which kids' everyday environments can be changed in order to allow them to best adapt by making positive use of such inborn personality traits.

When I set about writing this book, I knew that I wanted it to contain ample stories to which readers could relate. I wanted to describe the behavior of children who may be difficult, but who are not suffering from psychiatric disorders, in such a way that a parent could see his or her own son or daughter in them. For instance, it was paramount for me to really bring alive how ADHD symptoms often mimic normal childhood narcissism and to provide remedies for parents dealing with their kids' challenging developmental struggles. I labored to find evocative examples of the difference between true hyperactivity and a kid's habit of seeking needed attention and recognition in frenzied ways. I strove to highlight how sometimes a pattern of failing to finish tasks has little to do with a disordered brain and more to do with a child or teen approaching tasks with "magical thinking" about what can be accomplished. Similarly, I wanted to show how forgetfulness can sometimes be nothing more than a kid's underpracticing and underpreparing because he or she is overconfident. These scenarios, I thought, would help a parent discern whether his or her own child actually was afflicted with a disorder or was stressed for other reasons.

I felt it was necessary to include longer case descriptions in order for readers to confidently grasp the finer points of children's expectable, troubling reactions given their personalities and life circumstances, as compared with signs of a true psychiatric condition such as bipolar disorder. Readers will be introduced to seventeen-year-old Brandon, whose bipolar rages are best explained in terms of the harmful ways he deals with his tendency toward shame and the emotional flooding and reactivity that flares up when he and his mother are in conflict. Readers will also meet William, who was falsely diagnosed with autism spectrum disorder at age five. His case rather dramatically shows how brainy, introverted, individualistically minded boys with a passion for ideas and strong needs for interpersonal control can get mislabeled as autistic in their younger years.

In all the case snippets and studies that I've included, I changed names and disguised factual information for confidentiality reasons. But essential phenomena, meanings, and outcomes have been preserved. At no time do I use purely fictional accounts.

I've concentrated on success stories. These are the kids in my practice who appeared to be poster children for major psychiatric disorders when I first met them, but with family lifestyle changes, parenting interventions, play and talk therapy, and the passage of time, did not merit any such diagnosis. These sorts of cases are not rare. The reader will be reassured to learn about scientific evidence showing that upwards of a third of teenagers diagnosed with bipolar disorder are no longer diagnosable as bipolar by their mid- to late twenties and that approximately one in five toddlers diagnosed with autism spectrum disorder prior to age three don't meet the diagnosis when assessed a few years later. A National Institute of Mental Health study even shows that three-quarters of ADHD children outgrow their condition by the time they reach their midtwenties.

Lastly, at the end of the book, in a nonblaming, reasonable, highly practical way, I lay out dozens of strategies, tips, and lifestyle changes that parents can utilize to foster self-discipline, even-temperedness, and greater social competence in their kids. Guidelines are included for when to consider pursuing outside professional help and what to look for in a therapist.

My guess is that you picked up this book because you sympathize with the notion that as a society we have become too casual medicalizing and abnormalizing children's behavior. Chances are you eagerly wish to build your knowledge base of commonsense psychological and developmental explanations for children's emotional issues. Maybe you're a parent who is perplexed and exasperated by your child's wayward behavior. You urgently desire a deeper understanding of why your child behaves in a maddening way and what can be done about it. You want your child diagnosed with a psychiatric disorder only if he or she really has one. If you are aided by my book, the countless hours I have spent poring over research literature and magazine articles, reflecting on my work with clients, and taking solo writing trips on retreat in the desert at Joshua Tree, California, will have been well worth it.

CHAPTER ONE

Mad Science and Mad Medicine

Back in 1985, I was a lowly mental health intern at a community clinic in Seattle, Washington, when I experienced my first rude awakening about my chosen profession. I was on a crisis-intervention team. Most of the clients I was responsible for were severely mentally ill. George, a homeless eighteen-year-old young man, was no exception. On the dreary Seattle day on which I met with him, there was fire in his eyes. He told me with conviction that the KGB was plotting against him. He was being followed and harassed. The KGB had implanted a transistor in his teeth and was constantly monitoring his whereabouts. Disturbingly, George was even convinced that the KGB was determined to rape him. Weeks earlier, he had traveled across the Canadian border into British Columbia to escape KGB agents who were close on his tracks. But he returned, believing it would be harder for KGB agents to operate in the United States, given President Reagan's tough stance against the Soviet Union.

I did what most caring interns would do. I listened intently. I tried not to appear rattled. Most of all, I focused on winning George's trust so that he would agree to be hospitalized. On that score, I was successful. George voluntarily agreed to go to the local psychiatric ward at the University of Washington Medical Center.

Several days later, I put in a follow-up call to one of the psychiatric nurses at the hospital and asked how George was faring. I was dumbfounded to learn that his condition had worsened. He was in a full-blown catatonic state, refusing to talk, eat, or bathe. The medications he had been given seemed to be having no impact.

I asked the nurse to walk me through George's hospital-intake process. She told me that he had undergone a standard physical exam, which had been more invasive than usual because of the sores and scabs that had accumulated on George's body. She mentioned in passing that George required a rectal exam because his lack of hygiene had caused infections in that region of his body. Later, I asked the nurse for the name of his internist. It turns out that the doctor had an Eastern European name and a thick accent. It suddenly occurred to me that, in a sense, George's paranoid delusion had come true: he had been invasively probed by a foreign agent. It then made sense to me why George's condition had worsened.

George's case is a rather extreme and dramatic example of the blind spots and failures of common sense that can occur in the practice of mental health, particularly when a practitioner views a client as the embodiment of a diagnosis or the victim of a disordered brain and unquestioningly follows some treatment protocol. When the interaction is medicalized in this way, the practitioner can see it as essentially irrelevant to understand *why* a client acts the way he or she does.

Mental health professionals are often prone to look at kids' problem behaviors as something to be medicated, controlled, or changed. Yet problem behaviors always communicate something. If we fail to take the time to conscientiously explore what purposes or functions a behavior holds for a child, we may miss an opportunity for imparting genuine and lasting change.

The standard approach to hyperactivity, for example, explains it solely as the mere outcropping of a child's disordered neurophysiology. You would no more try to understand what purposes it serves a kid to be hyperactive than you would try to understand what purposes it serves a kid to have an elevated blood-sugar level. There are those kids whose hyperactivity is rooted in their compromised brain development. Arguably, for these individuals, medication and behavioral control are necessary and humane interventions. Yet most kids whose behavior is hyperactive exhibit such behavior for a cluster of reasons. Maybe it's because they have learned that their exhibits of hyperactivity will mean that an otherwise preoccupied and randomly available, though loving, parent will finally take notice. Maybe it's also their way of communicating that the sedentary demands of home and school life leave them desperately needing more kinetically mobile play experiences. Maybe it's because they have a flare for the dramatic and tend to be showy and loud when they have a strong desire to be recognized for demonstrating a skill or ability. To be of assistance in any thoughtful way, we have to understand the multiple meanings of what a child is trying to communicate through his or her hyperactivity.

Also, context is everything when trying to understand behavior. If we view a child's behavior as a symptom to be checked off and do not inquire about the everyday conditions under which it occurs, we can get a skewed picture of that child's functioning.

For example, the rages my ten-year-old client Cynthia has when at home are profound and may even seem bipolar. At least four or five times a month, Cynthia becomes unmanageably agitated for periods of up to half an hour. On the surface, she is set off by things like being forced to wear a floral dress or to attend an obligatory church event. In such instances, she screams at the top of her lungs, paces, and believes others have it in for her. Awkward, benign smiles by family members in these moments can leave Cynthia feeling mocked and ridiculed. She shrieks out threats to harm them if they do not stop laughing at her. Family members then try to appear sincere and somber. Nevertheless, Cynthia still believes they are mocking her.

Yet Cynthia is a straight-A student. She has never once lost her temper at school in a way that would elicit concern on the part of her teachers. She is high-strung and bossy with her friends, but she has never emotionally lashed out at them. Why does Cynthia rage in some contexts, but not in others? In my intensive parenting work with Cynthia's mother, we discovered some key contextual understandings: Cynthia is more likely to explode when she is suddenly expected to stop an enjoyable activity without being forewarned and to comply with a demand that she perceives to be highly undesirable. When Cynthia's mother "goes on the counterattack," Cynthia's episodes are more severe and prolonged. When Cynthia's mother is able to "get in empathy mode" or "play amateur psychologist" and softly mirror back what Cynthia is feeling and why, there's a better chance that the episode will be defused. Without these contextual understandings, it would be hard to imagine how to effectively handle the situation in a worthwhile way.

The public generally assumes that mental health professionals are trained to be interpersonally sensitive, to query with the right kind of questions so as to get at deeper meanings regarding kids' behavior, to always put behavior in context, to distinguish between normal and abnormal behavior in kids, to be well informed about kids' social and emotional development, and to diligently include parents in child therapy. As surprising as it may seem, these are skills and types of knowledge bases that are not typically emphasized in medical or graduate school.

TRAINED PROFESSIONALS
KNOW BEST, OR DO THEY?

A pediatrician is the professional who is most likely to be consulted when a child is suspected of having ADHD. While teachers often are the first to suggest to the parents of a child that the child should be assessed, a pediatrician is commonly sought out for a formal judgment. While many pediatricians are adequately educated and trained to assess and treat ADHD, this is more the exception than the rule. How many physicians who actually call themselves pediatricians have specialized training in pediatric medicine and/or pediatric mental health?

Several years ago, Gary L. Freed, MD, chief of the Division of General Pediatrics at the University of Michigan, initiated a survey of physicians listed as pediatricians on state licensure files in eight states across the United States: Ohio, Wisconsin, Texas, Mississippi, Massachusetts, Maryland, Oregon, and Arizona.[1] According to the survey, 39 percent of state-identified pediatricians hadn't completed a residency in pediatrics. And even for those who had, their training in pediatric mental health was minimal. Currently, the American Academy of Pediatrics (AAP) estimates that less than a quarter of pediatricians around the country have specialized training in child mental health beyond what they receive in a general pediatric residency. The latest data examining pediatricians who have launched themselves into practice reveals that 62 percent of them feel that mental health issues were not adequately covered in medical school.[2] Nevertheless, this lack of training doesn't seem to discourage them from identifying ADHD. Survey data publicized by the AAP indicate that upwards of 90 percent of pediatricians feel qualified to evaluate ADHD.[3]

Moreover, the average length of a visit with a pediatrician is sixteen minutes.[4] This small allotment of time surely precludes much, if any, deeper discussion of a child's worrisome behavior to make sure that any diagnosis arrived at actually applies.

These days the typical child psychiatrist is not trained to observe, listen to, and think deeply about a kid's behavior. In the 1960s and '70s, learning how to do psychotherapy was a core requirement for psychiatrists. Current numbers out of Columbia University suggest that only one in ten psychiatrists provide psychotherapy to all of their clients.[5] A 2005 report that looked at the attitudes toward psychotherapy training of psychiatry residents in seventy programs across the country produced an unflattering statistic.[6] Forty-three percent of those surveyed believed that learning how to do psychotherapy in medical school was somewhat of a burden. The majority of chief residents in this same survey indicated that trainees saw an average of one to four clients, taking up six hours of their time a week—hardly intensive training by any standard. Daniel Carlat, MD, whose book *Unhinged: The Trouble with Psychiatry—A Doctor's Revelations about a Profession in Crisis* brought him national acclaim when it was released in 2010, summarizes the situation: "As psychiatrists have become enthralled with diagnosis and medication, we have given up the essence of our profession—understanding the mind. We have become obsessed with psychopharmacology and its endless process of tinkering with medications, adjusting dosages, and piling on more medications to treat the side effects of the drugs we started with."[7]

Insurance reimbursement systems are set up to reward psychiatrists for performing medication evaluations and engaging in brief check-ins instead of time-consuming psychotherapy. The "fifteen-minute med check" is standard in the field. A psychiatrist can pack in four such med checks in the hour it takes to see one psychotherapy client; it is the more lucrative course of action. If a family finds its way to a psychiatrist, it is almost guaranteed these days that the discussion will center on symptom patterns, possible diagnoses, and available medications.

This brings me to my own cherished profession—psychology. The general public often is unable to define the difference between a psychiatrist and a psychologist. Both are doctors. However, psychiatrists attend medical school and have MDs. They learn mostly about anatomy and physiology. Psychologists attend graduate school and have PhDs or PsyDs. They take courses in such subjects as abnormal psychology and psychological assessment. They learn advanced statistics and research methods. In addition to taking these courses, psychologists obtain training in how to do psychotherapy. When they are finished with graduate school, psychologists are supposed to become what is called in the profession "scientist-practitioners."

In reality, most psychologists come out of graduate school heavy on the "scientist" end and weak on the "practitioner" end, because most psychologists are, ironically, trained to practice like scientists. The current generation of psychologists are being encouraged to utilize only what are called "evidence-based treatments." These are interventions university-based academic psychologists have found to be effective in controlled studies. Psychologists are supposed to refer to manuals to select specific actions to take to address a client's presenting problem or diagnosis. Dr. Catherine Lee, a professor in the clinical psychology department at the University of Ottawa, captures the fervor with which new psychologists are expected to embrace this new approach: "If students are to master evidence-based practice, then they need not only to be convinced of its benefits, they must also learn how to do it. This involves competencies in critical thinking and effective research skills, as well as relationship competencies that are informed by detailed guidance from treatment manuals."[8]

This is far from a humanistic way of approaching human problems. Scripts for interacting with clients are the new norm—scripts that rely on manuals and research protocols. Graduate schools of psychology are generally not in the business of promoting skills and processes like "clinical intuition" or "personal insights that might have relevance to understanding the human condition." Trainee psychologists are not encouraged to integrate "book knowledge" with "personal knowledge"—to integrate clinical concepts with insights derived from their own psychotherapy and life experiences, and to use their own subjective thoughts and feelings when they are with clients to arrive at clinical judgments.

Yet personal perceptions of a client, when sensitively utilized, can make or break an accurate clinical judgment. This happened in four-year-old Juan's case. I was consulted for a second opinion after an extensive evaluation at the University of California at Los Angeles Neuropsychiatric Institute concluded that Juan was autistic. All the prescribed evidence-based assessment measures and procedures had been used. Yet within two minutes of meeting Juan, I knew that he was not autistic. Sitting on the floor in front of a toy castle in my office, I motioned for him to join me as I picked up a plastic figure of a knight mounted on a horse. "Oh dear," I said. "I think little blue knight's horsey has to go poo-poo." Juan smiled. I smiled more vibrantly. We shared prolonged eye contact. I became more exuberant: "Oh *dear* . . . I think little blue knight's horsey is going to make a big . . . *big* . . . poo-poo." Juan smiled more broadly. I then made a huge raspberry noise simulating loud defecation. Juan and I laughed hysterically together. In my mind, the degree of emotional synchrony we experienced at that moment automatically ruled out anything on the order of autism.

What does survey data tell us about the current training of child psychologists? A 2010 study out of the University of Hartford in Connecticut provides such a snapshot.[9] The authors found the results encouraging. This was somewhat mystifying to me. Poring over their numbers, I discovered that 45 percent of graduate students in child psychology had either no exposure to, or had just an introductory-level exposure to, coursework in child/adolescent life-span development. It is in these college classes that students learn about what is developmentally normal to expect in children. Fifty-two percent of would-be child psychologists had either no exposure to, or had just introductory-level exposure to, conducting parenting interventions. Almost 60 percent of them had no exposure to, or had just introductory-level exposure to, social issues affecting children, adolescents, and their families. What the authors seemed to base their encouraging words on was the 72 percent of would-be child psychologists who were receiving a great deal of experience and expertise in learning about evidence-based interventions.

What I derive from this study is that a sizable percentage of newly minted child psychologists have questionable preparation in knowing what types of behavior in kids are developmentally expectable. They may be more apt to practice therapy with a child one-on-one and be at a loss to know how to involve parents in any intensive way. They may be devoid of a larger cultural lens that enables them to see "big picture" issues, thereby throwing contemporary kids' behavior into perspective. "Big picture" issues might include the changing nature of children's play in American society or how monitoring kids' video-gaming habits has added a new wrinkle to the parent-child relationship over the past several decades. Perhaps the most striking takeaway from this study is that myriad would-be child psychologists leave graduate school with a scientific and conceptual knowledge of kids' behavior. But a more humanistic, experiential, individualized approach is required to reach, comprehend, and help kids.

MEASURING, OR MISMEASURING, KIDS' BEHAVIOR?

For child psychologists, behavior-rating forms filled out by parents and teachers are tools of the trade. They are as much a key part of the child psychologist's assessment storehouse as the thermometer is for the family physician. There are a plethora of them. But they all more or less follow the same format. Parents or teachers are asked to select which of the terms "never," "sometimes," "often," or "always" applies to a given statement describing a child's behavior. The statements are typically concise, such as: "has a short attention span" or "follows directions easily." The responses are then counted and can be computer scored. Profile scores and graphs are obtained indicating whether the evaluated child scores at the clinically significant range, compared to his or her same-age peers, on general mental health categories such as hyperactivity, anxiety, and depression. There is a scientific veneer to the process and to the final product. Nevertheless, as we shall see, a behavior checklist is not an objective instrument in the way that a thermometer is an objective instrument, and measuring behavior is not like measuring body temperature.

In twenty years of practice using behavior checklists, I am often astonished by the radically different readouts parents and teachers provide on the same child. Of the hundreds of ADHD assessments I have conducted that have included behavior-checklist data, parents and teachers agree on a clear-cut perception of the child as ADHD at best a third of the time. My experiences tend to align with what researchers have noticed. A well-designed 2000 study that looked at fifty-five kids who had been accurately diagnosed with ADHD combined type (symptoms of hyperactivity and inattention) found that teachers and parents agreed in a meager seventeen cases.[10] Likewise, Dr. Desiree Murray at Duke University Medical Center and a host of colleagues from prestigious institutions around the country in 2007 compared the ratings of parents and preschool teachers and discovered they jointly agreed upon ADHD in approximately one in four cases.[11]

Indeed, one of the most robust findings in social science research is the lack of agreement between parents and teachers when they are rating children's behavior. There are many explanations for this divergence. A kid's behavior in the context of a classroom is generally different than in the context of a home. Teachers are required to run classrooms. They may be biased in the direction of overrating behaviors by students that cause social disruption—like being uncooperative or talking out of turn. At the same time, they may underrate behavior that is linked to a child's internalizing psychic pain. The moderately depressed teenager who sits at the back of the class but who has a clean attendance sheet, completes homework, and obtains above-average grades is less likely to show up on a teacher's problem-child radar. However, that same teenager's mother or father may be acutely aware of the pain that their child is experiencing.

Of course, parents and teachers are human. Their ratings of a kid's behavior will always to some degree reflect their own value systems, tolerance levels, and cultural sensitivities.

Given the starkly different ratings that parents and teachers often provide, experts caution against using only one source when evaluating a child. The multi-university research team headed by Dr. Murray was emphatic on this point: "Obtaining ratings from multiple informants is . . . critical for obtaining a full picture of a young child's functioning." This also is one of the "best practices" included in the American Academy of Pediatrics' guidelines for evaluating ADHD. It also is a safeguard against ADHD being overdiagnosed. When the two-informant requirement is strictly adhered to when diagnosing ADHD, studies show that the number of true cases of ADHD shrinks considerably—by up to 40 percent.[12]

How often is the mandate to obtain ratings from multiple informants followed by pediatricians? A study published in a 2005 edition of the journal *Pediatrics* found that only 20 to 30 percent of pediatricians gathered behavior ratings from multiple sources when assessing for the presence of ADHD.[13] An earlier 2002 survey in the *School Psychology Review* brought to light that a mere 12 percent of pediatricians obtain information on a kid's classroom behavior when conducting ADHD assessments.[14] These findings are quite disturbing for one important reason. In order for ADHD to even be officially diagnosed according to the *Diagnostic and Statistical Manual of Mental Disorders* (*DSM*), the handbook relied on by clinicians to arrive at a diagnosis, the symptoms have to be remarkable across two settings—usually home and school. Not obtaining information from teachers as well as parents should foreclose any reasonable judgment about ADHD.

Controversy surrounds another popular assessment instrument used with kids—the continuous-performance test. What makes this type of test appear scientific is that devices and computer screens are involved. The Conners' Continuous Performance Test (CPT) and the Test of Variables of Attention (TOVA) are the two most widely used. The basic testing principle is the same. Kids are told that a series of numbers or symbols will flow across a screen. They are instructed to press a button or click a computer mouse only when they see the target symbol or number—ignoring everything else. Scores are then generated for factors like "correct detection," or the number of times a kid accurately responded to the appropriate stimulus. "Omission error rates" are computed. These pertain to the number of times a kid failed to press a button or click a mouse when the appropriate stimulus passed along the screen. "Commission errors" refer to times when the kid pressed a button or clicked a mouse when the appropriate stimulus was not visible. The end product is a computer printout of these detection and omission/commission error rates. A chart is produced indicating where a kid falls relative to same-age peers. If the kid places above cutoff scores, he or she is considered to have clinical problems with attention and concentration.

Many psychologists and educational consultants reap the financial benefits of adding a continuous-performance test to their assessment battery. These tests add upwards of $500 to the cost of an evaluation. Yet there is no sizable body of evidence that confirms that they are any more accurate in detecting ADHD than behavior rating scales, which are a fraction of the cost to administer and score. In fact, a team of investigators from universities across the United Kingdom in 2009 revealed that teacher ratings of kids' classroom behavior on three different questionnaires accurately detected true cases of ADHD, while scores on the CPT did not.[15]

Wouldn't the level of fatigue a child experiences affect continuous-performance test scores? Isn't a tired kid a less mentally vigilant kid? Dr. Renee Lajiness-O'Neill from Eastern Michigan University hoped to answer this question a few years ago when she oversaw a study of twenty-five young adult males and females undergoing rigorous assessment for signs of ADHD.[16] Each of the recruits was administered the CPT before and after a battery of tests. It was brought to light that CPT scores were more likely to be in the ADHD range on the rerun of the test. It turns out that the sequence of when a CPT is administered relative to other tests during an assessment can have a bearing on whether a person gets diagnosed with ADHD.

I have always resisted using a computer performance test. I could never wrap my mind around how a child's ability to accurately respond to symbols floating by on a screen generalizes to everyday life challenges. When a child has difficulties with attention and concentration, this usually occurs in the context of a human interaction or in the context of a learning situation that involves reading, writing, or performing math calculations. Observing and gathering information on how attentive and mindful kids are in these everyday situations has always seemed to me to be the main data bank on which to rely.

DRUG COMPANIES AND
MARKETING REPS CALLING THE SHOTS

On December 13, 2006, paramedics arrived at the Plymouth County, Massachusetts, home of four-year-old Rebecca Riley only to find her slumped over on her parents' bed, dead. The medical examiner on hand identified the cause of death as heart and lung failure brought about by the medications she was on. Rebecca was being prescribed Depakote, Seroquel, and Clonidine by Dr. Kayoko Kifuji, a Tufts–New England Medical Center child psychiatrist. She had diagnosed Rebecca with ADHD and bipolar disorder when she was two years old. Rebecca's death provoked a national debate on how a child as young as two could ever be diagnosed with major mental illnesses and be put on powerful tranquilizers. Katie Couric eventually covered the story in a CBS *60 Minutes* segment.

Ultimately, Rebecca's parents were tried for and convicted of murder due to allegedly overdosing her. But this harrowing outcome didn't take the national spotlight off the shocking revelation that a toddler could be diagnosed with mental illness and put on not just one but three powerful tranquilizers. None of the drugs Rebecca was prescribed was approved by the Food and Drug Administration for use with kids her age—not then and not now. There was absolutely no robust scientific justification for Dr. Kifuji making the medication choices that she made. How could a reputable psychiatrist be so inclined to diagnose a child so young with diagnoses so severe and treat with medications so unapproved? The main answer lies with the spectacular success of twenty-first-century pharmaceutical marketing of psychiatric drugs.

In 2008, psychiatric drugs sold in the United States netted their makers $40.3 billion.[17] A good portion of that amount involved drugs commonly prescribed to kids. A *Wall Street Journal* report indicates that between 2002 and 2007, prescriptions for psychiatric drugs for kids rose by nearly 45 percent.[18] The most recent estimates suggest that up to eight million American kids are on one or more psychiatric medications.[19] Meds for kids are big business and highly profitable. Prices of ADHD meds at the middle dose for ninety pills on Drugstore.com in 2011 were Concerta, $540; Vyvanse, $532; Intuniv, $500; Adderall, $278; and Ritalin, $191. The price of the most common antidepressants, like Prozac, Celexa, Lexapro, Zoloft, Cymbalta, and Wellbutrin, for ninety pills, was around $380. Two of the drugs prescribed to Rebecca Riley by Dr. Kifuji happen to be quite pricey. Drugstore.com rates in 2011 for 180 500 mg tablets of Seroquel were $1,048 and for Depakote, $708.

Among drug reps, it is common knowledge that kids are a lucrative market. At the urging of doctors, parents, and teachers, kids are required to buck up and take their meds. In the words of Gwen Olsen, who worked for fifteen years as a drug rep with such pharmaceutical-industry mainstays as Johnson & Johnson and Bristol-Myers Squibb: "Children are known to be compliant patients and that makes them a highly desirable market for drugs, especially when it pertains to large-profit-margin psychiatric drugs, which can be wrought with non-compliance because of their horrendous side-effect profiles."[20]

Most large-profit-margin psychiatric drugs are approved by the FDA strictly for use with adults, not kids. However, doctors are allowed to use their discretion and prescribe them to kids for "off-label" purposes. Doctors can use their medical instincts to determine whether a drug approved for adults might also ease the suffering of kids. But there is no scientific backing for such use. The studies haven't been conducted. The FDA approval hasn't been obtained. Off-label prescribing relies on doctors' instincts alone. While drug manufacturers and their marketing staff are bound by law not to influence doctors' off-label prescribing habits, it's not the law that's foremost on the minds of drug reps fanning out to doctors' offices all over the country. It's upping sales.

The right to use adult meds with kids for off-label purposes has left many physicians easy prey to drug reps and pharmaceutical companies' marketing ploys. A glaring example of this was uncovered in the largest health-care fraud case ever handled by the US Department of Justice, in 2009.[21] Pfizer agreed to a $2.3 billion settlement for promoting off-label use of a variety of drugs, one of which was the antipsychotic medication Geodon. One of Pfizer's illegal actions was paying 250 child psychiatrists to promote its off-label use with teens. Dr. Neil Kaye, for example, was paid $4,000 a day in speaker's fees to give speeches to other physicians with titles like, "the off-label use of Geodon in Adolescents."[22] Geodon happens to be a highly expensive and highly profitable drug. At Drugstore.com in 2011, it cost $1,400 for 180 40 mg capsules. It currently nets Pfizer $1 billion a year.[23]

At the time of Rebecca Riley's death in 2006, the number of drug reps in the United States was at an all-time high: 102,000.[24] It was the heyday of doctor-seducing, trinket-driven psychiatric medicine. Carl Elliott, in his shrewd article in the *Atlantic* that year, titled "The Drug Pushers," spoke of drug reps ponying up sports tickets for doctors, televisions for their waiting rooms, and expensive tropical vacations. One drug rep revealed to Elliott that he constructed a makeshift putting green in a hospital and gave away a putter to any doctor who got a hole in one.[25]

Of course, doctors deny that their diagnostic decisions and medication-prescribing practices are swayed by drug reps' sales pitches, promises of lunches and gifts, or provision of free samples of the medications the drug rep is promoting. But the research doesn't back them up. Many doctors who take free samples of drugs are far more likely to later prescribe that drug, even when cheaper and equally effective drugs are on the market. One study that pored over psychiatry residents' chart notes found a high correlation between drug reps' sales visits and new prescribing habits involving the drug promoted.[26] The turnaround time in switching over to prescribing the freshly promoted medication was fast—within twelve weeks. An often-cited 2001 survey shows that 61 percent of doctors believe interactions with a drug rep have no influence on their medical decisions. Yet only 16 percent of them believe this is true of other doctors.[27]

A surprisingly high number of doctors actually rely on information drug reps provide to keep up with what is supposedly cutting-edge in the world of pharmaceuticals. Several years ago, a Kaiser Foundation poll of 2,608 doctors indicated that 75 percent of them found the information supplied by drug reps "very useful" or "somewhat useful."[28] More often than we'd like to think, drug reps are quasi-medical advisors. It's somehow overlooked that they're selling a product and that the information they provide to doctors detailing how their new medication might help certain patients with certain emotional problems, better than the alternatives on the market, is potentially biased. After all, they're trying to make a sale.

The conflict of interest inherent in drug reps supposedly providing objective information about the uses and effectiveness of medications, yet upping the sales of their own, mirrors what exists in the entire field of psychiatric-medication research. Take the case of Dr. Joseph Biederman. He has the honor of being chief of the Clinical and Research Programs in Pediatric Psychopharmacology and Adult ADHD at the Massachusetts General Hospital, the teaching hospital of Harvard University. Dr. Biederman's work is responsible for loosening our understanding of how manic-like behavior should be thought of in kids. Historically, manic behavior has been considered rare, especially in kids. When psychologists like me see it in a person, it can be identified right away. The manic person hasn't slept for days, believes he or she has inexhaustible energy and superhuman abilities, and, most prominently of all, talks a blue streak. Dr. Biederman redefined manic behavior in kids in terms of irritability, severe tantrums, and rapid mood swings. His work burst the doors wide open. This looser definition of manic-like behavior heralded a fortyfold increase in the diagnosis of bipolar disorder in youngsters, based on the latest data set we have.[29]

In a Senate hearing in 2008, it was revealed that Dr. Biederman had received $1.6 million in speaking and consulting fees from many of the pharmaceutical-industry giants manufacturing antipsychotic medications for use with children thought to have bipolar disorder.[30] It turns out that Dr. Biederman was on the payroll at AstraZeneca, the makers of Seroquel, which is among the most frequently prescribed drugs for bipolar disorder with kids today and one of the medications prescribed by Dr. Kifuji to Rebecca Riley back in 2006.

Dr. Biederman's case is just one example of the industry norm. Large pharmaceutical companies commonly fund psychiatric-research programs. Because of this, there is an inherent potential for biased reporting or for researchers to strictly report favorable findings on the medications they are funded to study. Results that are successful get published and end up on glossy brochures in doctors' offices. Results that are unsuccessful don't get published and are filed away in the basement. The Medical Products Agency in Sweden estimates that as many as 40 percent of clinical studies of antidepressants don't get published or publicized.[31] Before approving a drug, the FDA does, however, require a pharmaceutical company to release the results from all the studies it paid to be conducted, whether a drug's outcome proved to be successful or not. But to get at that information, sometimes bold action is required, such as making use of the US Freedom of Information Act to petition the FDA to obtain the full story on clinical drug trials—the ones that show the medication was effective, as well as the ones that show it is a dud.

This is exactly what Irving Kirsch did and reported on in his compelling book, *The Emperor's New Drugs: Exploding the Antidepressant Myth.* Dr. Kirsch and his staff accessed the FDA data available on a host of popular antidepressants and ran the numbers. Across thirty-eight clinical trials involving three thousand patients, the benefit of being on an antidepressant was only slightly better than being on a placebo. He sums up the results in his book with the following startling fact: "Improvement in patients who had been given a placebo was about 75% of the response to the real medication."[32]

Placebo-type studies are generally considered to be the most scientifically trustworthy ones. Two identical groups of depressed people might be divided up. One group is given the real pill, which is the medication that is being tested. The other group is given a placebo—a fake pill that is made to look like the real pill but has none of the psychoactive ingredients of the real pill. After a while, all participants involved may be interviewed by a research assistant on how much their depression has improved. The research assistant is unaware of who is taking the real pill or the fake pill. That is what makes a study a double-blind, placebo-controlled one. The research assistant is blind to who is taking what so that he or she does not arrive at a biased viewpoint.

Dr. Kirsch's discovery on the minimally higher effectiveness of antidepressants over placebos is actually not so controversial. Back in January 2003, when Prozac was approved by the FDA for use with children, the decision was based mainly on three studies. One study showed an unsuccessful outcome: depressed adolescents were as likely to get better taking a placebo, as they were taking Prozac. The response rates were extraordinarily high—65 percent. That means 65 percent of the adolescents became less depressed whether they were given Prozac or a sugar pill. The two other studies did indicate that depression in children and adolescents improved with Prozac, over placebos. In one, 56 percent of the respondents got better on Prozac, versus 33 percent on placebos. On the other, 41 percent of respondents got better on Prozac, as compared with 20 percent on placebos.[33]

Doctors are often unaware of the amazingly high improvement rates using just placebos. Patients can get better taking a sugar pill placebo, even when they are explicitly told that there is no medicinal ingredient in it to treat their ailment. This was the finding of Harvard Medical School professor Ted Kaptchuk and his fellow scientists in a recent study with patients complaining of irritable bowel syndrome.[34] He divided eighty patients into two groups. One got no pill. Members of the other group were told to take two pills a day that were openly described as "like sugar pills," with no medicinal ingredient in them. The bottles that contained the pills they were to consume had the word "placebo" clearly printed on the front. A stunning 59 percent of those taking the pills reported relief from taking them. For many people, the simple act of taking a pill, whether or not they know it has little medicinal value, can lead to improvement—particularly if the medical and psychiatric conditions for which they are taking it are vague or loosely defined.

What about Seroquel, the blockbuster antipsychotic drug that sells for over $1,000 for 180 500 mg tablets on Drugstore.com and has generated upwards of $17 billion in sales since 2004?[35] This was one of the medications Rebecca Riley was prescribed for bipolar disorder. How does it measure up against a placebo? Based on a pair of studies in the prestigious *American Journal of Psychiatry* and the *Journal of Clinical Psychopharmacology*, the response rate is close to 55 percent for Seroquel, as opposed to 37 percent for placebos.[36] This hardly inspires confidence. It's like saying Seroquel helps 19 percent of the patients who take it, the rest of whom would have gotten better by simply taking a sugar pill. Moreover, sugar pills, unless taken in mass quantities, don't produce weight gain, but Seroquel does. Antipsychotics like Seroquel have been associated with an average weight gain of twelve pounds a year.[37] The *New York Times* in 2010 reported that in civil lawsuits brought against AstraZeneca, this drug manufacturer knowingly hid the Seroquel–weight-gain link and instead published a study suggesting that the drug was linked with weight loss![38]

BLAMING THE BRAIN IS NOT SO BRAINY

Nowadays, brain-based explanations for kids' problem behaviors are so commonplace that even parents sound like medical experts when they are sought out for their opinions. Recently, when asked by an Ohio psychologist for her personal beliefs regarding the cause of ADHD, one mother commented:

> ADHD is a biological disorder of the brain where the chemical norepinephrine and dopamine are not produced in the proper amount. . . . The receptor sites in the brain, there's fewer receptor sites, there is . . . if you look at some of the PET scans, the areas which are affected, the blood vessels are narrower in those areas, and it's a medical disorder.[39]

This mother is clearly well schooled in the chemical-imbalance approach to ADHD, which goes something like this: ADHD is a biologically based brain disease. ADHD children are born with brains that are genetically preprogrammed to undersupply them with dopamine and norepinephrine, the brain chemicals that are responsible for helping them to stay alert, goal-directed, and motivated. Psychostimulant medications, such as Ritalin, are uniquely designed to correct for the imbalance of dopamine and norepinephrine in the ADHD child's brain. This chemical-imbalance explanation might be clear-cut and persuasive. However, it's far from scientifically correct.

Let's start with what we know about the neurochemical dopamine. Studies do reveal ADHD to be associated with lower levels of dopamine in the brain. However, we don't really know if the low availability of dopamine *causes* ADHD or is *the effect of having ADHD*. In other words, kids with ADHD may behave in ways and have lifestyles that contribute to the lower production of dopamine in their brains. For example, it's common knowledge that ADHD kids are distractible at school and tend to find traditional schoolwork unrewarding. Yet release of dopamine in the central nervous system depends greatly on people finding everyday tasks engaging, exciting, and rewarding. The low dopamine levels found in the brains of many ADHD kids may be related to how understimulated and undermotivated they are by classroom learning day in and day out.

Low dopamine levels also have been linked to a Western-style, high-fat diet.[40] ADHD kids are twice as likely as non-ADHD kids to have this type of diet and to eat processed, fried, and refined foods that are higher in total fat, saturated fat, refined sugar, and sodium.[41] These dietary habits may thus contribute to lower dopamine production in the brains of some supposedly ADHD kids. In other words, this finding also complicates the notion that ADHD is caused solely by a preexisting brain malfunction.

Lastly, boys are two to three times more likely than girls to be diagnosed with ADHD. Curiously, studies show that the male brain produces less dopamine than the female brain.[42] We have to be careful in automatically assuming that dopamine deficiencies are due to an ADHD brain, rather than a male brain per se.

Chemical-imbalance explanations for mental health problems are increasingly coming under fire. Kenneth Kendler, one of the most well-known psychiatrists in the United States and coeditor of the journal *Psychological Medicine*, stated a few years ago: "We have hunted for big simple neurochemical explanations for psychiatric disorders and have not found them."[43] The famed science writer John Horgan expressed the same sentiment in his award-winning book, *The Undiscovered Mind:* "Given the ubiquity of a neurotransmitter such as serotonin and the multiplicity of its functions, it is almost as meaningless to implicate it in depression as it is to implicate blood."[44] And Dr. Wayne Goodman, chairman of the Department of Psychiatry at Mount Sinai School of Medicine in New York, once wrote: "Biological psychiatrists have looked very closely for a serotonin imbalance or dysfunction in patients with depression or obsessive compulsive disorder and, to date, it has been elusive."[45]

Leading scientists are convinced that there is no solid evidence to assume that depression is caused by a serotonin imbalance. However, this hasn't stopped pharmaceutical companies from churning out ads making that claim. Take this press release put out by Forest Laboratories for its antidepressant Lexapro: "Research suggests that depression is caused by an imbalance of certain chemicals in the brain, most notably serotonin. . . . Lexapro is thought to work by helping to restore the brain's chemical balance."[46]

This is fairly typical as drug ads go—frame the mental health problem squarely as a medical condition with biological causes and solutions. It's as if only biochemical treatments have biological effects. However, with easier access to brain-imaging techniques for research purposes, we are continuously discovering how "nonbiological" interventions can alter the brain's neurochemistry. Torkel Klingberg, a Swedish neuroscientist, has conducted research with implications for how the brain activity and neurochemistry of ADHD people can be improved with memory training. Klingberg is the cofounder of Cogmed, a computer-based program where children are given memory training for thirty to forty minutes a day, five days a week, spread over five weeks. This regimen has been shown to enhance dopamine-receptor density in the brain, as well as frontal and parietal cortex brain activity.[47]

Even ordinary habits such as physical exercise and meditation can alter brain structure. A recent article in the journal *Brain Research* reporting on the physical fitness and brain development of nine- and ten-year-old children showed how the fitter ones tended to have a larger hippocampus.[48] The hippocampus is an area of the brain linked to memory and learning. Eight weeks of approximately thirty minutes a day of mindfulness meditation also has been shown to produce more gray matter in the hippocampus.[49]

It's no longer scientifically valid to think of the brain as an isolated organ, wholly dependent on genetic preprogramming for its development. Brains are affected by life experience. Nor is it scientifically valid to believe that emotional disorders are either biologically caused, due to "nature," or environmentally caused, due to "nurture." Rarely do brain experts studying such disorders speak of nature *versus* nurture anymore. It's all about nature *and* nurture.

Genes for emotional disorders passed onto us from our parents are not fixed blueprints guaranteeing we will develop that disorder. They are risk factors. Life experience impacts whether these genes will be turned on or off, and whether risk becomes eventuality. Walter Goldschmidt, the eminent UCLA anthropologist, stated this well: "Most genes that are said to cause a disease actually just increase the probability of its occurrence."[50]

We know that in the case of bipolar disorder, genes alone are not the sole cause, because the twin of a person with bipolar disorder who shares identical genes doesn't always develop the disorder. A child with a parent or sibling diagnosed with bipolar disorder is just four to six times more likely to be similarly diagnosed, compared to a child with no bipolar-disordered family members.[51] The Autism Speaks website succinctly spells out a nature *and* nurture causal explanation for autism: "Most cases of autism . . . appear to be caused by a combination of autism risk genes and environmental factors influencing early brain development."[52]

To say that clear-cut, one-sided biological explanations for childhood disorders like ADHD, bipolar disorder, and autism spectrum disorder are misguided is not the same as saying biology doesn't play a role. But if we think of these disorders as entirely brain-based, we run the risk of being overly seduced by medical and medicinal interventions, which have their place, but are not the only interventions at our disposal. If we think of them as entirely brain-based, we also are less inclined to meaningfully analyze the behavior that makes us consider a diagnosis in the first place. Since so many of the behaviors associated with these disorders mirror aspects of childhood itself, if we don't meaningfully analyze them, we have no genuine way of teasing apart examples of legitimate disorder from examples of slow maturation in social and emotional growth or any number of other normal developmental or psychological childhood phenomena.

Exclusively blaming children's brains for their emotional problems is every bit as skewed as the past habit of exclusively blaming parents. The causes of children's emotional problems definitely cannot be boiled down to questionable parenting *or* faulty brains. This should be good news for parents. Knowing they're not responsible for their kid's emotional problems in any absolute way, but that their parenting habits and lifestyle choices may play a part, helps parents to be proactive. We forget how liberating and empowering it can be for parents to acknowledge the part they play in their child's problems. Knowing that they have some control can provide parents with a sense of hope. If they can zero in on and correct what they are doing wrong or not doing right, they can make a real impact on their children.

When reaching out to professionals for help, then, parents need to have their eyes wide open. They need to realize that doctors' and therapists' education and training primes them to think in illness terms. It also primes them to categorize and medicalize kids' behavior instead of seeking to understand it in ordinary human terms. For example, it sets them up to think that a young child with delayed language skills probably has a mixed receptive-expressive language disorder. This despite the fact that the child in question has a full-time, non-English-speaking nanny and absolutely no preschool experience, and has been thereby deprived of adequate English-language stimulation.

Doctors are more influenced by drug reps than we want to believe. It is troubling that many doctors arrive at a diagnosis to justify prescribing medications that drug reps have persuaded them are cutting-edge and usable with kids having a variety of emotional problems. As astounding as it may seem, in the doctor's or therapist's office, parents may need to steer the discussion about their kid's problems in the direction of ordinary, commonsense understandings and solutions. Parents may need to wonder aloud whether their kid's problems are on the far end of normal or are due merely to slower social and emotional maturation. If they do not, parents can be fair game for getting sucked into a juggernaut of mental illness explanations and treatments for their kid's behavior that, in reality, don't apply.

CHAPTER TWO

The Rush to Diagnose

A few years ago I met a family whose story crystallized for me how commonplace it has become in our society to rush in and diagnostically categorize children's behavior rather than step back and humanistically understand it, as well as to assume that a child's difficult behavior must indicate a psychiatric disorder.

Sarah and her husband, Rob, sat on my office couch. Sarah leaned forward and asked: "Have you heard of Ring of Fire?" My instincts told me that she was probably probing my credibility as a child psychologist, but I was baffled by her reference. I guessed: "Is it a song?" She shook her head dismissively: "No, it's a type of ADHD I learned about on the Internet." To lessen my ignorance, after the consultation I researched "Ring of Fire" online and discovered it was a type of ADHD popularized by media personality and proprietor of psychiatric clinics nationwide, Dr. Daniel Amen. Turns out the "Ring of Fire" Sarah and Rob referenced did not pertain to the Johnny Cash song but to a peculiar red ring Dr. Amen found in the brain-imaging results of ADHD individuals who were on the aggressive end.

Educators at the school that their five-year-old son, Charlie, attended had referred them to me for an evaluation. The week before our meeting, Charlie's kindergarten teacher had pulled Sarah aside during a morning drop-off and offhandedly commented: "I think Charlie might have ADHD, Asperger's, or some sort of learning disorder. It's worth looking into." The learning specialist at the school had taken a more direct approach, stating baldly: "We need an assessment to see if this school is the best fit for Charlie." These events made Sarah and Rob understandably anxious, and they began to scour the Internet for information on what might explain Charlie's behavior. The teacher had mentioned that Charlie could be impulsive, willful, and moody. Surfing the Internet on causes of impulsivity, moodiness, and willfulness in children, Sarah and Rob happened upon "Ring of Fire" ADHD and surmised this diagnosis might fit Charlie.

I knew that the concerns expressed by the teacher and the learning specialist would worry most parents. I tried to put Sarah and Rob at ease and to ally myself with them. I encouraged them to discuss their concerns candidly and fill me in on the details of the situation. They explained that Charlie's teacher was finding Charlie to be immensely difficult to manage, as he "marched to the beat of his own drum" in class. Raising his hand and waiting to be called on were challenging tasks for Charlie. He also found it difficult to stay in his seat and follow directions, never mind transitioning between workstations. One day, Charlie had ignored his teacher's instructions to the class to remove their art aprons, insisting upon wearing his art apron long after his classmates had removed theirs. He had stuffed the bottom part of the apron into the waist of his pants and proudly announced that he had a "new bra." The teacher had mentioned this to Charlie's parents as evidence of Charlie's tendency to act strangely.

Charlie's parents acknowledged that, at home, Charlie could be "strong willed." But after a few warnings, or a strong reprimand, he usually complied with parental wishes. At the preschool Charlie had attended, his teachers reportedly adored him and praised his leadership skills. His positive preschool experience had convinced Charlie's parents that he was ready for kindergarten, even though he would be young in relation to his peers.

I suggested that it would be helpful for me to observe Charlie in his classroom prior to meeting him in my office. In the classroom, I would be anonymous, so Charlie might be less influenced by his perception of me as an evaluator. On the scheduled day, his teacher introduced me as "a guest." I sat off to the side of the class and observed.

I was astounded by the regimented atmosphere in the kindergarten classroom and by the explicit focus on academics. As students moseyed through the front door, they grabbed different-colored folders from their backpacks and placed them in color-coordinated trays: blue for math homework; red for science homework; and yellow for reading homework. After a rather rushed five-minute circle time, in which most of the twenty students had their hands raised the entire time but only four were invited to speak, students were instructed to gather in their preassigned groups (Lions, Tigers, and Zebras) and walk quietly to their workstations: *OK, Lions, you will be with me, making shapes with rubber bands on our geoboards. Tigers, you will go to the reading station. Zebras, you will go to the math station. I want everybody to work quietly. Remember the rules: no talking and raise your hand if you need help.*

Charlie's group was the Lions. He was required to sit in a seat directly in front of the teacher so that she could keep a watchful eye on him, while other members of the group were allowed to sit cross-legged on the carpet with their geoboards on their laps. The teacher demonstrated how to make a rectangle: *I'm going to count to ten. See if you can make it just like mine. Good. Now this is a line segment. Before you make it, I want you all to say "line segment" out loud.*

Charlie made three rectangles and became more engrossed in making rectangles than he was in listening to the teacher: *Charlie, you did not say "line segment." Let's all say it together again, and give Charlie a second chance.* The teacher's tendency to experience Charlie's benign expressions of autonomy and testiness as deliberate acts of defiance persisted throughout the observation. For instance, after Charlie pulled off what I considered the impressive feat of engaging in independent, sustained silent reading for fifteen minutes, he remained buried in his book. Meanwhile, the rest of the Lions had transitioned to the math workstation: *Charlie, you are not where you need to be. Did you not hear me when I told all the Lions that it was time for math?*

Later, Charlie held his hand up to signal to the assistant teacher that he needed help. After two minutes of not being acknowledged, Charlie stood up and gruffly announced: *I hate this math stuff.* Several girls in the Zebra group giggled. Charlie was promptly and sternly told by the assistant teacher to sit in his seat: *Charlie, you are not speaking appropriately. Sit down and hold your hand up until I am ready to help you.* He sat down and instead folded his arms and rested his head on the desk, swinging his legs vigorously under the table. He was in this irate posture when it was time for me to leave.

I later conducted a formal assessment of Charlie in my office. On measures of intelligence and academic achievement, he was multiple age and grade levels ahead. In my report, I concluded that Charlie's social and emotional functioning varied depending on how much his need for autonomy was honored. When he experienced some control and an activity interested him, he was cooperative, attentive, and content. Threats to his need for autonomy arose in structured situations with set rules and social protocols. Aspects of his kindergarten experience were highly challenging for him: an emphasis on acquiring academic skills through teacher-guided activities, group learning experiences with prescribed tasks, and quick and efficient transitioning between workstations. Charlie's work slowdowns and shutdowns, off-the-cuff comments, and off-task behaviors were in direct proportion to the degree of control he felt he had over whatever activity was permitted, whether that activity interested him, and how long he wished to pursue it. Charlie needed help with finessing verbal expressions of dissatisfaction, so that his expressions would not be seen as disrespectful. I concluded that Charlie did not warrant a mental health diagnosis.

I listed specific steps Charlie's kindergarten teacher could take to improve Charlie's school performance, knowing that she might see this as me telling her how to do her job and that school administrators might think that I had downplayed signs of child pathology. I recommended that educators at his school build rapport with Charlie by warmly welcoming him in the morning with hugs, assigning him special tasks to do, and praising his efforts to complete tasks. I felt this would enhance his overall willingness to cooperate. I also encouraged educators at the school to provide occasions for Charlie to receive positive attention rather than negative attention by making comments along the lines of, *Charlie, you are so tall and your arms are so long. It might be harder for you to hold your arm up and wait to be asked because your arms are so long! If you can hold that long arm up and wait to be asked, it will tell me your arm is not just long but strong!* or by reframing off-task comments and behaviors in positive ways that would redirect Charlie, such as, *Charlie, I can see that you are using your good brain to solve those math problems and you want to make sure you get them right. But now is the time to put your math workbook away and get your cute self over to the reading station.* I urged educators to expect that Charlie would be slow to transition between tasks and activities and encouraged them to offer praise and encouragement as a way to help him move more quickly, perhaps even encouraging him to compete against himself: *How fast can those strong legs get you over to the math station, Charlie? My adult legs can get me there pretty fast! I know you can do it.*

It was absurd that after umpteen hours of formal assessment and a healthy fee paid to me by Charlie's parents I was reduced to merely recommending what I considered to be obvious and practical ways of improving Charlie's classroom experience and participation. It was even more absurd to me that school personnel had considered, rather casually, that Charlie might be classified with a mental health diagnosis in the first place and steered his parents to my office. The entire experience confirmed for me how necessary it is to contextualize children's behavior, especially those on the younger end, who are more likely to react sharply and intensely when what is being asked of them cognitively, emotionally, and socially is developmentally beyond them. By "contextualizing" I simply mean considering how their behavior might be an expectable reaction to unfavorable life circumstances.

THE KINDERGARTEN PSYCHIATRIC DRAGNET

Charlie's predicament is far from unique. Using a twelve-thousand-strong sample of children from the Early Childhood Longitudinal Study Kindergarten Cohort, economist Dr. Todd Elder of Michigan State University recently ran some statistics using children's birthdates and ADHD medication use.[1] He calculated that as many as one million kindergartners are misdiagnosed with ADHD merely because they are the youngest and most immature in their class. He went on record with the implications of his study: "If a child is behaving poorly, if he's inattentive, if he can't sit still, it may simply be because he's 5 and the other kids are 6. There's a big difference between a 5-year-old and a 6-year-old, and teachers and medical practitioners need to take this into account when evaluating whether children have ADHD."[2] Dr. Elder particularly noted the financial waste that occurs due to misdiagnosis and needless medication use, which he estimated to be $320 million to $500 million annually.

More problems are cropping up for preschoolers who are transitioning to kindergarten than ever before. Several years ago, researchers at the Yale Child Study Center analyzed data from forty different states across the United States and found that prekindergartners were more likely to be expelled from school than students in grades K–12 due to troublesome behavior.[3] In a study commissioned by the mayor of Springfield, Missouri, in 2005, three-quarters of 101 kindergarten teachers and 39 elementary school principals polled had seen moderate to severe increases in the frequency of aggressive behavior in their kindergarten students.[4] Such behavior largely comprised hitting, shoving, name calling, and using profanity. One teacher wrote: "I have noticed these [aggressive] students are also subject to frequent tantrums or meltdowns. The tantrums can range from dropping to the floor yelling, crying, and kicking, to knocking things off tables, to running away."[5]

As the rates of problem behavior have risen in the transition to kindergarten, so too has our willingness as a society to put kindergarten students under a diagnostic lens. The latest epidemiological data reveal that one in five kindergartners manifests a psychiatric disorder.[6] Dr. Alice Carter from the University of Massachusetts–Boston, the lead scientist on this study, told *Medscape Medical News*: "What it suggests is that we really need to be screening for social-emotional problems because a significant number of these children are already having difficulties that will likely interfere with their learning and building of relationships at a pretty critical juncture."[7]

No doubt this early-intervention approach is well intentioned.

Much good has come from public-health campaigns and media spot-lights that have emphasized early intervention. Legions of children with clear-cut cases of autism and other severe disorders have benefit-ted greatly from early identification and treatment. However, children who have no clear-cut psychiatric condition, but who are mercurial in their mood, expressiveness, and activity levels, are ill-served by a diagnostic, early-intervention mind-set and are particularly at risk for being misdiagnosed in kindergarten. These are the kids who rage and tantrum at school but not at home—or vice versa. With a warm but firm teacher, they cooperate, communicate, and socially connect, but with a stern or overwrought teacher, they tune out or act up. During the regular school day, in the controlled chaos of the classroom, they tend to be organized and attentive, but in the uncon-trolled chaos of the after-school program, they can become disorga-nized and unmanageable. The diagnosis/early-intervention mind-set ill serves such kids because it separates them out from the classroom and home conditions that contribute to them exhibiting problems in the first place and forces parents, teachers, and other professionals to think that any emotional issues that exist are due to some disease en-tity located inside the child. The diagnosis/early-intervention mind-set puts the *child* under the microscope instead of where that child is developmentally and the appropriateness of what is being demanded of her cognitively, emotionally, and socially in kindergarten. We need to adjust our mind-sets so as to avoid the tendency to exclusively view children's problem behavior as a set of psychiatric symptoms to be read in isolation. We need to hone our skill at scrutinizing the interaction between where children are developmentally and what the kindergar-ten environment demands, and take a close look at the classroom con-ditions that affect children's behavior.

What do we see when we put today's kindergarteners under the microscope? In Bellevue, Washington, kids enrolled in public schools are expected to "write without resistance when given the time, place and materials" and engage in "repeated independent readings of a fa-vorite book or simple text."[8] In Lynbrook, New York, budding learners should be able to "recognize and describe positional words (over, under,

above, below, on, off, between)" and "measure length and height using standard units of measure."[9] In O'Fallon, Missouri, little ones sally
forth each day to "differentiate between a letter, word and sentence;
identify capitalization and punctuation; locate elements of printed
material, count 1 through 100, and recognize and write numerals 0
through 20."[10]

In 2009, Molly Holloway, a mother of twins who attend a well-
heeled school in Bowie, Maryland, wrote to Jay Mathews, the education
columnist for the *Washington Post*, about her children's kindergarten
experience: "They have tests at least monthly in math, reading, social
studies and science. The tests are multiple choice so that they can practice filling in the little bubbles to be ready for the Maryland State Assessment in three years."[11] Is it any wonder that the syndicated advice
columnist Amy Dickinson jested in a *Time* magazine article a few years
back that kindergarten should be renamed *kindergrind*?[12]

Enormous changes in the average kindergarten classroom curriculum have occurred in the wake of the No Child Left Behind legislation. Many programs that were once rooted firmly in child-centered
play have been replaced with ones that are academically oriented and
rely heavily on teacher guidance. Kindergarten today is all about kids
learning the rudiments of reading and writing. Opportunities for unstructured or semistructured play in kindergarten are on the decline,
and our young children are being deprived of the lessons in sharing,
cooperating, turn taking, and burning off aggressive energy that are
built into naturally occurring childhood play. Further, we forget how
by its very nature play is pleasurable. When we remove play from kids'
first encounters with school, we stifle the early pleasurable associations
kids then usually attach to school. This is not the right start we want
to give our children.

How do we know with any certainty that play in kindergarten has
become a scarce commodity and that textbooks and worksheets are
replacing blocks and art supplies on classroom shelves? The Los Angeles Unified School District's approach to kindergarten is likely to
be similar to that used in kindergartens across the country. Scholars
Allison Fuligni and Sandra Hong, at the University of California at

Los Angeles, surveyed 112 kindergarten teachers and learned that 79 percent of them allot either no time or only up to thirty minutes of play during the school day.[13] Sixty-two percent of them, on the other hand, spend ninety minutes or more teaching reading. It's no longer provocative, but humdrum, to propose that kindergarten has become the new first grade.

Cautionary tales about this shift are being told by public policy experts and teachers alike. In 2009, a "who's who" of child-welfare scholars gathered by the Alliance for Childhood published data that underscored the importance of active play and social-emotional learning in kindergarten for kids' long-term development.[14] Dr. Stephen Hinshaw, a highly regarded developmental psychologist on the faculty at the University of California–Berkeley, put it succinctly: "It's a mistake to focus exclusively on academic readiness. Even more vital than early reading is the learning of play skills, which form the foundation of cognitive skills."[15] Pushing reading before age seven, Dr. Hinshaw claims, "puts undue pressure on a child."

A veteran teacher during a Policy Analysis for California Education interview several years ago weighed in on what it was like in the field: "The kids are developmentally in the same place where they were, but the expectation is for them to be doing academic work; and for some of these kids, you are stepping all over their developmental foundations to teach something they are not ready for."[16]

Kindergartners these days are being dealt a double whammy. Their overall stress is elevated due to their being confronted with academic tasks and social expectations that are beyond their developmental capacities. Then they are deprived of the means to cope with that stress—animated, kinetic, imaginative play. The younger students, or those less socially and emotionally advanced, pay the price. When they wander off, tantrum, hit, dillydally, squirm, squeal, or cuss, they are at risk for being caught up in the kindergarten psychiatric dragnet, when their behavior is often merely a negative reaction to stress.

TEACHERS: FRONTLINE DIAGNOSERS

Surveys reveal that teachers are typically the driving force behind kids being given a diagnosis—particularly with respect to ADHD. Forty-seven percent of physicians in one study identified teachers as the most likely to first suggest a kid might have ADHD (versus 30 percent identifying parents as the most likely to first suggest this).[17] Pediatric specialists also have found that over 55 percent of physicians feel pressured by teachers to assign a diagnosis of ADHD to kids sent to them.[18]

It is not surprising that teachers tend to step into the role of frontline diagnosers. After all, classrooms, along with homes, are the main venues where kids usually show problem behaviors. For many kids, the challenges they face in the classroom far exceed anything they face at home.

These challenges include sitting, listening, and staying still for extended periods of time; working independently without ready access to one-on-one help from an adult; sharing the attention of an adult with many other students; and cooperating with large numbers of relatively anonymous peers. Day after day, teachers observe how kids manage these challenges. With a finite amount of time, energy, and resources, teachers have to make judgments regarding whether kids' unusual or unexpected reactions to these challenges are somehow abnormal.

It's easy to accept that teachers have some say in identifying whether the behavior of a student rises to the level of a significant problem, but is it possible that teachers have too much say? Are teachers—particularly novice teachers—undertrained to tease out normal from abnormal behavior in kids? Is it possible that teachers' more vague ways of defining mental disorders like ADHD lead them to inappropriately label kids? Perhaps conditions in the average classroom are such that teachers feel pressured to push for a diagnosis, urge medication, and suggest special-education services for "problem" children—factors that contribute to the overdiagnosing of kids?

Teachers don't always have the sort of educational background that enables them to distinguish between what is developmentally typical and atypical in children. As many as a third of teachers in a Los Angeles sample had not taken any coursework in child development or early-childhood education.[19]

On the topic of whether teachers are more apt to overdiagnose than underdiagnose ADHD, researchers in the Department of Psychology at Eastern Illinois University offer a clear answer: ADHD is overdiagnosed by teachers. Michael Havey and his team analyzed teachers' ratings of students' behavior. They learned that nearly 24 percent of students were viewed by teachers as having ADHD. This percentage is well above the generally accepted 5–10 percent prevalence rate.[20]

Teachers' tendency to overdiagnose ADHD is probably due in part to the overly broad set of behaviors they associate with the disorder. This is reflected in information distributed to educators through the website of the National Association of Special Education Teachers, which lists the following behaviors as evidence of the clinical presentation of ADHD:

- Waking slowly or, especially in young children, being disorganized and/or grumpy in the morning unless anticipating high excitement activity
- Unexplained irritability or easy frustration over minor issues or matters, often described as "things bug me"
- Falling asleep slowly and with great difficulty at night
- Impulsivity (difficulty staying focused on an immediate task because other thoughts often intrude and race through the mind)[21]

As I see it, describing supposed ADHD behavior in such a broad and folksy way always raises the risk that an inappropriate diagnosis will be applied to a child whose difficult behavior is unrelated to ADHD.

Oftentimes, a kid seems to be on a teacher's ADHD radar when he or she falls short of what is considered an ideal, teachable student. Teachers have very clear ideas about what an ideal, teachable student looks like: "passionate," "assertive," "outspoken," and "energetic" are not words that most teachers would use to describe such a student. Instead, research shows that teachers seem to prefer having students who listen, follow instructions, comply, control their emotions, and transition well between tasks. In a study of 717 teachers from a socio-economically and culturally diverse school district in Tennessee conducted by Peabody College professor Dr. Kathleen Lane, the key social skills the vast majority of teachers zeroed in on as crucial for success in school were the following: complies with directions; attends to instructions; controls temper in conflicts with peers and adults; ignores peer distractions when doing class work; and easily makes transitions from one classroom activity to another.[22] The ideal, teachable student, based on these criteria, would be one with compliant personality traits. By extension, students who have more spirited personalities, who are assertive, action-oriented, outspoken, quick-tempered, slow to transition, demand individual attention, and learn by talking things out more than by thinking things through exhibit traits that a teacher might be inclined to see as evidence of ADHD.

To be fair to teachers, the pressures they face in the classroom almost favor pathologizing children's behavior; a referral for medication or special-education services often seems like the only viable solution.

In the wake of the No Child Left Behind Act, "accountability" is the buzzword in school districts across the country. States are now required to define and enforce academic standards in each grade in order to secure federal funds. Teachers are under mounting pressure to bolster student test scores. Increasing the amount of homework is one avenue that is being used by teachers to make sure that students get enough practice to master essential academic materials. Several decades ago, it was rare to assign homework to kids prior to the third grade. Nowadays, upwards of 64 percent of six- to eight-year-olds have daily homework.[23] Moreover, listening to parents suggests that the amount of and difficulty of the homework being assigned has increased in recent years. A parent of a third grader at Marengo Elementary School in South Pasadena, California, recently told me about one particularly demanding homework assignment that was given to her son that made her head spin. In advance of a test covering thirty types of angles (e.g., right angle, acute angle, obtuse angle), she had spent the better part of a week drilling him. She even allowed him to stay up late on the night before the test so that he could practice some more. His test score indicated that twenty-nine of his thirty answers were correct, but achieving this result put a great deal of stress and strain on the mother-child relationship.

Schools also now seem to stress organizational skills much more than they stressed such skills in the past. Children are required to be their own executive secretaries. They are expected to keep track of all homework assignments and, when they are due, to hand them in on time, to assertively ask for makeup work when they return to school after being out sick, and to follow up on a homework assignment that was handed in but not checked off by a teacher. Such skills might be helpful life skills for a teenager to master as he or she ventures into young adulthood. However, for your average second or third grader, such organizational demands can be incredibly stressful. Teachers are placed in a quandary regarding kids who lack organizational skills or who aren't provided with the kind of support and structure at home that facilitates good work habits—not to mention those students who don't take well to a chalk-and-talk/drill-in-the-skills educational approach. Often teachers have no choice but to consider a special-education referral for these students in order to help them get the individualized attention they need.

Since the No Child Left Behind Act was passed over a decade ago, the number of children nationwide who have qualified for special-education services under the "Other Health Impairments" category has more than doubled.[24] This is the category under which kids with ADHD are placed. A mammoth study of almost ten thousand seven- to eleven-year-olds across the United States that was conducted by public policy scholars out of the University of Texas–Austin and the University of Michigan–Ann Arbor found that students in states where there were stricter academic accountability laws had a greater chance of being diagnosed with ADHD.[25]

It may be that as academic standards are increased and organizational skills emphasized at younger and younger ages, teachers became more inclined to view a struggling student as a disabled student. This is the perspective of Jay P. Greene, head of the Department of Education Reform at the University of Arkansas. In a September 2009 interview on National Public Radio, Dr. Greene spoke candidly:

Public schools have been using special education as a remedial-education program. Students who are struggling academically but have no true disability are being wrongly placed in special education. The students may be struggling because they have been taught poorly or because they have a difficult home life, but these are not disabilities. . . . If we blame processing problems in children's brains for academic struggles rather than poor instruction or issues outside of school, we'll fail to take the necessary corrective steps.[26]

In this same interview, Dr. Greene highlighted the importance of public funds being made available to school districts to offer academic remediation and support services to struggling students. The present system is set up so that school districts need to designate a student as disabled and serviceable in special education in order to get funds from state and federal governments. Unless reforms are made, Dr. Greene wryly stated, "It won't be long before we live in a Lake Woebegone where all children are above average, and the ones who aren't are labeled 'disabled.'"[27]

Teachers are often helpless to change the classroom conditions in which they work. They feel overwhelmed by larger public policy directives that impinge upon their daily educational practices. Consequently, circumstances favor an attraction to brain-based theories of disability and medication solutions. Seeing the singular cause of a child's problems as a disordered brain is a fairly cut-and-dry approach; the cause and effect are simple and clear-cut. The medication solution is a convenient and efficient one. Secretly, teachers may feel that if they had fewer students in their classroom, a coteacher, and less homework to correct, they would have the time and energy to provide individualized attention to a moderately troubled student.

Studies show that teachers are often strong supporters of psychostimulant usage for ADHD. Several years ago, a group of scholars affiliated with the University of Wisconsin studied first- and second-grade teachers and concluded that they had very positive attitudes about the use of stimulants to treat ADHD. They were neutral as to any potential negative side effects or to the use of behavioral strategies to address ADHD behaviors. Somewhat disturbed by their findings, these scholars made the following cautionary remark: "One has to wonder if medication has become the alternative to least restrictive environmental efforts in managing classroom behaviors. It seems important to emphasize that children do not learn from medication, it only controls symptoms while they are being treated."[28]

This last point made by the University of Wisconsin scholars is worthy of elaboration. Taking a stimulant does not chemically download social and academic information into the supposed-ADHD child's brain. An abundance of evidence shows that stimulant use helps a child focus for longer and stay calmer in his or her body. Nevertheless, there is no convincing body of evidence showing that stimulant use improves a kid's academic and social functioning over the long haul. In addition, teachers' neutrality about the side effects of stimulant medications is a concern. Common side effects, such as appetite impairment, sleep irregularities, and mood swings coming off a dosage, are often pronounced enough to create conflict in parents about whether to put their child on a stimulant.

Many states legally forbid teachers from weighing in on whether a student has a mental disorder and needs medication. However, in practice, teachers still remain the frontline diagnosers. Their judgment often tips the scale on whether a student ends up being prescribed medication. As long as this remains the standard, teachers' ratings of a kid's behavior will always carry weight when a diagnosis of ADHD is being entertained. However, for ADHD to be diagnosed correctly the symptoms must occur in two different everyday environments— typically home and school—and this requirement is often overlooked.

Technically, teachers should not be making formal judgments anyway regarding a student's disability status and eligibility for special-education services. That falls within the professional domain of school psychologists and other mental health professionals. Yet the norm is otherwise. Studies show that in 73 to 90 percent of cases, a teacher referral for a special-education evaluation results in eligibility for services.[29]

For better or worse, teachers influence what behavior in kids gets seen as proof of a diagnosable condition. As long as teachers are swayed by our society's obsession with brain-based explanations for kids' problems with self-control and academic underachievement, there is a good chance that the rates of misdiagnosis and overdiagnosis of mental health conditions will persist.

MENTALLY GIFTED, NOT MENTALLY DISORDERED

One of the most fascinating books I have read in recent years is by Dr. James Webb and a handful of coauthors titled: *Misdiagnosis and Dual Diagnosis of Gifted Children and Adults.*[30]

The book is a treasure trove of information on the subtle ways that mentally gifted children and adults are often misperceived as emotionally disturbed. The authors cite the following clever study that highlights how tricky it is to distinguish between mental giftedness and ADHD.

What does a gifted child look like? Would the average teacher consider the following kid gifted?

Sam is a 7 year old and a second grader. He is a student in your class. He has a high activity level and appears more restless than other children his age. Sam has difficulty restraining his desire to talk in the classroom and interrupts you frequently. You have repeatedly tried to change Sam's behavior, but Sam questions authority and he has a difficult time accepting rules and regulations. Sam's homework is frequently messy because he appears careless and inattentive to details. Sam has a poor attention span, especially when he is bored. Sam's home environment appears to be normal.[31]

This vignette was given to 132 teacher trainees by social scientists Anne Rinn and Jason Nelson. The trainees were then asked the following questions: (Form A) "If this child were a student in your class, what do you think the underlying explanation for his behavior would be?" and (Form B) "If this child were a student in your class, do you think the cause of his behavior could be attributed to ADHD or due to his being gifted and talented?" Participants also were required to back up their answers with explanations.

Regardless of the question asked, the vast majority of trainees attributed Sam's behavior to ADHD. Only one in five perceived Sam as potentially gifted on the Form A question. Nearly a third thought Sam might be gifted when provided that option on the Form B question. Teacher trainees who were strictly of the mind-set that Sam had ADHD provided reasons such as "If Sam was gifted and talented his work would be neater than it already is and he would care more about doing his homework than he does"; "Talented students do not question authority or act up in class"; and "Because he seems to be very active and excited but gets bored with the work. If gifted and talented he would do the work and get bored afterwards."

These rationales reflect the stereotypes of gifted children, who are assumed to be nerdy and quirky, academic buttoned-down types who take to school like a duck to water. But the behaviors exhibited by Sam (which are commonly associated with ADHD) are actually fairly typical of gifted kids—especially when they are underchallenged or bored.

Some gifted kids are intellectually restless and excitable. Bursting with ideas, they are eager to display their abundant knowledge. They may ask questions incessantly—even ones that are off-topic. This speaks to a genuine curiosity that is both ardent and shifting, causing the mind to dart off in different directions. Gifted kids may be three steps ahead of the teacher, anticipating questions and prepared with answers. Containing their excitement until they are called upon may feel like torture. A gifted kid may want to blurt out answers that seem patently obvious or become overtly resentful because of the accumulated frustration of having to wait while classmates cobble together answers that he or she can arrive at with lightning speed. It is estimated that most gifted kids placed in regular classrooms spend up to one-fourth to one-half of their school day waiting for their classmates to catch up to their level. Not surprisingly, all of this waiting can cause fidgetiness and agitation, which can get misconstrued as ADHD-like behavior.

Some gifted kids may come across as haughty and aloof; they do not suffer fools gladly. They may use their remarkable verbal and logical reasoning skills to question the actions of authority figures and see no reason why they should refrain from pointing out when a teacher contradicts him- or herself or fails to apply a rule consistently. They tend to believe that logic should always guide actions and often have a blind spot for social tact.

Fourteen-year-old Jim is one such kid. He was brought to see me by his physician parents because of an alarming interaction he had with a teacher that had caused her to feel unsafe in his presence. During a midterm exam, Jim asked his teacher for extra time. She casually stated something to the effect of, "Take all the time you need," knowing that Jim was a talented student who routinely aced tests. Jim took her comment literally. He saw it as an opportunity to settle in and answer his American history essay questions with painstaking detail. He was the last one left in the classroom, and the allotted test time had long since passed. His teacher eventually required him to hand in his test. Jim had only answered three of the five questions. He became livid because this was in violation of what his teacher had told him. He followed her all the way to the teachers' lounge, arguing with her over the unfairness of her actions. For days afterwards, Jim could not shake off his resentment.

It would be a mistake to view Jim's trouble with authority figures and rules as oppositional, impulsive ADHD behavior or Asperger's-like social rigidity. The issues with Jim are rooted more in his accelerated logical thinking skills and his need for acquisition of greater social tact.

Many gifted kids manifest terrific feats of engrossment and motivation on tasks that interest them. On tasks that fail to capture their interest, they can become easily bored, distractible, and unmotivated. Typically, the tasks that excite them are mentally taxing and passionately pursued. They might plow through a book in the Harry Potter series in one sitting, while leaving their algebra homework untouched. They may believe that it is pointless to do algebra homework for practice and reinforcement reasons when they are already confident in their grasp of the assigned material. They may fall behind academically after losing grade points for failing to turn in homework consistently. Points also may get deducted for not being a "good citizen." Coming off as indifferent when confronted with a spotty homework record does not curry favor with teachers. Not uncommonly, these students hit the ball out of the ballpark on in-class tests—that is, as long as these tests do not contain obscure information that could only have been obtained from doing a homework assignment.

Take Jared. Of the hundreds of kids I have administered intelligence tests to over the years, he yielded the highest IQ—156. On tests of verbal comprehension, visual-spatial analysis, and attention/active concentration, he placed above the 99.9th percentile. If he was in a room with a hundred kids his age, he would be smarter in all of these areas than 99.9 of them. Yet Jared's grade point average at the prestigious private high school he attended was hovering around a C. His homework was weighted so heavily into his grades in all of his classes that the As and Bs he received on tests failed to compensate for the low scores. When I spoke with Jared's school counselor, she pulled no punches, fervently arguing that Jared's organizational issues around homework were due to ADHD. She noted that her son had exhibited similar problems. However, his homework habits had improved after he was prescribed a stimulant for ADHD.

I mentioned to her that my testing showed that Jared was mentally gifted. In my estimation, his lackluster grades were due to his overall mind-set about homework, not ADHD. In my mind, he was not forgetful in the ADHD sense. I felt that he was consistently choosing not to do his homework, which, given his intelligence, he probably experienced as distasteful busywork. I added that it didn't help that his parents traveled a great deal and were not always on hand at night to enforce good homework routines.

The school counselor became more adamant. She questioned my resistance to seeing Jared's behavior as ADHD. She pleaded with me to agree to have him evaluated by a psychiatrist for the purpose of his potentially undergoing a trial dosage of ADHD medications. Instead, I recommended that she make herself available each day to check in with Jared around assigned homework that he needed to attend to that night. Friday-afternoon sessions with her to review his efforts on a given week might build in some necessary, school-based accountability. Meanwhile, in therapy with Jared, I agreed to work with him on his attitude toward homework and to try to coax him into buying into the essential value of homework and its impact on his grade point average. If Jared's long-term goal of enrolling in an Ivy League university was to be realized, he simply could not sidestep homework. His school counselor eventually circumvented me and went directly to his parents, urging the need for a medication evaluation. They complied because they did not want to make waves at the school.

Jared's story highlights how single-minded school personnel can be around framing organizational difficulties exclusively in terms of ADHD. It also underscores a taboo among educators in our democratic society; some kids are extraordinarily talented, and the kind and amount of homework they need may differ from what is assigned to the typical student.

In the teenage years, many gifted kids become highly idealistic and nonconformist. They may rant about the "rat race," "the machine," "the system," or how mainstream society sucks the soul out of them. However, these kids are not "rebels without a cause" who angrily defy adults out of a sense of alienation they can barely articulate. These are the kids who might pore over texts by Karl Marx and Friedrich Nietzsche and engage in discussions that are coherent and well informed. They may get As in English, history, and art yet fail a geography class because the teacher emphasizes areas of study that they find dull and uninspiring. They may be genuinely insulted and alienated by grading practices that overemphasize organizational skills, compliance, preparedness, and showing good citizenship.

One gifted teen I saw recently had a high school science teacher who insisted upon students taking notes with different-colored pens: red ink was for definitions of terms and concepts, blue ink was for drawings of biological cells and cellular processes, black ink was for graphs and charts, and green ink was for review notes. At random throughout the school week, the teacher stopped her lessons and asked students to take out their notebooks. She deducted grade points for students who had not followed her note-taking specifications. This bright kid experienced the teacher's actions as so absurd and arbitrary that he gave up trying altogether in the class.

Some gifted kids emerging into young adulthood question the very relevance of attending high school. This is especially true if they have all-consuming intellectual interests that are being insufficiently tapped at school. Mabel was one such kid. When I met her she told me, "I'm not letting school get in the way of my education." She had dropped out of high school midsemester in the twelfth grade. Her parents and several teachers suspected that she might be clinically depressed or have bipolar disorder. They inferred from her complete academic disaffection that she must somehow be suffering from a mood disorder. However, Mabel claimed to be, and acted like, she was quite content with her life. She slept until noon, rode her bike to the local coffee shop, and read prominent works of literature there all afternoon. In the evening, she took martial arts and pottery classes. During our therapy sessions, she quoted lines from Walt Whitman and Henry Thoreau, and waxed eloquently on the central dilemma of life, which she conceived of as: "Do you want to be successful? Or do you want to be happy?" She had airtight reasons for why attending high school put a person on track for being professionally successful but personally unhappy. Mabel eventually took courses at her local junior college and transferred to a prestigious four-year college in her early twenties.

If Mabel was depressed, it was more of an existential than a clinical depression. It was the type of depression that she was determined to think and feel her way through, instead of medicating. Her academic disaffection in high school had to do with her desire to pursue her own intellectual interests more rigorously, strictly on her own terms. The organizational demands of high school, at that juncture in her life, were experienced by her as off-putting and alienating. Her parents, rightly or wrongly, allowed her to opt out of high school on the condition that she build her day around meaningful and constructive pursuits.

When gifted kids appear restless, fidgety, distractible, argumentative, aloof, alienated, or unmotivated, educators need to overcome the taboo against questioning the quality and type of schooling these kids are receiving. To not do so, as the saying goes, is "akin to not checking a car's fuel level when it has unexpectedly stopped running."

UPDIAGNOSING TO GUARANTEE
TREATMENTS AND SERVICES

In October 2008, Congress passed the landmark Mental Health Parity and Addiction Equity Act. This new law was seen as a giant leap forward in recognizing that mental health and substance abuse coverage ought to be on par with regular medical coverage. Prior to this law, insurance companies had placed arbitrary limits on the number of office visits for which a client might be eligible. Charging higher copayments for mental health and substance abuse services also was common. There was much fanfare in Washington, since the new legislation was popular among Republicans and Democrats alike. In remarks made to the *Washington Post*, Democratic congressman Patrick J. Kennedy from Rhode Island, who was a chief sponsor of the legislation and had been treated for drug and alcohol addiction himself, summed up what many felt: "We've always had a stigma, sort of like mental illness is a character flaw. But now science has moved forward, and we can see the complexities in the brain that lead to eating disorders, compulsive disorders. All these connections are being made, the science is just becoming so firm. And it destroys the myth that this stuff is a choice."[32]

As with all laws, the devil was in the details. The law left it up to the discretion of health plans to classify which mental health diagnoses they covered. There also was no provision that restricted a health plan from excluding or limiting coverage for a lesser diagnosis. Many health plans in states that had enacted parity laws prior to the federal legislation had clear guidelines regarding what did or did not constitute a "serious mental illness." The number of therapy visits a health plan authorized and the copayment amount a patient was responsible for varied depending on the severity of the diagnosis. This is still pretty much the practice.

Historically what is considered a "serious mental illness" and therefore deserving of more intensive treatment and lower copayments has varied, depending on a health plan's adherence to preexisting state parity laws. The honorable Patrick J. Kennedy might be flummoxed to discover that eating disorders are considered a serious mental illness worthy of maximum coverage in California, but not in Maine,

Nebraska, Hawaii, or Oklahoma—to name but a few states.[33] Apparently, the science of mental illness is not supremely objective and fluctuates depending on the preferences of state legislators.

Limiting maximum coverage to serious mental illnesses has led to the practice of "upcoding." This was the conclusion of a team of researchers charged with analyzing the implementation of the California mental health parity law during 2000–2005.[34] The mental health providers they interviewed acknowledged a tendency to skew diagnoses toward the severe end to ensure reauthorization of psychotherapy treatment visits and lesser copayments for clients. The parity versus nonparity diagnostic system had simply provided an incentive for mental health providers to assign more severe diagnoses to clients.

Speaking as a psychologist, upcoding is not exactly akin to fabricating a more severe diagnosis. Often one has to make subjective judgments about how to group symptoms. There are choice points where even the most skilled clinicians are left with a variety of diagnostic options. For instance, inattention, poor concentration, and being revved up and on edge can point to an anxiety disorder or to ADHD. The teenager who has periodic temper outbursts and is unmanageable at home could be classified with intermittent explosive disorder, temper dysregulation disorder (a new *DSM*-5 diagnosis), or a form of bipolar disorder. There are mild to severe diagnoses for depression ranging from adjustment disorder with depressed mood, to dysthymia, to major depressive disorder. When pressured by parents to schedule ongoing therapy visits with a kid and preserve a productive therapy relationship, there is understandably the temptation to frame symptoms in ways that indicate a more severe diagnosis so that ongoing visits will be paid for by the client's insurance and be less of a financial burden to the family.

In general, under managed care, the rationing of services appears to promote updiagnosing by mental health professionals. This way there is greater likelihood that needed treatment will be approved. One survey of mental health counselors discovered that 44 percent of them would alter or had altered a diagnosis to ensure additional managed-care reimbursement.[35] In fact, the skyrocketing rates of bipolar disorder diagnoses in kids and teens may be due in part to updiagnosing within the managed care system to ensure that needed services are covered.

Drs. Joseph Blader and Gabrielle Carlson from the Department of Psychiatry and Behavioral Science, Stony Brook State University of New York, examined a representative sample of the psychiatric hospital records of American children and adolescents from 1996 through 2004.[36] During the eight-year span, the rates of kids and teens ascribed a discharge diagnosis of bipolar disorder had increased four- to fivefold. The authors surmised that the surge in bipolar disorder was due to what they called "rebranding." In the 1980s and early '90s, an explosive, unruly, acting-out kid or teen who was hospitalized was typically diagnosed with a conduct disorder (not considered a true mental illness in most state parity statutes). That was sufficient for his or her health plan to cover the cost of the hospitalization—even a prolonged hospitalization. As managed health care spread in the mid- to late '90s, the payment rules changed. If even a brief hospital stay was to be paid for by a health plan, nothing short of a severe diagnosis would guarantee it. Explosiveness and high-conflict in the parent-child relationship somehow became part of the clinical phenomena loosely associated with bipolar disorder.

Updiagnosing also may be responsible for the surging rates of Asperger's syndrome and autism spectrum disorder. This is the perspective of none other than Dr. Allen Frances, the person who had officially approved of Asperger's inclusion as a mental disorder in the *DSM-4*. In a recent National Public Radio interview, Dr. Frances asserted:

> In order to get specialized services, often one-to-one education, a child must have a diagnosis of Asperger's or some other autistic disorder. And so kids who previously might be considered on the boundary, eccentric, socially shy, but bright and doing well in school would mainstream into regular classes. Now if they get the diagnosis Asperger's disorder, they get into a special program where they may get $50,000 a year worth of educational services.[37]

Dr. Frances's assertion is not far-fetched when we look at the education and income levels of the parents of kids who are labeled autistic. A 2010 study out of the University of California–Davis un-

covered a peculiar phenomenon.[38] The ten locations in California
with the highest-density rates of autism happened to be areas where
more educated and high-income families lived. An extrapolation
from this finding can be made. It is well within the comfort level of
most educated, higher-income parents to interface with professionals. They may be more apt to get in action mode when their youngster shows worrisome signs of language delays, social awkwardness,
and temper tantrums. Seeking out early intervention may come
naturally to them. Pressuring educators and health-care professionals to ascribe diagnoses and advocating for their kids to receive
high-quality services might even be seen as virtuous parental actions.

It seems, then, that the way our school and mental health systems
are set up today necessarily leads to kids being assigned diagnoses to
receive the help they need. To obtain intensive and specialized services
that are attractive to parents, kids are being assigned ever-more severe diagnoses. There are many unintended consequences to this. The
mere mention of a diagnosis, especially a severe one, primes parents
and teachers to accept powerful psychoactive medications as a plausible
intervention. As discussed later, medications certainly have their place
in treating childhood problems. However, what about the financial
and health costs of putting kids on medications unnecessarily? What
if kids are left to languish on medications? Studies show that the average length of time a kid is kept on a stimulant is fifty months, with few
physician check-ins.[39]

Mental health professionals may think they are playing a benign
bureaucratic game when they attribute a more severe diagnosis than is
warranted to a kid simply to ensure that treatment and services are authorized. But once in a data bank, these diagnoses tend to follow kids.
And as we'll see, the consequences can be surprisingly problematic.

CHAPTER THREE

Casualties of Casual Diagnosing

It's rare that I find myself arguing with a kid over a diagnosis—even rarer if the kid is a teenager. Teens tend to be painfully self-conscious. They do not want to appear odd. A mental health diagnosis is not something a teenager typically flaunts. However, seventeen-year-old George was an exception. He sat across from me in my office and swore that he had bipolar disorder. The source of his self-diagnosis was a TV clip in which Dr. Drew, the host of *Loveline*, tagged Mel Gibson, the actor, as bipolar because of his outbursts of rage. George also had occasional outbursts of rage. To be certain of the accuracy of his self-diagnosis, George went online and purchased a copy of *Bipolar Disorder for Dummies*. Now George, with a dog-eared copy of *Bipolar Disorder for Dummies* at home, was pressing me, the doctor, to accept that he had this condition. The conversation went something like this:

DR. GNAULATI: *George, I think the reasons why you're experiencing so much depression, confusion, and anger are complicated. There is no single reason. You were raised to be a good Catholic boy and toed the line for years, but at the expense of so many underlying*

*feelings. Adulthood is just around the corner and I think you feel to-
tally underequipped to face it. You don't have any big future career
dreams that link up with what you are studying at school, so high
school seems totally irrelevant to you. You have begun and ended
two painful relationships with girls over the past six months. Do
you want me to go on?*

GEORGE: *But it has to be more than that. I think my uncle was bipolar. Doesn't it run in families?*

DR. GNAULATI: *I'll tell you again how I see bipolar disorder, and you
tell me if any of it applies. The short version is that it is usually a
debilitating mental illness where there could be days of sleeplessness,
boundless energy, euphoria, and a feeling like you could conquer the
world. Bipolar depression is sort of the opposite: extreme fatigue,
lethargy, and feeling completely defeated as a person.*

GEORGE: *I thought bipolar was when you could get real mad for no
reason. Anyway, I still think I have it, and I need to talk to Dr.
Hamilton about upping my meds.*

George remained unconvinced. He had already identified himself as
bipolar on his Facebook page.

As a society, we have become remarkably casual about tossing
around mental health lingo and embracing diagnoses and disorders as
if they are just faddish labels. The same company that publishes *Candy
Making for Dummies* and *Gifts from the Kitchen for Dummies* not only
publishes *Bipolar Disorder for Dummies* but also *ADD & ADHD for
Dummies, Understanding Autism for Dummies, Postpartum Depression
for Dummies*, and the *Anxiety and Depression Workbook for Dummies*, to
name but a few.

Mental health jargon has also found its way into music lyrics and
song titles. "ADHD" is the title of one of most requested songs at live
concerts by the English alternative rock band Blood Red Shoes. MC
Frontalot, a San Francisco–based hip-hop artist, has a song called
"You Got Asperger's." The flamboyant rapper Krizz Kaliko's song
"Bipolar" is so trendy that it can be downloaded as a cell-phone ring-
tone. Krizz often collaborates with Prozak, a performer on the same
Strange Music record label. Blogs and online forums are in turn rife

with fans' diagnostic speculations involving their favorite musicians. For instance, on Captain Cynic, an online discussion forum, a question was posed in October 2009: "Eminem: Schizophrenic or bipolar or both?" A respondent going by the name of Zachfrenzel replied: "I'm a pretty big Eminem listener. I got Relapse the day it came out, it is really dark. . . . I feel he works out a lot on the album. . . . As far as being mentally screwed, it's known that he's OCD and ADD which would put him statistically at a higher chance of having some sort of depression. Depression is (at least I think) bi-polar to a lesser degree."[1]

Top-rated animated television shows have dedicated entire episodes to childhood diagnoses. Although these shows deal with the subject matter in an ironic way, children don't always grasp the implied critique. The ultimate takeaway is that childhood diagnoses are simply fodder for a good laugh. In a recent episode of *South Park* crudely titled "Ass Burgers," Stan, one of the central characters, is haphazardly diagnosed with Asperger's after presenting as forlorn in the school counselor's office due to his parents' divorce. Always looking for an angle to avoid doing schoolwork, Cartman, the show's likable antihero, mishears Stan's condition as "ass burgers" and tries to pull one over on the school nurse by showing up in her office with hamburgers stuffed in his underwear.

Bart Simpson, often considered TV's iconic ADHD boy because of his impulsivity and distractibility, was officially diagnosed as such in an episode of *The Simpsons* titled "Brother's Little Helper." During a fire-safety class Bart takes off with a fire hose and floods the school gym. Principal Skinner meets with Bart's parents and recommends that he be put on a drug called Focusyn or face school expulsion. Bart becomes paranoid after taking Focusyn, steals a tank, and shoots down a Major League Baseball satellite that he is convinced is spying on everyone in town. There is a "happily ever after" ending to the story, with Bart being prescribed Ritalin, regaining his sanity, and singing a variation of the Popeye song:

> *When I can't stop my fiddlin'*
> *I just takes me Ritalin*
> *I'm poppin' and sailin', man*

Even A. A. Milne's *Winnie-the-Pooh* characters have been utilized in folksy ways to increase parents' understanding of ADHD. On the ADHD Information Library website, Winnie-the-Pooh is flagged as a classic case of the inattentive type of ADHD: "Although Pooh is very lovable, loyal and kind, he is also inattentive, sluggish, slow-moving, unmotivated. He is a classic daydreamer with brain fog. In other works we have called this 'Space Cadet' style ADHD." Tigger has "the bouncy type of ADHD . . . the classic form," and even fastidious Rabbit doesn't escape the diagnostics. He's the "Over-Focused" type of ADHD, because, mystifyingly, "Rabbit tends his garden."[2]

We are ostensibly casual, even cavalier, as a society admitting to and discussing mental health conditions; yet, paradoxically, most Americans retain negative attitudes and stereotypes about kids and teens with diagnosable conditions. In 2007, Dr. Bernice Pescosolido from Indiana University and her five-member research team released a cluster of findings on adults' perceptions of children with depression and ADHD. Thirty-three percent of adults surveyed considered a child who has ADHD as either somewhat likely or very likely to be a danger to him- or herself. Eighty-one percent thought the same thing of a depressed child. The research team summarized their findings: "Large numbers of people in the United States link children's mental health problems, particularly depression, to a potential for violence and support legally mandated treatment."[3]

A few years ago, social work expert Dr. Tally Moses took the time to really get to know fifty-six adolescents from cities across the Midwest who were diagnosed with a variety of emotional disorders. Her extensive interviews uncovered how 62 percent of them felt judged and ostracized by peers to the point of friendships often being ended.[4]

Similarly, a 2010 study out of the School of Pharmacy at the University of Maryland, headed up by Dr. Susan dosReis, revealed that 77 percent of parents who sought treatment for their child's ADHD felt stigmatized.[5] Almost half the parents cited concerns about an ADHD diagnosis possibly negatively impacting their child's self-esteem and life prospects. As we shall see, parents have good reason to give these matters due consideration.

A host of rewarding careers are potentially off-limits to young adults who have been diagnosed with a mental health condition. The Los Angeles Police Department website states: "Candidates with a history or prior diagnosis of a psychological or psychiatric condition, including learning disabilities or attention-deficit disorder, or who have been treated with psychotropic medication or therapy, will be asked to provide relevant medical records before a final psychological determination will be made. . . . In some cases these conditions/diagnoses are accompanied by functional limitations that might necessitate a psychological disqualification."[6]

Obtaining information on whether ADHD renders a young adult ineligible to join the military is a veritable turkey shoot. The best answer that the National Resource Center on ADHD can supply is "maybe." But the consensus is that any person currently taking Schedule II drugs (those regulated by the federal government because they have a high potential for abuse), like Ritalin, needs to be off it for a year or longer and demonstrate no functional impairments to be considered for active duty in the armed services. Hiring practices for government and private sector high-security jobs often involve close scrutiny of mental health records. In many states across the country, it is extremely difficult for individuals with a history of mental illness to obtain a trucking license. "Bipolar disease" is listed by the Federal Aviation Administration as a medical condition that could disqualify a person from securing a pilot's license. A mental health diagnosis is reason enough for many life and disability insurance companies to put a person in a high-risk category resulting in heftier premiums or denial of coverage altogether. The most astonishing fact by far, at least for me, is that it took a constitutional amendment in Kansas in 2010 to remove mental illness as a possible reason to negate a person's voting rights in that state; 38 percent of the voters who turned out that November 2 still wanted to keep the language in the constitution the same: "The Legislature may, by law, exclude persons from voting because of mental illness."[7]

We live in the Internet age. Guarantees of privacy and secure medical records don't always hold up. We might brush aside concerns about a diagnosis that was hastily penciled in during an office visit, forgetting it is in a data bank somewhere. However, in order for psychologists and therapists to get paid for services by insurance companies, a diagnosis has to be supplied. Electronic record and billing exchanges are pro forma in the medical and insurance industries. But their computer systems are no less vulnerable to security lapses than a network set up by a teenage computer whiz-kid. Take the spyware mishap that compromised the computers at Ohio's Akron Children's Hospital several years back. For a meager $115, Scott Graham purchased SpyAgent and installed it on the computer of a hospital employee who had been a former love interest. In just over a week, IDG News Service reported, Graham was sent more than a thousand screen messages of medical procedures and notes on sixty-two patients.[8] Then there is the more notorious security breach that occurred at Health Net's Connecticut office in 2009.[9] A portable external hard drive containing medical information on approximately 1.5 million Health Net members went unaccounted for. Connecticut attorney general Richard Blumenthal sued Health Net for improper record storage. This incident gained national attention because it was the first time a state attorney general took legal action based on HIPAA (the Health Insurance Portability and Accountability Act), the federal law passed to ensure privacy and security of medical records. These are just a few examples of illegal leaks of confidential information clients desire to keep private.

What if a kid or teen has an air of indifference about a diagnosis and discloses it on his or her Facebook page? Maybe it's a confessional announcement ("I'm bipolar, but it doesn't make me uncool. I'm still chill.") or a reference tucked away in a blog. Such liberal disclosures can be a liability in the information age. A couple of years ago, CareerBuilder.com requisitioned the services of Harris Interactive to interview 2,667 managers and human resource workers at various companies on their hiring practices.[10] Forty-five percent of them acknowledged using social-networking sites like Facebook, MySpace, Twitter, and LinkedIn to screen applicants. Thirty-five percent of the employers denied job offers to applicants based on content in their social-network sites. With the stigma most people attach to mental health conditions, a bare-your-soul pronouncement about, or even an innocuous reference to, a psychiatric disorder could close doors. In a competitive work environment, with multiple qualified applicants, employers are always looking for ways to thin out the applicants.

A mental health diagnosis is also a label. As with any label, it can define for kids their role in life. To use a term that has fallen out of fashion, it can be a "self-fulfilling prophecy." This term was coined back in the 1940s by Robert Merton. It refers to inaccurate beliefs that someone might have about a person, which that person then accepts as true. Self-fulfilling prophecies usually carry negative stereotypes and lower the expectations of the person being labeled. In general, a mental health diagnosis carries the connotation that a person can't help behaving the way he or she does because of illness. If Frank, who believes he has ADHD (or has been led to believe this by his parents, teachers, or doctor), gets up five times from the kitchen table in a span of ten minutes while doing his homework, it's not because he won't stop himself; it's because he can't stop himself. To the extent that a kid believes a diagnostic label applies to him or her, he or she is less likely to take personal ownership of and responsibility for his or her actions and his or her potential to actively and purposively strive to change. Scientific evidence backs up this claim. The teenagers in Dr. Tally Moses's interviews who were apt to self-label as psychiatrically disturbed—really buying into having a disorder—felt the most socially stigmatized, depressed, passive, and lacking in a sense of mastery over their own destiny.

As we saw with George earlier in the chapter, a mental health label can also be latched onto and coveted. It can be used as an easy narrative to explain one's behavior. For boys who struggle with fluid communication, it can be a default position that obviates the need for further communication: "Duh, I'm ADHD. I just get hyper. That's why I take meds." Such an explanation serves to cut short further discussion of an individual's behavior, steering clear of such topics as what he might do to self-calm, for example, or persevere in his attempt to complete uninteresting homework. Dr. Peter Breggin, a national spokesperson on abuses in the psychiatric profession, eloquently captured this dynamic in an article in *The Huffington Post* a few summers back: "Something more subtle occurs when we accept a psychiatric diagnosis for ourselves or a loved one. We lose empathy for ourselves and our loved ones. Instead of learning about and identifying with the sources of our emotional pain and suffering, and our failures in life, we ignore our real lives and explain ourselves away with the diagnosis."[11]

Well-intentioned mental health advocates try to reduce the stigma surrounding mental illness by framing it as a brain disease. But rightly or wrongly, as Ethan Watters put it in a *New York Times Magazine* article that was a spin-off of his book *Crazy Like Us: The Globalization of the American Psyche*: "We treat people more harshly when their problem is described in disease terms. . . . A brain made ill through biomedical or genetic abnormalities is more thoroughly broken and permanently abnormal than one made ill through life events."[12] This may explain the unfavorable reactions teachers sometimes have toward ADHD kids. Believing an ADHD kid suffers from a brain disease can engender compassion. By the same token, it can lead to a sense of futility that nothing fundamental can be done on the teacher's or the kid's part to bring about lasting change. There may be the sense that the kid's hyperactive behavior must be simply tolerated, managed, or controlled (whether through medication or behavioral methods)—not changed. This can lead to negative reactions, whether openly expressed or just ruminated on.

Some scientific evidence shows that many teachers do have unfavorable beliefs about ADHD kids. A 2010 study in the *Journal of Attention Disorders* sheds light on this.[13] A group of nearly three hundred K–12 teachers were presented with a mostly positive description of a hypothetical youngster named Katie. One group of teachers was randomly given the description with a brief reference at the end that Katie had been recently diagnosed with ADHD. The description given to another group referenced that Katie had ADHD, but was taking stimulant medication. Yet another group got the identical description of Katie without any reference to her having ADHD.

The teachers were asked to comment on Katie's behavior, IQ, and personality. They rated the ADHD-labeled Katie much less favorably than the nonlabeled Katie, even though the descriptions were otherwise identical. This was true with the ADHD-labeled Katie on stimulants as well. It is important to note that over half of the teachers in this study had received professional training on ADHD as part of their teacher education.

Rational or irrational, most people tend to think that a mental health diagnosis is something permanent. They think of it as indicating a lifelong illness that needs to be managed, something that's a hindrance to living a full life. Tragically, when a serious diagnosis like bipolar disorder truly applies, this is not far from the truth. None other than Dr. Allen Frances, one of the panel of experts commissioned to approve diagnoses on the *DSM-4*, has gone public with his concerns surrounding loosening how we define and discuss bipolar disorder. In a *Psychology Today* editorial piece, he wrote:

> The label Bipolar Disorder . . . carries considerable stigma, implying that the child will have a lifelong illness requiring lifetime treatment. The diagnosis can distort a person's life narrative, cutting off hopes of otherwise achievable ambitions. People worry about getting married, having children, or taking on stressful ambitions, jobs, or work challenges. . . . An incorrect diagnosis of Bipolar Disorder may reduce one's sense of personal responsibility for, and control over, undesirable behavior.[14]

As a society, we need to reduce the stigma of mental illness. We need to be more accepting of and offer a wide range of support to people who are truly afflicted with mental illnesses like ADHD, bipolar disorder, and autism spectrum disorder. Casually talking about and liberally ascribing these diagnoses does not help this situation. When such diagnostic phrases are bandied about nonchalantly, and questionably and liberally ascribed, we trivialize the substantial sorrow and hardship of those kids and teens who truly warrant them. This contributes to the general public's questioning the validity of mental health conditions and being less than sympathetic to those who are disabled by them.

Our culture's easygoing attitude toward discussing and assigning childhood disorders also sends the wrong message to parents as they contemplate putting and keeping their child on medication. After all, most people think that a diagnosis and a medication go hand-in-glove. If a diagnosis of bipolar disorder is no big deal, then surely use of a prescription for Seroquel, Risperdal, Abilify, or Geodon (names of so-called atypical antipsychotic medications commonly used to treat mood swings and agitation associated with bipolar disorder) is the solution and should be no big deal either. Yet, as we are about to see, all of the psychiatric medications prescribed to kids and teens have detrimental side effects that parents are often unaware of. Rarely, if ever, is a psychiatric medication a "magic bullet," pinpointing and eradicating symptoms without any unpleasant side effects.

On the one hand, if we are too casual in our approach to diagnoses and medications, there's the risk that a child will be falsely labeled and put on a powerful psychoactive drug unnecessarily, harmed by having to suffer the unpleasant side effects; on the other hand, in those cases where a diagnosis does apply, a casual attitude makes it more likely that parents will be oversold on the supposed benefits of medications and underconcerned about the potential drawbacks.

KIDS' PSYCH MEDS: THE GOOD, THE BAD, AND THE UGLY

Amphetamines (Adderall) and methylphenidates (Ritalin, Concerta, and Focalin) are by far the most commonly prescribed children's medications. They are referred to as stimulants because they are thought to stimulate neurotransmitters in the brain that improve attention and concentration, as well as impulse control. Some three million children in the United States take stimulants for ADHD, and they have been used for therapeutic purposes with youngsters for over fifty years.[15]

Stimulants are fast acting, and parents often report sudden and dramatic positive changes in the outward behavior of their medicated child. Once a stimulant goes to work on a child's brain he typically is able to sit in his seat longer, stay focused and on task, and keep from talking out of turn. The sudden and dramatic turnaround leaves many parents reasoning backwards that their child must have ADHD because of the positive effects of the stimulant medication. However, this manner of arriving at a diagnosis has been discredited, since anyone who takes a stimulant achieves quick gains in attention and concentration. This is why stimulants like Ritalin are a hot commodity on high school campuses, going by the names "Vitamin R" and "R-Ball," bought and passed around illegally by teens to enhance their homework endurance and boost their concentration on all-important tests. A recent Massachusetts Department of Public Health study found that 13 percent of six thousand high schoolers surveyed acknowledged an "illicit, unprescribed use" of Ritalin.[16]

Typical side effects of stimulant medications are appetite and sleep problems, mood swings, and heart irregularities. However, it is difficult to obtain accurate information on how often such side effects occur and how severe they are. This is because pharmaceutical companies often cherry-pick studies to promote medications that emphasize their benefits and downplay their hazards. It is estimated that almost 40 percent of studies on psychiatric medications conducted by drug companies are stashed away in the basement vault because they don't yield favorable results.[17]

What does a careful review of the research uncover about the frequency, type, and severity of stimulant side effects? In a 2010 study reported in the journal *Psychiatry*, 48 percent of kids taking a stimulant experienced side effects, 21 percent reporting them to be either very bothersome or extremely bothersome.[18] Appetite issues and slower rates of physical growth are more prominent adverse reactions than pharmaceutical companies and the medical establishment care to admit. In the highly regarded Multimodal Treatment Study of Children with Attention Deficit Hyperactivity Disorder, the average growth rate of medicated children was 2.0 cm less in height and 2.7 kg less in weight compared with unmedicated children, with no noticeable signs of any growth rebound in the medicated children three years into the study.[19] Similarly, preschoolers prescribed stimulants have been found to have annual growth rates 20 percent lower than normal for height (-1.38 cm/year) and 55 percent lower for weight (-1.32 kg/year).[20]

Even though sleep issues are formally recognized as a standard stimulant side effect, it is extremely difficult to get one's hands on information detailing the problem. This is partly because researchers rely on parents to assess the amount and quality of children's sleep, and parents happen to be poor judges of this. You really need to do controlled experiments and carefully observe the sleep of children on and off stimulants to get an accurate picture. A few years ago sleep experts in New Zealand did just that. On two separate nights in a hospital room, ADHD children were hooked up to polysomnograph equipment. During one of the nights, the children had been on Ritalin for the preceding forty-eight hours; during the other, they had been off Ritalin for that time period.[21] Their sleep patterns were closely examined and compared to a control group of nonmedicated children. All participants agreed to be caffeine-free while involved in the study. Compared to that of the nonmedicated children, and even when they were off Ritalin, the sleep onset of children on Ritalin was delayed by an average of twenty-nine minutes, and their sleep duration was shorter by an average of 1.2 hours. The authors of this well-designed study concluded that stimulant medications like Ritalin did not affect the quality of children's sleep but definitely did affect the quantity of it, resulting in the potential worsening of daytime concentration— ironically, what stimulants are administered to treat.

Over the past twenty years that I have worked with ADHD kids and their families, one of the most personally disclosed, yet least officially acknowledged, adverse reactions to using stimulants reported to me by parents pertains to negative mood states shown by their medicated children. I have heard report after report of children put on short-acting stimulants like Ritalin and Adderall becoming emotionally undone when their medication wanes in the late afternoon, turning grumpy, irritable, and even belligerent. Many parents view their medicated child's unruly behavior as evidence of them having ADHD in the first place. But parents need to consider whether their child's negativity is medication related rather than ADHD related. After all, based on one reputable study, as many as one-third of children on stimulants emotionally unravel and become moody when the effects of the medication taper off.[22]

In 2007 the FDA required stimulant makers to warn patients of the cardiovascular risks associated with taking these pills. The requirement was based on a large study revealing twenty-five cases of sudden death due to heart failure in children who had used methylphenidate or amphetamine products.[23] Experts deduced that the children likely had preexisting heart defects to begin with. The controversy resulted in the American Heart Association recommending that all children undergo an electrocardiogram to check for heart irregularities before being put on stimulant medication. There was backlash from pediatrician groups around the country because this was considered by them to be a burdensome and largely unnecessary medical procedure. A compromise was reached in which pediatricians agreed to assess for a family history of heart problems and check the heart rate and blood pressure of children before prescribing a stimulant.[24] There is merit to doctors taking these precautionary steps. Children receiving stimulants have been shown to have higher heart rates[25] and there is a 20 percent increased risk for emergency-room visits due to heart-related complaints (fainting, tachycardia, heart palpitations, hypertension) when using a stimulant.[26]

Pediatricians seem to have gotten the message. Over 90 percent of them when surveyed say they perform a routine cardiac history and physical exam before writing a script for a stimulant.[27] But, curiously, in this same survey by a team of researchers from Boston-based Tufts Medical Center, 54 percent of pediatricians did not discuss stimulant-related cardiac risks with parents. Apparently, most children being assessed for ADHD medication in the doctor's office get their heart checked, but parents accompanying them are not routinely informed as to why.

A less recognized stimulant-related adverse reaction is tic behavior. This more often than not comprises repeated eye blinking, grimacing, mouth twitching, nose wrinkling, or throat clearing. In one study, Dr. William Frankenberger, a nationally acclaimed ADHD expert, put the following question to a sample of junior high school and high school students using a stimulant for ADHD: "Do you have any tics (muscle twitches) that you did not have when you first started taking the medicine?" Thirty-five percent of the teenagers answered in the affirmative.[28] Reported rates of stimulant-related tics have even been as high as 60 percent.[29]

Parents are often convinced that ADHD medicines bolster academic achievement. It is logical to presume this to be true. If taking a stimulant results in a child staying seated in class and paying attention longer, it is natural to conclude she is more primed to learn. Direct-to-consumer ads and brochures distributed by drug companies try to capitalize on the perception that stimulants bolster academic achievement. One ad for Concerta, which appeared in the world's best-selling health, fitness, and beauty magazine, *Shape*, depicts a cherub-like boy sitting pensively at a desk with the following tidbits of information on his failed progress on a book report on US presidents streaming off to the side: "Leaves backpack on bus . . . Disruptive in library . . . Doesn't finish book . . . Teacher calls mom." Printed in the middle of well-ordered gold stars above the boy's head are the following statements: "Starts CONCERTA . . . Reads quietly in library with Matt . . . Finishes report before dinner . . . Turns in report with classmates."[30]

But what does the science tell us about any long-term academic gains from stimulant medication usage? There are few long-term studies out there, but the trend among those that do exist confirm that the academic functioning of ADHD children does not significantly improve over time with medication use. For instance, researchers conducting the Early Childhood Longitudinal Study–Kindergarten (ECL-K) followed a nationally representative sample of children from kindergarten through fifth grade and discovered no significant gains in reading and mathematics scores associated with ADHD medications.[31] And, in the decade-old Multimodal Treatment Study of Children with Attention Deficit Hyperactivity Disorder, tracking the progress of six hundred ADHD children as they enter young adulthood, the most recent data at the eight-year mark provide no real evidence of any academic benefits from taking ADHD medicine.[32] Actually, by the eight-year mark over 60 percent of the ADHD children who had been taking medication in this study discontinued it. This seems to suggest that most parents and children decide over time that the disadvantages of taking ADHD medicine eclipse the advantages, and prescriptions don't get refilled. Overall, the consensus is that stimulants help ADHD children concentrate better and act less impulsively over the short run (up to two years), although whether this translates into better academic achievement is inconclusive.

The medications most frequently prescribed for bipolar and autism spectrum disordered kids and teens are called atypical antipsychotics and include Abilify, Risperdal, Seroquel, Zyprexa, and Geodon. The name "antipsychotic" can be misleading, since even though they are utilized to treat schizophrenia-related psychotic experiences, when it comes to children and adolescents they are mainly prescribed to quell the agitation, aggressiveness, and moodiness that frequently accompany a bipolar or autism spectrum disorder diagnosis. These medications are among the most profitable ones on the market right now. Their use with children has increased sevenfold in the past decade.[33]

When you talk to parents whose child has been started on an atypical antipsychotic like Risperdal or Seroquel, they usually cite reductions in the frequency and intensity of the child's rage attacks and agitation. When this medication is working well it can make family life much more tolerable with a highly disruptive child. However, we are just now learning about the unpleasant side effects of these medications.

Weight gain is perhaps the most pernicious one. Dr. Christoph Correll of Zucker Hillside Hospital in New York investigated the weight and metabolic changes of 272 patients ranging in age from four to nineteen when put on atypical antipsychotics and discovered some alarming results. In less than eleven weeks, patients on Zyprexa gained an average of 18.7 pounds, while those on Seroquel averaged 13.5 pounds, Risperdal 11.7 pounds, and Abilify 9.7 pounds. Further, 10 to 36 percent of the patients became overweight or obese within eleven weeks.[34] In truth, little is known about the long-term metabolic risks for diabetes and hypertension due to antipsychotic-medication weight gain.

Antipsychotics have also been associated with what are called hyperprolactinemic reactions. In boys this can take the form of female-like breast development, and in girls it can delay and disrupt menstruation.

Several years ago, psychiatrists in Spain noticed that over three-quarters of the sixty-six children they were studying developed hyper-prolactinemic reactions to short-term antipsychotic medication use.[35]

The new antipsychotics are often touted as being much less likely to cause extrapyramidal side effects compared with the previous generation of such drugs. Extrapyramidal side effects usually take the form of muscle tremors, coordination problems, and jerky body movements. However, studies show that such reactions are still a real risk when using the newer antipsychotic drugs. A recent article in the journal *Psychiatry* put the rate of tremors, muscle spasms, and coordination problems among patients using atypical antipsychotics at 5–10 percent.[36] In the Spanish study cited above, nearly 38 percent of the medicated teenagers exhibited unusual physical movements.

DON'T ASK, DON'T TELL

The mind-set most doctors and their patients seem to adopt when it comes to medication side effects is one of "don't ask, don't tell." Studies show that only 20–25 percent of patients bring side effects from using stimulants and antipsychotic medicines to the attention of their doctor.[37] And an up-to-date online survey of more than one thousand parents directed by the Child Mind Institute for *Parenting* magazine found that 50 percent of parents experience doctors as downplaying the risks associated with putting kids on medication for psychiatric reasons.[38] I would argue that this tacit don't ask, don't tell arrangement is a consequence of how loose-minded and casual we have become regarding the whole enterprise of discussing, assigning, and treating childhood disorders. We want to believe that diagnoses like bipolar disorder and ADHD are so widespread among children, and the medications used to treat them so safe, that critical reflection and tell-all discussions are unessential. When our kid's doctor proposes tagging on a different type of medication to treat a symptom that we have a sneaking suspicion may be a side effect from the one originally prescribed, we want to believe the doctor knows best. (This polypharmacy approach is on the rise, and there is evidence to suggest that there's been a 150 percent increase in the use of multiclass psychotropic medications with children over the past ten years.)[39] But if we are to prevent children from being falsely diagnosed, put on an unnecessary regimen of meds, or, for that matter, put on a necessary regimen of meds where the benefits outweigh the side effects, critical reflection and tell-all discussions are precisely what are called for.

I'll end with a description by Joanna Moncrieff, author of *The Myth of the Chemical Cure*, that captures what I believe to be the ideal type of relationship that parents should strive to have with their kid's doctor around the issue of prescribing of medications. In this case, of course, "the patient" is the child and his or her parent or parents, and together with the doctor they collectively assess the efficacy of any medication:

> Instead of acting like a medical doctor, telling the patient what disease they have and what is the appropriate treatment, the psychiatrist or prescriber needs to act more as a pharmaceutical advisor. They should inform people about the range of effects a drug can induce, both those that might be useful and those that are likely to be harmful in order to help people evaluate the benefits of taking a particular drug for themselves. However, the user's experience of a drug's effects will be the key determinant of the drug's utility and thus they become a more equal partner in the consultation.[40]

CHAPTER FOUR

Abnormalizing Boys

On a rainy March morning in 2012, a statistic reported in the *Los Angeles Times* caught my eye. It was based on a study out of the Centers for Disease Control and Prevention and involved the latest prevalence rates of autism spectrum disorder in young children. An astounding one in eighty-eight kids was presumed to have this disorder. For boys, the breakdown was one in fifty-four, five times the rate for girls.[1]

Alarmed, I decided to dig around for more information on how boys' mental health and school behavior compared with that of girls'. These are some of the statistics I unearthed:

- Approximately 75 percent of students labeled emotionally disturbed and referred for special-education services are male.[2]
- Boys are more than twice as likely as girls to be diagnosed with ADHD.[3]
- First- and second-grade boys are three times more likely than their female peers to be put on medication for mental health issues.[4]
- Preschool-age boys are expelled four and a half times more often than preschool-age girls.[5]

• By age seventeen, 42 percent of boys have been suspended from school at least once, compared with 24 percent of girls.[6]

We could extrapolate from these statistics that boys are simply the more emotionally unstable or behaviorally unmanageable sex and call it a day. But a more sensible approach may be to examine whether as a society we are abnormalizing typical masculine behavior in boys.

Let's begin with boys and aggression.

When my son was twelve years old, he and his tribe of male friends hit upon a new pastime. It involved recording their favorite "kills" on *Call of Duty: Black Ops*. This is a first-person, military-style shooter video game that sold over seven million copies worldwide within twenty-four hours of its release in November 2010. The video-gamer can maneuver a special-forces soldier behind enemy lines, using an assortment of weapons and explosive devices to kill off combatants. My son excitedly recorded his most stealthy and acrobatic kills, tinkered with the graphics, added his favorite music, and posted the end products on YouTube for his friends to enjoy. His friends did likewise. The refrain I heard over and over that spring while they pursued their craft was: "Awesome kill, dude." Now, I should add that my son and his friends at that age were all boys who liked to be tucked in and kissed goodnight, to show off their flannel jammies, and to talk in baby voices about how cute their pet dogs and cats were.

Just how common is it for boys to be fascinated by aggressive acts, violence, and war? We tend to assume that boys who enjoy aggression must be antisocial. But scientists are beginning to corroborate what parents of boys observe on a daily basis: even the most well-adjusted boys derive pleasure from aggressive fantasy and play. A study out of Plymouth, England, on normally developing kids by British and American scientists confirms this. Joyce Benenson and her fellow researchers conducted open-ended, one-on-one interviews with 209 boys and 126 girls, whose ages ranged from four to nine. The kids were asked about their activities with their three favorite toys and friends. They were invited to discuss how much they liked to play childhood games like dress up and killing or catching bad guys. Fifty-three percent of the boys spontaneously mentioned using their toys to enact physical aggression, compared with 6 percent of the girls, and 39 percent of the boys spoke of being physically aggressive in their play with friends, compared with 8 percent of girls. The authors went on to caution the general public against assuming that boys who were fascinated with aggression had malfunctioning brains or were displaying abnormal behavior.[7]

It is often difficult for parents and educators to appreciate the role aggression plays in boys bonding and caring for one another. I have in mind here classic rough-and-tumble play. This is when young boys tackle and shove each other, chase and flee, shadowbox, mock wrestle, and the like. These behaviors are often frowned upon by educators and forbidden on the playground. Yet in the view of Mac Brown, a nationally recognized education professor at the University of South Carolina, rough-and-tumble play is crucial for young boys' social and emotional development. Over the span of ten days, he videotaped dozens of boys engaged in free play at a youth center. Afterward, each boy had an opportunity to sit down and review the tapes with Brown and candidly discuss his play experiences. The taped and interview data overwhelmingly support the idea that boys recognize the difference between rough-and-tumble play and real aggression. Much of the time, the boys took turns chasing and being chased, shoving and being shoved, and checking to see if real hurt was occurring or aggression was being carried too far. Laughing uproariously and putting their arms around each other after physical contact was the norm. Interestingly, there was only one minor injury requiring adult intervention during the 119 hours of videotaped rough-and-tumble play. This should dispel the notion that rough-and-tumble play always leads to somebody getting hurt. Brown then detailed the benefits of rough-and-tumble play for boys: "A place for negotiation, problem solving, fulfilling their need to belong to a group, having intimate contact with friends, experiencing friendly competition, and developing a sense of community somewhere between the warmth and closeness of family and the isolation and indifference of the adult masculine world."[8]

Sadly, young boys' normal fascination with playful aggression is being increasingly thwarted and abnormalized. In a 2010 article appearing in the *Journal of Research in Child Education*, the vast majority of pre-K teachers surveyed reported immediately stopping or redirecting the rough-and-tumble play of four-year-olds almost always or usually always.[9] Almost half of the ninety-eight teachers in the study were bent on stopping or redirecting boys' rough-and-tumble play several times a week or daily. Girls' play needed to be stopped or redirected a fraction of this time. Comments by teachers contained in the study are as revealing as they are discouraging:

> *Rough play is too dangerous—if allowed, someone is almost always hurt, so we just try to eliminate it as much as possible.*

> *At recess, the children may play chase. If it gets rough, the play is stopped. Superhero play is allowed as long as it doesn't get rough. Power Rangers are not allowed.*

> *I personally don't like play fighting and never permitted it at home with my own children. My superintendent does not allow any outside play.*

The focus in most pre-K and early elementary schools is on controlling and eliminating aggressive play in boys—not on accepting, working with, refining, and providing constructive outlets for boys' natural aggression. Peg Tyre, the author of a hard-hitting book covering this topic, *The Trouble with Boys*, put it bluntly in a recent interview:

> In the wake of Columbine, we're uncomfortable with fantasy violence and play violence so we have zero-tolerance policies. But, in many schools, zero-tolerance is taken way too far, and when a kid stretches his forefinger and goes 'pew-pew' we suddenly look at him like he's a potential Columbine. Many boys, whose natural fantasy life revolves around action and violence, start to feel like school is not for them.[10]

Peg Tyre is not exaggerating. Periodic, highly publicized school shootings do seem to have created a measure of hysteria and rigidity, driving a zero-tolerance approach to all forms of aggression, playful or otherwise, on school grounds.

Take the case of six-year-old Mason Jammer, a kindergartner at Jefferson Elementary in Iona, Michigan. On March 3, 2010, he faced a two-day suspension from school for curling his fist in the shape of a gun and pointing it at a fellow student. Apparently, little Mason had been previously warned on several occasions to curb this behavior. One gets the impression from reading the account in the *Grand Rapids Press* that Mason was given the two-day suspension for being a "repeat offender."[11] School officials went on record as saying Mason's fist-curled gun gesture made other students feel uncomfortable. Mason's mother proposed that there might be more effective ways of instructing Mason to not make a gun with his fist. She was of the opinion that an appropriate consequence would have been to deprive him of recess.

Mason's case gets to the very heart of the matter with young boys and aggression. None of the grown-ups involved mentioned how Mason's fist-qua-gun gesture might be his playful way of expressing anger at a peer. If other students felt uncomfortable, there might need to be an educational focus on helping inhibited kids skillfully handle being the object of another kid's playful aggression—the sort of right-back-at-you style that scores points with boys. Some time also could be devoted to emphasizing the difference between pretending to hurt and actually hurting. Another topic that might be explored is Mason's need for more recess time to work off aggressive energy, or his probable lack of age-appropriate access to rough-and-tumble play during recess time to indirectly work out any conflicts with fellow students he might be experiencing. Expecting Mason to smoothly talk out his angry feelings would be holding him to a standard that might come easily to the average girl, but not the average boy.

Which brings me to a subject that must be broached, even if it raises hackles in some quarters. To what degree as a society are we using standards of behavior that are typical of the average girl, but not of the average boy, to judge boys? Do we label boys as mentally unstable, behaviorally unmanageable, academically underachieving, in need of special-education services, or displaying behavior warranting school suspension just because their behavior deviates noticeably from that of the average girl?

In a sense, girl-behavior has become the standard by which we judge all kids. Nowhere is this truer than when we judge kindergarten readiness in kids. Claire Cameron Ponitz, from the Center for Advanced Study of Teaching and Learning at the University of Virginia, has dedicated her professional career to studying what contributes to kindergarten readiness in kids. According to this professor, the little ones who are destined to do well in the run-of-the-mill twenty-first-century kindergarten class are those who manifest good "self-regulation." This is a term that is bandied about a great deal these days by teachers and psychologists. It mostly refers to everyday behaviors like remembering to raise one's hand in class; wait one's turn; pay attention; listen to, recall, and follow instructions set down by teachers; and refrain from blurting out answers. These self-regulation skills have become nothing short of a prerequisite for basic functioning in the average academically oriented kindergarten across America—not to mention a prerequisite for success.

As it turns out, kindergarten-age girls are far more advanced than boys in self-regulation. A few years ago, Cameron Ponitz and her colleagues confirmed this by putting several hundred five- and six-year-old boys and girls through a type of Simon Says game called the Head-Toes-Knees-Shoulders Task. Trained research assistants rated the kids' ability to follow the correct instruction and not be thrown off by a confounding one, as when needing to touch their toes when asked to touch their heads. Curiously enough, remembering such rules as, "touch your head really means touch your toes," and actually inhibiting the urge to touch one's head and instead touching one's toes, amounts to a nifty example of good overall self-regulation. The researchers combined the results of boys' and girls' scores on the Head-Toes-Knees-Shoulders Task with parents' and teachers' ratings of these same kids' capacity to pay attention, follow directions, finish schoolwork, and stay organized. The outcome was quite remarkable. They discovered that boys were a whole year behind girls in all areas of self-regulation. By the end of kindergarten, boys were just beginning to acquire the self-regulatory skills with which girls had started the year.[12]

This self-discipline edge for girls persists on up into middle school and beyond. Look in the window of any classroom and you will rapidly witness more girls than boys paying attention to the teacher instead of daydreaming; taking notes and organizing them; and carefully reading instructions before launching into a test. Ask parents and they will tell you it's their daughters who are more likely to be burning the midnight oil to complete homework, check it for errors, and slot it into a well-kept, color-coordinated binder. On average, at every age, girls try harder in school and obtain better grades in all subjects than boys. It's not that girls are necessarily smarter. It's that they tend to "do school" better.

"Doing school" these days seems to play right into most girls' strengths—and most boys' weaknesses. Gone are the days when you could blow off a series of homework assignments throughout the semester but cram for and ace that all-important midterm exam, thus preserving a respectable grade. Getting good grades is far less about acing important tests than it used to be; it is more about keeping up with and producing quality homework—not to mention handing it in on time. In one landmark study on eighth-graders out of the University of Pennsylvania, it was shown that girls are apt to start their homework earlier in the day than boys and spend almost double the amount of time completing it. In this same study, girls' grade point averages across all subjects were higher than those of boys, even in basic and advanced math—traditional strongholds of boys. Nevertheless, boys obtained higher IQ scores than girls.[13]

Gwen Kenney-Benson, a psychology professor at Allegheny College, a liberal arts institution in Pennsylvania, would say that girls succeed over boys in school because they tend to be more mastery-oriented in their schoolwork habits. They are more apt to plan ahead, set academic goals, and put effort into achieving those goals. They are also more likely than boys to feel intrinsically satisfied with the whole enterprise of organizing their work and impressing themselves and their teachers with their efforts. On the whole, boys approach schoolwork differently. They are more performance-oriented. Studying for and taking tests taps into their competitive instincts. For many boys, tests are quests. Tests get their heart pounding. Doing well on them can be an occasion for a high-five and is a public demonstration of excellence. In contrast, Kenney-Benson and some fellow academics provide scientific evidence that shows that the stress many girls experience in test situations can artificially lower their performance, giving a false reading of their true abilities. These researchers arrive at the following overarching conclusion: "The testing situation may underestimate girls' abilities, but the classroom may underestimate boys' abilities."[14]

As the research demonstrates, we do most boys a great disservice when we tie grades more and more to staying on top of homework and pleasing teachers with demonstrations of preparation and effort. This is essentially grading them on schoolwork habits that come easier for girls, who, granted, may falter when grades are tied excessively to test scores.

Robert, a client of mine, is a prime example of a boy who loves tests but hates homework assignments. The public school he goes to is a National Blue Ribbon School and is ranked among the top ten in California. Around Valentine's Day, his eighth-grade English teacher handed out an assignment that, at first, Robert found amusing. She required all forty students in the class to design Valentine's Day cards for each other. She was emphatic about wanting them personalized. Names had to be spelled correctly and compliments written up genuinely, based on real knowledge of classmates. If personalizing the cards meant interviewing someone in the class you barely knew, so be it. Robert told me in the private confines of my office that he thought this assignment was a total joke. Each week, when he came to his therapy session with me, he ruminated on the ridiculousness of this assignment. He spoke of how there were a handful of classmates he had absolutely no interest in getting to know. He spun dozens of sarcastic compliments he wished he could have used. I told him my personal favorite was this: "Anthony, I admire the way you drill up into your nose with your finger when you pick it." Most of all, Robert was livid over the unfairness of the Valentine's Day card homework assignment being worth 100 points in the class, when the final exam was worth only 180 points.

Granted, Robert's predicament in his eighth grade English class is a rather glaring example of a type of assignment and grading practice that is female-friendly and male-unfriendly. Truth be told, it is impossible to know for sure how widespread these more female-friendly curriculum choices are in classrooms around the country. What we do know with a measure of certainty is that the teaching profession is overwhelmingly female. The latest numbers out of the National Education Association indicate that in excess of 75 percent of teachers are women.[15] This is the greatest gender imbalance in the teaching profession since the NEA began compiling such statistics forty years ago. The numbers climb when we zero in on the percentage of elementary school teachers who are female. In New York State, for example, over 90 percent of elementary school teachers are women.[16]

Obvious, yet uncomfortable, questions arise with numbers this skewed. Is what is considered normal for kids' schoolwork habits and levels of self-discipline being defined and judged primarily by women in ways that favor girls and set up heaps of struggling boys to appear emotionally troubled or learning-disordered? If so, it is clear that it is not being done in any malicious or overtly biased way, but rather as an unintended consequence of thinking and acting from within a female gender identity.

Teaching is not the only child-serving profession that is fast becoming female dominated. In 1970, about 20 percent of pediatricians were women. Today, the figure stands close to 53 percent.[17] Likewise, in 1970 women made up 20 percent of psychologists. That figure now is 72 percent.[18] An even higher number of school psychologists are female—75 percent, which is noteworthy since the primary role of school psychologists is to assess kids' learning style and behavior to detemine eligibility for special-education services.[19] Women also comprise about 80 percent of licensed clinical social workers in the United States.[20]

When kids are being evaluated to determine whether their behavior rises to the level of a clinical problem, the odds are the professional making that judgment will be a woman. If the kid is a boy, the odds also are that he will be viewed through the lens of what is normal for a girl. If he is a kindergartner who is further from the middle on the bell curve in being restless, squirmy, distractible, and aggressive, chances are this behavior will be not be perceived as an aspect of his emerging masculinity that needs to be constructively worked with and refined; instead, this behavior may be seen as evidence of a clinical problem like ADHD.

What if he is a young boy who is socially awkward, intellectually oriented, keeps to himself, and insists on communicating his detailed knowledge of subjects—other masculine traits? This behavior will have teachers and professionals wondering about high-functioning autism spectrum disorder. What if that boy is in middle or high school and tests well but yields lackluster grades because he noticeably spaces out in class, has a cluttered backpack, randomly forgets to hand in homework, or blows off collaborative group work? Chances are that boy will be viewed as an underachiever or possibly depressed, as opposed to behaving in a crudely masculine way in a girl-friendly school environment.

It is easy to be cynical about how alienated most boys feel in their school worlds. But the educational tide may be turning in ways that give boys more of a fighting chance. An example of this is what occurred several years ago at Ellis Middle School, in Austin, Minnesota.[21] Teachers realized that a sizable chunk of kids who aced tests trundled along each year getting Cs, Ds, and Fs. At the same time, about 10 percent of the students who consistently obtained As and Bs collapsed on important tests. The grading policy that existed seemed to give undue weight to organizational skills and compliant behavior, more so than to showing effectively what you know about academic material on tests. Curiously, there was no mention of this being unfair to boys. However, that was essentially the case. Grading policies were revamped. School officials smartly decided to furnish kids with two separate grades each semester. One grade was given for good work habits and citizenship, which they called a "life skills grade." A "knowledge grade" was given based on average scores across all important tests. Tests could be retaken at any point in the semester provided a student was up to date on homework. In my mind, this step merely corrects for the potential damage caused to an academic record by girls' greater propensity for test anxiety. It is the ethical step for school administrators to take.

Staff at Ellis Middle School also discontinued the hallowed practice of factoring homework into a kid's grade. Homework was framed as practice for tests. Incomplete or tardy assignments were noted but didn't lower a student's knowledge grade. The whole enterprise of severely downgrading kids for such transgressions as occasionally being late to class, blurting out answers, doodling instead of taking notes, having a messy backpack, poking the kid sitting in front of you, and forgetting to have parents sign a permission slip for a class trip was reconsidered.

These sorts of steps would keep many boys in the game at school. They are necessary to counteract the potential for less than endearing, immature masculine behaviors getting misperceived as signs of a behavior disorder.

CHAPTER FIVE

The Normalcy of Problem Behavior

One of the great delights of doing therapy with a child over the long haul is that you get to see how problems work themselves out over time. You can witness whether a kid lands on his or her feet when he or she enters young adulthood, or continues to struggle mightily. It also provides an opportunity to do a retrospective analysis as to whether a diagnosis ascribed to a kid early on really applied and to tease apart the degree to which troublesome behaviors in childhood and adolescence just reflected delayed development—or were evidence of a true, lasting disorder.

To illustrate, let me introduce Brad. Brad was fifteen years old when his parents first brought him to see me because of his unruliness. He was hot-tempered, argumentative, and willful with his parents. Conflict had become a way of life at home. Brad and his parents battled over his curfew, chores, homework completion, and excessive video gaming. They also argued about his involvement with several shady teenagers in the neighborhood. Academically, in middle school Brad had coasted. He had been mostly a straight-A student. By midsemester of his freshman year in high school, Brad was at best pulling Cs. Both of his parents were accomplished college instructors. In their minds, maintaining academic excellence was nonnegotiable.

At times, Brad's emotional outbursts nearly erupted into violence. On one occasion during a family therapy session in my office, Brad stood over his father and vociferously berated him. He demanded permission to move out of the house and live with one of his shady friends for the week. His father refused. Brad loudly threatened to punch him. I got out of my seat and stood between them. I calmly, but firmly, told Brad to back off or I was going to call the police. Thankfully, he stood down.

Then again, Brad surely was capable of violence. He had told me during an individual therapy session that he had fought off two kids in the neighborhood with a baseball bat. He was liking his "badass" reputation more and more. It was starting to go to his head. He began carrying a knife to school "just for protection." Another kid ratted him out. A school administrator discovered the knife. Brad was summarily expelled. That was midway through his junior year in high school.

Brad's high school expulsion was the catalyst for a more intensive therapeutic approach. Up until that point, I had been seeing Brad weekly for individual therapy, with bimonthly family sessions. Early on, I had referred him to a psychiatrist. All along, he was taking both Ritalin and Seroquel (a medication commonly used to treat bipolar-type agitation). He remained on these medications. I recommended to Brad's parents that he be enrolled in an intensive day program for troubled teens. Brad complied, albeit very reluctantly. He was home-schooled during the early hours of the day and dropped off at the treatment center later in the afternoon.

At the day program, Brad was expected to swear off all outside contact with friends and to socialize only with teens in the program. This was a requirement because it created a form of peer surveillance. During the intensive group-therapy sessions, the emphasis was on showing concern for each other and holding each other to high standards of conduct. If one of the students was about to go off the rails, it was just a matter of time before that kid would be outed.

Brad's parents met weekly with the other kids' parents in sessions run by a parenting coach. They found the sessions to be immensely supportive. The program functioned like a hermetic community. There was group pressure at all levels for kids to show respect for parents, maintain a sober lifestyle, and make healthy life choices. Brad stuck with the program for two years. He became a leader and a positive influence for dozens of other kids.

He also remained in weekly therapy with me the whole time. He used the sessions mainly to rant and vent about the rules in the program. Perhaps he needed this emotional experience with me to enable him to follow the rules in the program, while at the same time "saving face." Being able to verbally express and process the range of different, intense emotions he was feeling about daily events resulted in his acquiring more expressive mastery. Steadily, over time, Brad became less likely to experience intense emotion as a diffuse force that overcame him, as though he was possessed by violent emotional energies.

Brad enrolled in a local community college by the time he turned eighteen. He was determined to be a lawyer. He researched courses that would be helpful in furthering his professional ambitions. He did extremely well in community college and transferred to a prestigious university by the time he turned twenty. He secured off-campus housing, was off medications, and had a girlfriend.

Now that he was living away from home, Brad preferred to meet with me on an as-needed basis. Typically, he would call if he had had a fight with his girlfriend or needed academic advice. He knew that I had been a college professor. I functioned more like a life coach for him than a traditional psychologist. By the time he turned twenty-three, Brad was accepted into a prestigious law school. The explosive episodes and profoundly unruly behavior he had shown in his early teens were history. He could be testy, high strung, and quick tempered, but he did not exhibit any behaviors that resembled his emotional style as a teen. At this point, he had been off medications for about four years.

Readers with a working familiarity of mental health diagnoses will see the fifteen-year-old Brad as a poster child for many different disorders. ADHD and bipolar disorder might be the ones considered by the savvy diagnostician. Nevertheless, how can it be that the fifteen-year-old Brad fit the criteria for a variety of different diagnoses—thought to be long-term, brain-based, debilitating conditions—but the twenty-three-year-old Brad didn't? Is it possible that the fifteen-year-old Brad was afflicted by some combination of severe adolescent storm and stress, slow maturation, and a highly conflictual relationship with his parents, rather than having ADHD or bipolar disorder?

DISORDERED? OR SLOWER TO MATURE?

Brad's case is typical of the 35–40 percent of teenagers who are diagnosable with bipolar disorder in their mid to late teens, but who shed the diagnosis by the time they reach their mid to late twenties. In a thought-provoking study conducted by social scientists at the University of Missouri, the scholars analyzed the responses of tens of thousands of Americans who had completed an online survey on personal health matters. They concluded that an extraordinarily high number of eighteen- to twenty-four-year-olds (35–40 percent) essentially outgrow their bipolar diagnosis by the time they are twenty-five- to twenty-nine-year-olds.[1] What are we to make of this? Is there a form of "pediatric bipolar disorder" that is not a lifelong condition, but is still quite disabling when it takes hold in mid to late adolescence? This was the conclusion of these scholars. Other experts have formed an entirely new diagnosis for these preteens and teens—temper dysregulation disorder. This new *DSM-5* diagnosis is thought to apply to those who have attacks of rage several times a week. The intensity of the rage has to be in excess of what one would expect in a given situation. But how is that judgment to be made; how do we differentiate temper dysregulation disorder from an extreme case of adolescent storm and stress?

A similar controversy is brewing in the ADHD world. It relates to the work, conducted over a fifteen-year time span, of Dr. Philip Shaw and his staff at the National Institute of Mental Health.[2] They scanned the brains of 223 children and teens at three-year intervals using magnetic resonance imaging equipment. The brains of an identical number of children and teens without ADHD were scanned at similar intervals. It was discovered that the brains of the ADHD children and teens were normal but matured more slowly. To be exact, the brain development of ADHD kids and teens was about three years behind that of their non-ADHD counterparts. Dr. F. Xavier Castellenos, one of the investigators in this study, speculated that this sheds light on why ADHD kids often prefer younger playmates. He told *Los Angeles Times* reporter Denise Gellene, "They may be 11 but their brain is 8. They can't act their chronological age. This lets parents know that having younger playmates is OK and to be expected."[3]

Dr. Shaw was almost exuberant in his comments on the study findings: "I think it is good news. I think that it means that this basic brain biology is intact. All that's different is the timing of it. If ADHD was a complete deviation away from normal brain development, you'd expect the sequence to be completely disrupted. It wasn't. So we think this is pretty strong evidence that ADHD is more of a delay in brain development."[4] The implications of this NIMH study are profound. What many ADHD children and teens may need are cognitive and emotional enrichment experiences—and the passage of time.

Dr. Shaw even went on record to say that as many as three-quarters of ADHD kids outgrow the disorder as they emerge into young adulthood.[5] On the face of it, this sounds like a remarkable figure. Was Dr. Shaw speaking out of excessive enthusiasm, perhaps? There happen to be very few longitudinal studies of ADHD children from which to draw inferences. However, those that do exist point to ADHD being outgrown in high numbers. One such data set shows 95 percent of people who had ADHD as kids self-report not having it by ages nineteen to twenty-five.[6] When parent reports are utilized, instead of those by young adults, the figure slips to 66 percent. This finding was yielded by none other than Dr. Russell Barkley, one of the world's leading spokespersons on ADHD. In the scholarly article in which he published these results, he discredits the 95 percent recovery rate. He does so by questioning the accuracy of the nineteen- to twenty-five-year-olds' self-reports. Rather, in characteristic fashion, Dr. Barkley implicates their brains: "ADHD is associated with smaller areas of prefrontal cortex. . . . It is therefore reasonable to suppose that ADHD, being associated with diminished frontal lobe activity, may interfere with accurate self-appraisal."[7]

It's possible that a good number of the nineteen- to twenty-five-year-olds in Dr. Barkley's study did fudge in judging their current ADHD status—although those were probably people closer to age nineteen than to age twenty-five, who did so not because they had disordered brains but rather, more likely, immature ones. Highly reputable developmental psychologists, including Laurence Steinberg of Temple University, now believe that it is not until people enter their early to mid-twenties that skills like impulse control and avoidance of risky behavior reach full maturity.[8] Lifespan-development scholars Brent W. Roberts and Kate E. Walton at the University of Illinois even define young adulthood as twenty to forty years of age. They claim it is not until people are comfortably ensconced in this phase of their life that real personality maturation takes hold.[9]

Adult-like levels of emotional stability, goal-directedness, and productivity are acquired later in life than we may want to believe. The idea that this happens before age eighteen is fast becoming outdated. We have to be careful about upholding distorted notions of what is developmentally appropriate. There are risks associated with the fixed idea that self-control, goal-directedness, and high productivity should be well formed in the teenage years—we may pathologize and medicalize the behavior of kids who are not on that timetable.

Of course, as we've seen, imposing unrealistic developmental demands on younger kids has similar risks. An inability to wait one's turn, cooperate, follow directions, and stay focused and on task may be ADHD phenomena, but they are also developmental challenges with which all kids have to contend. Imposing greater expectations for acquisition of these skills onto little kids, at younger and younger ages, can be a setup for a false diagnosis. One well-designed study showing how almost a third of kids diagnosed as ADHD did not have the disorder when reassessed at age six prompted the authors to comment: "An approach is needed that does not unnecessarily label children whose problems are transient or expose them to treatments with potential side effects."[10] And mistaking developmental differences for organic disorder is not unique to an ADHD diagnosis. A study with autism spectrum disordered kids was conducted by Dr. Jamie Kleinman and a team of researchers. A group of seventy-seven kids with this disorder were assessed between the ages of sixteen and thirty-five months. They were then reassessed between the ages of forty-two and eighty-two months. Almost a fifth of the kids no longer merited the disorder when reassessed.[11]

We want to believe that all kids march along some developmental highway where the milestones are unchanging and reached by each kid at more or less the same chronological age. There may be some basis to this as far as kids' cognitive development goes. But in the social and emotional realm, things are very different. In this realm, kids develop at uneven rates. Knowing what feelings are appropriate to express in what situations is a talent acquired at different stages among children. So too is knowing what level of emotional intensity is socially allowable, what level of intensity of emotion will help achieve a desired social goal, or how to handle others' emotions.

Reduced mastery of these types of social and emotional challenges often underlies diagnoses such as ADHD, bipolar disorder, and Asperger's. For instance, there are young children who scream when they don't get their way, grab at toys they don't want to share, and shove peers away who suddenly enter their physical space. Sometimes reduced social and emotional mastery like this means a kid has one or more of these disorders, but sometimes it just means the kid is slower to mature. What the slower-to-mature kid then needs is not an undue diagnosis, course of medication, or special-education referral. What he or she needs may be more ordinary than that—like a better-quality preschool experience. Confidently expected, prolonged, one-on-one contact with a parent who gives him or her doses of undivided attention will also help. So too will verbal prompts and suggested word choices when a child is excessively or inappropriately mad, sad, or glad. Exemplary emotional expressiveness can be achieved when children are surrounded by kids and adults who are able to demonstrate mastery of the skills that they lack. Ample opportunities for unstructured, animated, imaginative play also are helpful.

Social and emotional maturity is not something that lies dormant inside a kid, awakened by chronological age alone. Parents who believe their ADHD kid is really a slow-maturing kid can't just sit back and count on time passing for developmental catch-up to occur. As I am trying to demonstrate throughout this book, maturation is as much an interactive process as it is something that unfolds inside a child as he or she ages. It is aided by sensitive interactions with caring parents at home. It is also aided by interactions with conscientious, reliable, patient, tactful, and affectionate—but firm—educators, coaches, counselors, ministers, priests, and so on. Maturation depends on favorable psychobiological events, and time. It also takes a village.

THE DELICATE PARENT-CHILD
ATTACHMENT DANCE

A single mom named Pamela came to visit me to talk about her five-year-old son, Elmer. Elmer was frequently oppositional with her. Pamela was climbing the executive ladder in the music entertainment industry and kept long work hours. Her client responsibilities changed from day to day. Decisions regarding Elmer's kindergarten drop-off and pickup schedule often had to be made on a moment's notice. Work travel also was part of Pamela's job. She confessed that on mornings when she was required to fly out of town, she'd sneak out of the house and have the nanny tell Elmer she'd left. She did this to avoid the "huge scenes" that erupted when Pamela informed Elmer that she'd be leaving on a business trip.

Elmer's dad was mostly uninvolved. He lived across the country. The handful of annual visits Elmer had with his dad usually occurred without planning and preparation. His dad believed surprise visits would make his time with Elmer more exciting and fun. He would telephone Pamela out of the blue to let her know he'd be in town the next day and wanted time with Elmer. Inquiries would be made about the types of toys and games Elmer was enjoying. Elmer's dad would eventually show up showering gifts on Elmer. Dad and son would take off together for the day, typically to an amusement park or the beach. Sometimes Elmer would be taken out of school for the purpose of seeing his dad. Pamela was furious that Elmer's dad was so unreliable and erratic, but she mostly hid her feelings because she was happy to have a break from parenting. Besides, on the surface, Elmer seemed to enjoy his visits with his dad. Strangely, Elmer did not exhibit any of the difficult behavior he exhibited with his mother when he was with his dad. Elmer's dad would leave as capriciously as he had arrived. For days afterwards, Elmer's behavior would be far worse than usual.

Pamela's most challenging times with Elmer were in the morning when she was trying to get him out the door and to school on time. Elmer sometimes adamantly refused to eat the breakfast he was served and pressed Pamela to make a different breakfast. At least two days a week, when it came time to leave the house, Elmer threw himself on the ground and rolled around on the floor, whining and uttering sounds using a baby voice.

Nights also were difficult. Elmer refused to take a bath unless his mother got in the tub with him. Attempts by Pamela to leave Elmer's bedside before he was sound asleep would be met with Elmer protesting loudly or getting out of bed and following her downstairs.

The kindergarten teacher reported that Elmer complained of tummy aches several days a week. He also couldn't go to the bathroom alone and often asked his teacher to stand just outside the door while he went about his business.

Pamela was open-minded and genuinely curious about child development. It was easy for me to switch into the role of parenting consultant with her, instead of therapist per se. She desired concrete advice on how I perceived Elmer's noncompliant behavior and what she could do about it. I told her that Elmer's oppositional behavior was normal *under the circumstances*; it was his desperate way of signaling that something was amiss in his attachment bond with her and his dad. I explained to Pamela that Elmer's morning antics around refusing to eat breakfast and rolling around on the floor were his way of trying to prolong his contact with her. Through no fault of her own, Pamela had found herself in a career where the scheduling demands imposed a great deal of randomness on her availability for Elmer. At the same time, Elmer's relationship with his dad was erratic. He had very little control and predictability over when and for how long he would get to see either parent. Naturally, when separations loomed, like them gearing up for the morning school drop-off, Elmer would amp up his behavior to force her to stay around longer. This was his desperate way of trying to assert some control over when and for how long he'd get to be with his mother.

As for Elmer's strange lack of difficult behavior with his dad, I suggested that this was how Elmer was adapting to his impoverished relationship with his father. The nicer, more pleasant, and more fun he could be around his dad, the more he might be able to seduce him into visiting more often. All things considered, it was safer for Elmer to let his frustrations spill out with his mother. She could be counted on to stick around—regardless of whether he was pleasant or unpleasant.

My analysis of the situation resonated with Pamela. Acting on my advice, she tried to eliminate as much randomness as possible around Elmer's pickup and drop-off times. She committed to having him picked up from the after-school program he attended by 5:00 p.m. every day. She picked Elmer up herself on Mondays, Wednesdays, and Fridays. To allow her to leave work early on these days, she worked late on Tuesdays and Thursdays and had the nanny pick Elmer up from school. On Tuesdays and Thursdays, she made sure that she was home in time for Elmer's bedtime ritual. I reassured her that, for the time being, it was wise for her to lie down with Elmer until he was sound asleep. In a near-sleep state, his anxiety would be percolating. Being there with him, and for him, on his terms during this anxious time would be very comforting. It might even undo the emotional effects of some of the troubling separation experiences he had undergone in the past. I cautioned her against sneaking out of the house on the mornings when she had to travel. Instead, Pamela was to let Elmer know of her departure plans days in advance, with frequent reminders of when she would be leaving and returning. Father-son visits would have to be redesigned. At the very least, the "surprise element" had to be banished, and Pamela should insist on a week's notice to emotionally prepare Elmer. Lastly, I proposed that Pamela spend fifteen minutes each day with Elmer playing a game of his choosing; she should be emotionally present and attentive to Elmer during this time.

Pamela's actions paid off. Within the month, Elmer was much more manageable. The frequency of his oppositional behavior had tapered off. On two occasions, he even stayed in his bed and fell asleep on his own when Pamela had to break away from the bedtime ritual to take some important phone calls.

Parents often intuitively get it when I explain how a kid's disruptive behavior can signal a need for more predictable contact and involvement. They may intuitively get it because these types of parent-child attachment dynamics are actually innate. They are hardwired in parents' and kids' brains. We have the late British psychologist Sir John Bowlby to thank for this idea. He wrote widely on how young children are experts at behaving in ways that entice, if not force, parents to be physically and emotionally present during moments of need. It is part of their evolutionary biology. In the ancestral environments in which humans lived for millennia, the survival of young kids depended greatly on their success at alerting caregivers to stay physically close by. Young children were prime targets for predators. They were also completely helpless in the face of hostile attacks by enemies and sudden, dangerous climate events. Behaviors that enticed and forced parents to stay close by were of great survival value. Kids who were less effective at making parents pay attention and come running were at risk. The better a young kid was at signaling a parent to stay close by, the greater were his or her chances of being protected when the inevitable danger struck. Bowlby called these behaviors "proximity seeking."

Some proximity-seeking behaviors that kids' brains are hardwired to perform are cute and charming. The "social smile" occurring around the first month or two of life that is universal among infants is one such example. Parents witnessing their infant's first smile are filled with awe and love. The infant's smile is nature's way of making parents bond with their infant. Bonding simply means strongly desiring to be with and around one's lovable baby.

Other proximity-seeking behaviors that kids' brains are hardwired to perform can be mildly frustrating for parents. Take "stranger anxiety." At around six months, and lingering throughout the first year of life, infants become frightened by unfamiliar people. They show a primal distrust of them. They stare at them warily. They can violently resist being left with them. This can be embarrassing for parents, especially if the stranger is a grandmother or other relative, who is essentially unknown to a child because of their infrequent visits.

Nevertheless, it is supremely normal for kids to express such stranger anxiety. Nature has equipped the child to communicate that at this age, primary caregivers are the only ones who can really be trusted and the only ones who are truly intent on keeping him or her safe.

"Pit stop" type proximity-seeking behavior by toddlers can also flummox parents. It's as if the toddler has an emotional radar system in place, tracking Mom's whereabouts at all times. As long as he or she knows Mom's location, the toddler can crawl or walk off into the living room to climb around on the couch with glee. Surges of anxiety can be dealt with by checking in, or pit-stopping, with Mom. A gentle back rub or kiss on the forehead from Mom can fill the toddler's emotional tank. Then it's off Mom's lap and back to explore the living room. Older toddlers don't need bodily pit-stops as much. A shared glance with Mom from across the room is enough to reassure them. Confidently expecting Mom to be there to check in with physically and emotionally is what lessens the child's anxiety over exploring his or her surroundings. It's what releases the kid's adventuresome spirit.

As kids age and mature, they still need a certain amount of control over the comings and goings, and emotional presence, of parents. Global distress reactions like crying, whimpering, irritation, anger, and resentment can be a kid's brain-inspired way of communicating to parents that they are preoccupied or absent too much of the time, or that separations and reunions are too sudden, random, and emotionally troubling. Such reactions also may communicate that the child feels he or she has too little say over when and for how long contact occurs with parents. Under these circumstances, global distress reactions like these can be very normal. They are nature's way of inviting and demanding corrections to the quality of attachment in a kid's relationship with his or her parents. If we medicalize them and treat them exclusively as evidence of ADHD, depression, or a mood disorder, we miss nature's call.

LESS BEAUTY SLEEP, MORE UGLY BEHAVIOR

Two Swedish sleep experts recently provided scientific backing for the notion of beauty sleep. They talked a few dozen young men and women into being photographed in a well-lit room on two different occasions in the middle of the afternoon—once after a good night's sleep and again after a period of prolonged sleep deprivation. They were carefully instructed to wear no makeup and maintain identical grooming across photo shoots. Sixty-five observers who had no idea about the sleep status of the subjects went to work rating how attractive— tired versus rested, and healthy versus unhealthy—the young men and women in the photographs looked. Lo and behold, the faces of the sleep-deprived were assessed as being less attractive, less healthy, and less rested.[12]

A good night's sleep might help you look your best. But what does science say about a bad night's sleep, or a pattern of them, for kids feeling and behaving their best? Before attacking this question, some statistics on the current sleep attitudes and behaviors of Americans will help frame the issue.

According to a Sleep in America Poll, the typical sixth grader sleeps about 8.4 hours on school nights and the typical high school senior a mere 6.9 hours.[13] Only 20 percent of teens get the recommended 9 hours of sleep nightly. Over 50 percent of this age group admit to getting insufficient amounts of sleep and feeling tired during the day. The authors point to the "awareness gap" that exists between parents and teens, since 90 percent of parents insist that their teenager gets enough sleep during at least a few nights of the school week.

What many parents also don't fully comprehend is how rapidly children's self-control and mood can deteriorate when they obtain less sleep or suffer from poor-quality sleep. Under such circumstances, kids can become very ADHD-like—mentally foggy, cranky, irritable, and overactive. In fact, one of the best-kept secrets in psychiatry is the strong correlation between ADHD and sleep problems. Depending on the study, 20–70 percent of ADHD kids have co-occurring sleep problems. In a 2009 article that appeared in the journal *Sleep*, Reut Gruber found that the seven- to eleven-year-old ADHD kids in his sample slept an average of eight hours and nineteen minutes nightly—thirty-three minutes less than the kids in his sample without ADHD.[14] Experts say kids in this age range need nine to ten hours of sleep a night. That means Gruber's ADHD kids were getting close to an hour's less sleep a night than the ideal.

Naturally, we have to wonder if a group of kids who are hyperactive are really just chronically sleep-deprived. This question was asked of Dr. Seema Adhami, a sleep expert at the University of Massachusetts Memorial Medical Center, when interviewed by the editor of the *Carlat Child Psychiatry Report*. Dr. Adhami answered in the affirmative: "Yes, absolutely—in children, hyperactivity and moodiness may be symptoms of poor sleep. Sometimes it can be hard to differentiate the cause of these symptoms, but considering sleep as a possible factor is important. For instance, if you have a child who was doing well and is going through a period of inattention, hyperactivity, moodiness, and irritability, it is worth finding out if anything has changed in regard to sleep."[15] This perspective is echoed by Jim Horne from across the Atlantic, at Great Britain's number one sleep lab, the Sleep Research Centre at Loughborough: "Children who persistently go to bed late get into hyperactive states and learning becomes a problem at school the next day."[16]

Poor sleep habits are also linked to negative moods and depression in kids. At the annual meeting of the Associated Professional Sleep Societies in 2010, Dr. Mahmood Siddique reported that high school seniors with excessive daytime sleepiness have very high rates of depressive symptoms like irritability, low motivation, and low self-worth.[17] In the Sleep in America poll mentioned above, 73 percent of teens who reported being often unhappy and tense believed that they didn't get enough sleep at night.

Sleep deprivation may be one of the most common causes of poor attention, poor concentration, and moodiness in our kids. What are we doing about it as a society? Unfortunately, we are treating it as a medical problem and turning to pills. In 2005, one-third of the $1.9 billion spent on direct-to-consumer advertising by pharmaceutical companies was related to sleep medications.[18] Doctors are writing more and more prescriptions for sleep meds for kids. Dr. Judith Owens, a sleep specialist at Hasbro Children's Hospital in Rhode Island, has followed this trend. A few years ago, she and her colleagues surveyed close to thirteen hundred members of the American Academy of Child and Adolescent Psychiatry about their treatment practices with kids presenting with sleep problems.[19] What Dr. Owens and her team found was that one in four kids presenting with sleep problems at a psychiatrist's office leave with a prescription for a sleep medication.

We know very little about how safe and effective sleep medications are for kids. As for adults, we know there are risks. The results of a Canadian study should deter anyone from casual use of sleep medications.[20] Every two years from 1994 to 2007, over fourteen thousand people aged 18 to 102 were asked about their health and lifestyle. Those using sleeping pills or anxiety medications commonly prescribed for sleep problems had a mortality rate of 15.7 percent, compared with a rate of 10.5 percent among those not using such medications. The explanations given by the author for this increased risk of death varied. Sleeping pills and antianxiety medications can lower reaction times and reduce alertness and coordination, leading to falls and accidents. They can also dampen central nervous system activity, leading to impaired judgment and, as such, an increased risk of suicide.

The safer, more obvious solutions to kids' sleep problems really boil down to three lifestyle factors: less caffeine, less screen time, and later school start times.

The older kids get, the more likely they are to reach for a soda in the refrigerator. The more often they do this, the less they sleep. That is the conclusion reached by Dr. William Warzak, who has the most current scientific data available on kids' caffeine use and sleep habits.[21] He discovered that the average daily caffeine intake of kids between the ages of five and seven is 52 mgs. This is the equivalent of one and a half twelve-ounce cans of soda every day, if that can of soda is a Coca-Cola or Pepsi; if it's a Mountain Dew, the more exact number would be one. The average daily caffeine intake of kids between the ages of eight and twelve is 109 mgs, equal to a hefty three twelve-ounce cans of Coca-Cola or Pepsi every day. Kids guzzling down sodas at that rate slept about 8.47 hours a night, anywhere from half an hour to an hour less than what is ideal. Amanda Chan, covering this newsworthy study for MSNBC, pulled no punches with the title of her piece: "Chuck the Sodas If You Want Kids to Sleep."[22]

Generation Z is the new name given to kids in the thirteen-to-eighteen age range, who have grown up in the Internet age. These are the kids who are really plugged in. We are only just learning how plugged in they actually are and how much their use of new technologies affects their health and well-being. A 2011 press release by the National Sleep Foundation offers some clues.[23] Upwards of 55 percent of Gen Z-ers surf the Internet or send/receive text messages on their cell phones within an hour before settling in to sleep. Dr. Lauren Hale, a Princeton-educated sleep expert, sees this as a major public-health concern: "The higher use of these potentially more sleep-disruptive technologies among younger generations may have serious consequences for physical health, cognitive development, and other measures of well-being."[24] She may be onto something. As it turns out, the artificial light put out by screens can trick the brain into suppressing the release of melatonin, the hormone responsible for sleep. And surfing the web or playing video games are more mentally active pursuits than watching television. It is easy to conjure up an image of a baby boomer nodding off in front of the tube. Gen Z-ers are not nodding off staring at their cell-phone screens, punching away at the keys on their laptops, or scrutinizing the television monitor wired up to their Xboxes. Their use of these more interactive technologies close to bedtime is keeping them awake. Gen Z-ers sleep an average of seven hours and twenty-six minutes on school nights, at least one and a half hours less than their bodies need.[25] Perhaps MSNBC's Amanda Chan should do a sequel to her caffeine piece with the title: "Chuck the Screen Time—An Hour before Bedtime—If You Want Kids to Sleep."

Do earlier high school start times interfere with teens getting adequate sleep and, therefore, impair their functioning? Robert Vorona, a leading doctor at Eastern Virginia Medical School, and some of his sleep medicine colleagues set about doing some detective work on this topic.[26] They studied Virginia Department of Motor Vehicles teen automobile crash rate data for 2008 and uncovered a peculiar bit of information. The teen crash rate was approximately 41 percent higher in Virginia Beach than in neighboring Chesapeake. They determined that the higher teen crash rate in Virginia Beach was probably due to high school classes there beginning at 7:20 a.m., unlike in Chesapeake, where classes began at 8:40 a.m. The Virginia Beach high schoolers were forced to get up much earlier. They were getting less sleep, and their driving suffered.

With the onset of puberty, changes in the brain result in teens not feeling sleepy until later. Most teens will start to feel sleepy up to two hours later in the evening than preteens. In technical terms, this is known as the "sleep-wake phase-delay" that occurs with puberty. However, teens still need more than nine hours of sleep a night. In the sleep squeeze play that occurs between their biology keeping them up later and their schools demanding that they get up earlier, teens sleep less. Adding just thirty minutes to the start time of high school classes in the morning can pay big cognitive and emotional dividends. That was the message contained in a study published in the July 2010 issue of the *Archives of Pediatric and Adolescent Medicine*.[27] Over two hundred ninth through twelfth graders attending a private school in Rhode Island were allowed to start school at 8:30 a.m., rather than the usual 8:00 a.m. time. The number of teens who subsequently got at least eight hours of sleep jumped from 16 percent to 55 percent. In the process, there were significant reductions in daytime sleepiness and depressive and irritable feelings. Large numbers of teens also rated themselves as more motivated to pursue schoolwork and extracurricular activities.

The science is there. When kids and teens appear mentally foggy, moody, irritable, academically unmotivated, hyperactive, and impulsive, it is important to exercise common sense and see if poor sleep might be a factor. It's perfectly normal for sleep-deprived kids to behave in these ways. If we really want to zero in on safe and effective remedies for ordinary sleep difficulties, it's crucial to see the problem as less of a medical one and more of a lifestyle and educational-policy one.

MENTAL DISORDERS? OR ANCIENT COPING MECHANISMS?

Shortly after my son's twelfth birthday, we hopped in the car and took a jaunt to the Spider Pavilion on the South Lawn of the Los Angeles Museum of Natural History. I had a hidden agenda for taking the trip. From an early age, Marcello was prone to becoming emotionally undone at the sight of spiders. It was seriously interfering with his taking on the chore my wife and I had assigned him when he turned twelve: taking out the trash. He complained bitterly that there were spiders in the garage where the trash cans were kept and that this was an unfair work detail. Miffed, I assumed that this professed fear was a ploy to get out of performing a family duty. No son of mine was going to be a slacker. The test, and possible cure, would happen at the Spider Pavilion. Marcello stood back from, but still ogled, the Brazilian tarantula housed in a brick-size, thick glass container. However, when we parted the plastic curtain flaps to enter the garden where spiders were dangling freely from myriad leggy plants and wooden rafters, Marcello became petrified and scurried to the exit.

Why are so many kids deathly afraid of spiders, snakes, the dark, open spaces, enclosed spaces, and, during infancy, strangers and sudden departures by parents? Evolutionary psychologists would say that these fears are innate and carried huge adaptive value in ancestral environments. Dr. Robin Fox, best known for founding the anthropology department at Rutgers University, has written widely on how our biosocial makeup as humans is designed to respond best to hunter-gatherer conditions that existed for over 95 percent of human history—not our contemporary automobile-filled, crowded, noisy, artificially lit, urban surrounds. In fact, many human characteristics that are currently classified as psychiatric disorders have helped us survive and cope as a species.

Thom Hartmann, the radio host, business entrepreneur, and public intellectual, caused a mild stir back in the early 1990s with his speculative, but intriguing, hunter versus farmer theory of ADHD. In a nutshell, he proposed that ADHD traits such as distractibility, impulsivity, and aggressiveness bolstered the survival of preagricultural humans. Hunters "think visually," he explained, "and if you see a flash in the darkness, or an object move from the corner of your eye, it is likely potential food or a predator."[28] Restlessness, constant visual scanning, and being amped up for quick and aggressive action happen to be attributes of fine hunters. If Ritalin had been around 150,000 years ago and taken in mass quantities, our survival as a species might have been uncertain. Traits such as patience and a flare for organizing and planning are needed more by farmers. ADHD children, Hartmann postulated, had ancestors with these hunter-enhancing traits in abundance. By implication, ADHD children do not have a mental disorder but are accidently endowed by nature with traits of their ancestors that make them good hunters but not particularly adept at sitting for long periods of time in a chalk-and-talk classroom.

The notion that ADHD produces better hunters may be more than just speculative and has some scientific backing. A few years ago, Dan Eisenberg, an anthropology graduate student from Northwestern University, curried favor with various nomadic and recently settled Ariaal tribesmen in Kenya, who allowed him to draw their blood for research purposes. Eisenberg discovered that the tribesmen with the DRD4 gene, associated with ADHD, were more physically nourished in the nomadic population, but less so in the settled one.[29] It turns out that being ADHD in actuality gives you a leg up under nomadic conditions when you have to forage and hunt but acts as a hindrance when you have to slow down and plow the soil.

ADHD traits might make kids effective hunters, but the modern American classroom is surely no African savanna. What is the solution? At the very least, it seems to me, during periods of the day all young children, and those manifesting ADHD traits in particular, need to have access to open green spaces and be given permission to run wild. This is no romantic proposition. Dedicated professors at the Human-Environment Research Laboratory at the University of Illinois have shown how ADHD children can undergo enhancements in attention and concentration after being able to romp around in outdoor green spaces and places.[30] We should not be shocked when on the grassy knolls, our ADHD hunter-type kid's pretend play gravitates toward hunting and killing, chasing and being chased, eluding capture, dominating others or being dominated by them, submitting to others, or forcing others to submit.

Anxiety is also a trait that has offered and still offers people an adaptive edge. We may be endowed by nature to be irrationally anxious, to see danger where it does not exist, until the evidence is to the contrary, rather than the reverse. It is easy to forget that catastrophic losses due to disease, war, famine, and predatory and climatic events were the norm in human history until fairly recently. In the Middle-Ages, one-fifth of women died in childbirth.[31] Perinatal infant death rates were about the same.[32] The bubonic plague in the fourteenth century wiped out an estimated 75 million people.[33] The influenza epidemic of 1918–19 killed more than the Great War—an estimated 20–40 million.[34] Until the early twentieth century, the average life expectancy hovered around age forty.[35] In classical Greece and Rome, a person was lucky to live until he or she was thirty.[36] Worrying about and anticipating the worst was a reflection of the tenuousness of human life. Our brains are designed with this protective "anticipate danger" response, even though, in actuality, the probability of catastrophic loss is, in the twenty-first century, far less than it once was.

For kids, psychological health and well-being does not entail an anxiety-free state of mind. In ancient environments, an unanxious kid was a dead kid. Better to automatically interpret that a twig blown by the wind was possibly a poisonous spider and flee, than to idly stand around during one unfortunate moment and be mortally bitten. Being psychophysiologically prepared for danger is always preferable to being unprepared. This anxious energy exists in all kids, but in some more than others. When we view anxiety as written into the human genome in this way, it should make us more tolerant of and patient with kids who worry about what lurks in the dark, what physical harm might be (but probably is not) due to weird bodily sensations, how being away from the protective presence of loved ones during times of perceived danger can be highly upsetting, and how actual and imagined creepy-crawly things send them into a tizzy.

In their severe forms, conditions like ADHD, bipolar disorder, and autism spectrum disorder disadvantage a child under most life circumstances. However, in their mild forms symptoms can wax and wane across life circumstances, sometimes to the point where the very accuracy of the diagnosis is in question. It is in these milder forms that we would do better to talk about dysfunctional behavior than disorder per se. By calling a behavior dysfunctional, we hold open the possibility for the very same behavior to be functional under different circumstances. We respect that if change is to occur, we need to address not just the behavior, but the environmental demands that contribute to its being dysfunctional—or some combination of both. For example, instead of saying, *Melinda has ADHD*, we can say, *Melinda demonstrates dysfunctional levels of impulsivity and distractibility in her current classroom, where there is an emphasis on group work, long periods of sustained silent reading, short recesses, and heavy homework requirements.* Or, instead of saying, *Brian might have bipolar disorder*, we can say, *Brian's moodiness, emotional reactivity, and explosiveness are dysfunctional when he is in conflict with people who become easily agitated in his presence, especially when he is chronically sleep-deprived.* Or, instead of saying, *Phil is probably on the spectrum*, we can say, *The degree to which Phil shuts down and socially isolates himself when he is unable to find and interact with peers who share his narrow interest in space travel is dysfunctional.*

Sometimes even small changes in a kid's environment can have a big payoff. We tend to lose sight of how environmentally sensitive kids are, especially younger ones. On any number of occasions in my practice over the years, I have seen how a mildly depressed or ADHD-like kid can be transformed by a change of teacher, a change of school, signing up for a sport, a reduced homework load, a summer abroad, a front-of-the-class seating arrangement, a month living away from home with an even-tempered aunt, or any of a host of other everyday steps.

An evolutionary perspective on children's problem behavior, curiously enough, should ease the guilty consciences of parents who believe they are to blame for their kid's difficulties. We have our ancestors to blame, or rather to credit! Calling ADHD traits and anxious behavior a form of disease is extremely disrespectful to our ancient ancestors, who got better and better over the millennia honing their behaviors to take down big game and anxiously anticipate danger so those who came after them had more of a shot at survival. Having this profoundly historical perspective makes me sit back and smile when parents come to me in my office and say, "I think I screwed up my kid."

CHAPTER SIX

ADHD? Or Childhood Narcissism at the Outer Edges?

In a typical American classroom, there are nearly as many diagnosable cases of ADHD as there are of the common cold. In 2008, researchers from the Slone Epidemiology Center at Boston University found that almost 10 percent of children use cold remedies at any given time.[1] The latest statistics out of the prestigious Centers for Disease Control and Prevention estimate that nearly one in ten school-age children have ADHD.[2]

The rising number of ADHD cases over the past four decades is staggering. In the 1970s, a mere 1 percent of kids were considered ADHD. By the 1980s, 3–5 percent was the presumed rate, with steady increases into the 1990s. One eye-opening study showed that ADHD medications were being administered to as many as 17 percent of males in two school districts in southeastern Virginia in 1995.[3]

With numbers like these, we have to wonder if aspects of the disorder parallel childhood itself. Most readers of this book will recognize the core symptoms of ADHD. After all, the disorder and its associated symptoms are practically legendary: problems listening, forgetfulness, distractibility, prematurely ending effortful tasks, excessive talking, fidgetiness, difficulties waiting one's turn, and being action-oriented. Many readers also may note that these symptoms encapsulate behaviors and tendencies that all kids seem to find challenging. So what leads parents to dismiss a hunch that their child may be having difficulty acquiring effective social skills or may be slower to mature emotionally than most other kids and instead accept a diagnosis of ADHD?

The answer may lie, at least in part, with the common procedures and clinical atmosphere in which ADHD is assessed. As I've previously discussed, conducting a sensitive and sophisticated review of a kid's life situation can be time-consuming. Most parents consult with a pediatrician about their child's problem behaviors, and yet the average length of a pediatric visit is quite short. With the clock ticking and a line of patients in the waiting room, most efficient pediatricians will be inclined to curtail and simplify the discussion about a child's behavior. That's one piece of the puzzle. Additionally, today's parents are well versed in ADHD terminology. They can easily be pressured into bypassing richer descriptions of their kid's problems and are often primed to cut to the chase, narrowly listing behaviors along the lines of the following:

Yes, Amanda is very distractible.
To say that Billy is hyperactive is an understatement.
Frank is impulsive beyond belief.

All too often, forces conspire in the doctor's office to ensure that any discussion about a child's predicament is brief, compact, and symptom-focused instead of long, explorative, and developmentally focused, as it should be. The compactness of the discussion in the doctor's office may even be reassuring to parents who are baffled and exasperated by their kid's behavior. It is easy to understand why parents may favor a sure and swift approach, with a discussion converging on checking off lists of symptoms, floating a diagnosis of ADHD, and reviewing options for medication.

CHILDHOOD NARCISSISM

In my experience, the lack of a clear understanding of normal childhood narcissism makes it difficult for parents and health-care professionals to tease apart which behaviors point to maturational delays as opposed to ADHD.

What is normal childhood narcissism? It can be boiled down to four tendencies: overconfident self-appraisals; craving recognition from others; expressions of personal entitlement; and underdeveloped empathy.

Let's start with overconfident self-appraisals. The veteran developmental psychologist David Bjorklund says the following of young children:

> Basically, young children are the Pollyannas of the world when it comes to estimating their own abilities. As the parent of any preschool child can tell you, they have an overly optimistic perspective of their own physical and mental abilities and are only minimally influenced by experiences of "failure." Preschoolers seem to truly believe that they are able to drive racing cars, use power tools, and find their way to Grandma's house all by themselves; it is only their stubborn and restricting parents who prevent them from displaying these impressive skills. These children have not fully learned the distinction between knowing about something and actually being able to do it.[4]

It is normal for preschoolers to think big and engage in magical thinking about their abilities, relatively divorced from the nature of their actual abilities. Even first graders, according to research by psychologist Deborah Stipek of the University of California at Los Angeles, believe they are "one of the smartest in the class," whether this self-assessment is valid or not.[5] The play of young children is full of references to them being all-powerful, unbeatable, and all-knowing. As most parents intuit, this overestimation of their abilities enables young children to take the necessary risks to explore and pursue activities without the shattering awareness of the feebleness of their actual abilities. For maturation to occur, kids need to get better at aligning their self-beliefs about personal accomplishments with their actual abilities. They also need to get better at realizing how a desired outcome is fundamentally connected to how much effort and commitment they put into a task. The ways in which caregivers deal with kids' successful and not-so-successful demonstrations of supposed talents have a bearing on how well kids form accurate beliefs about their true abilities. This brings us to the next ingredient of normal childhood narcissism—recognition craving.

The eminent psychoanalyst Dr. Heinz Kohut had much to say about kids' showiness and its role in the acquisition of self-esteem. He was the one who brought the concept of narcissism into the spotlight during the 1980s. He proposed that adequate handling of a kid's "grandiose-exhibitionistic needs" is one pathway toward establishing a kid's basic sense of self-worth. Consider, for example, a toddler who discovers for the first time that she can run across the living room unassisted. She brims with pride and is delighted by her masterful display. Her mood is expansive. She turns to caregivers for expressions and gestures that mirror back her sense of brilliance. Appreciation and joy shown by caregivers during these moments of exhibitionistic pride are absorbed like a sponge and become part of the child's self-experience. Such praise becomes the emotional glue that she needs to hold together a basic sense of aliveness and self-worth.

Disappointment, of course, always lurks around the corner. Kids cannot always flawlessly swing across the monkey bars or execute a perfect cartwheel. Parents are not always able to pay undivided and sensitive attention to their kids' efforts. And parents cannot, and should not, be constant sources of unqualified praise. They only need to be good enough in their recognizing efforts. It is also important that parents do not emotionally rescue their kid when his or her pride gets injured. Gushy statements aimed at putting Humpty Dumpty back together again should be avoided. When a narcissistically needy seven-year-old loses in a footrace with Joey, a neighbor, it's better to avoid saying, "You are a great runner. Your dad and I even think you'll be a wide receiver one day. Come on now. Wipe off those tears." What his emerging sense of self needs is something more like this: "Honey, I'm so sorry you lost. . . . I know how bad you must feel. . . . It feels so great to win. . . . But you know Joey is on the all-star soccer team and has been practicing his running for months. It's gonna be tough to race against him anytime soon. You can always jog with your dad on Saturday mornings. That will surely make your legs stronger, and who knows what might happen?" This sort of measured response ensures that kids will develop realistic self-appraisals. It also aids with the sort of self-talk that kids need to acquire to help them restore their self-esteem in the face of failures and setbacks, without crumbling in shame or lashing out at others because their pride has been injured.

Caregivers usually find kids' exaggerated claims of what they can perform and witness-my-brilliance moments tolerable, if not cute and amusing. However, when encountering kids' expressions of personal entitlement, most caregivers bristle. It is tempting for most caregivers to think that something is morally or medically wrong with their six-year-old when he or she stubbornly refuses to eat pasta for dinner as everyone around the table chows down with gusto, or when their five-year-old defiantly runs down the driveway rather than files into the minivan with the rest of the family to see a movie at the mall. What are we to make of such extreme attempts on the part of kids to stubbornly insist upon things going their way or to act like they deserve special attention or treatment?

One way of thinking about this involves kids' need for autonomy. They need to have a measure of control over what happens to them and around them, to have access to sources of pleasure that arouse and enliven them, and to have the means to avoid sources of pain. Throughout their childhood, kids also need a measure of control over the pace of life to which they are required to adapt, without becoming excessively understimulated or overstimulated much of the time. The proverbial "morning rush to get out the door" often sets the stage for kids' most bothersome displays of personal control. A sudden "fashion crisis" necessitating a last-minute dash to the clothes hamper, or a refusal to turn off the television and leave for school, can signify how exasperated a kid is over the mandate that he or she move at a pace that may be convenient for grown-ups but is immensely stressful for him or her. These types of defiant behaviors can also signify how effective a kid has been at pressing his or her agenda in the past, knowing parents will ultimately surrender to his or her wishes.

The final dimension of normal childhood narcissism I will discuss is empathy underdevelopment. Empathy is fundamentally an emotional experience. It involves "feeling along with others." It entails a capacity to join with others and be sensitized to their emotions. Young preschoolers often hover nearby a crying friend and make awkward attempts to be comforting. This shows a rudimentary emotional connection that is the basis of empathy. By the time kids reach age four or five, caring behaviors become much more refined. By this age, most kids are well on their way to naming and verbally elaborating upon the feelings others are manifesting. Of course, the greater the spectrum of emotions a kid is allowed to experience—and allows him- or herself to experience—the more fully he or she is able to empathize with others across a range of feeling states in a variety of emotional situations.

Maintaining a healthy degree of empathy is a balancing act. Often the struggle for young children is to be sensitized to another person's distress, anger, or excitement without becoming oversensitized or desensitized by it. When children become overly upset in the face of another kid's negative feelings, they experience what developmental psychologist Nancy Eisenberg calls a "personal distress reaction." These types of reactions tend to make kids more self-focused because, once distressed, a kid is more concerned about his or her own self-comfort instead of how to be a friend to someone in need.

Empathic concern for others and feeling connected to them makes a kid "ruthful." It dissuades a kid from engaging in "ruthless" acts of aggression. Where there is empathy, there is the experience of another's suffering as being one's own to some degree. In conflicts, the emotional pain caused by aggressive actions reverberates back to the child via empathic connection. It acts as a deterrent against wilder acts of aggression. It spurs the motivation to back off, make up, and make amends.

Empathy maturation, more often than not, is something that needs to be coaxed along by parents, caregivers, and educators. Kids should be prodded into elaborating on how they think a friend might be feeling: "Marissa has a frown on her face. How do you think calling her a witch made her feel?" They need to be reminded of the importance of sometimes putting their needs aside for the time being. At Bob's birthday party, for example, it is Bob's time to be the focus of everybody's enjoyment.

CHILDHOOD NARCISSISM AND ADHD-LIKE BEHAVIOR

When I listen carefully to how parents describe their kid's ADHD-like behavior, their descriptions often touch upon normal and not-so-normal levels of childhood narcissism of the sort I have just discussed.

If he can't solve a problem immediately, Jonah has a meltdown.

Maria is so emotional. When she's calm she can focus and get homework finished. When she's doing her drama-queen thing, forget about it. The night is a write-off.

It's bizarre. Frank insists that he is a good planner, puts his full effort into his homework, and keeps track of when his assignments are due, when all the evidence is to the contrary. Is he a pathological liar? Maybe he is suffering from amnesia or something?

It is like I am a short-order cook. Samantha will stubbornly refuse to eat pasta one night, then the next claim it is her favorite dish. On her off days, I throw together a meal so she will eat something. She is wafer-thin. Despite constant reminders to pick up her dirty clothes, I went upstairs last night only to find them strewn all over the floor. On top of this, just before bedtime she announced to me she had a science test she had not studied for. Welcome to my world!

During his regular school day when there is set structure and routines, Ernesto does fine. But in his after-school program, the daycare worker jokingly told me he acts like a Tasmanian devil. He can't handle unstructured play situations where the other kids are out there with their behavior and feelings. He seems to need a tame classroom environment where the other kids are calm and sit peacefully for him to behave right.

Evidence of childhood narcissism—overconfident self-appraisals, attention-craving, a sense of personal entitlement, empathy struggles— are nestled in these snippets I have collected over the years in my work with kids who have been brought to me because of suspected ADHD. In the pages that follow, I will painstakingly go through most of the core symptoms of ADHD and show how closely they resemble aspects of childhood narcissism. For now, let me give you a flavor of this approach by analyzing a few of the above examples.

Take Jonah's situation. He falls apart emotionally when unable to immediately master a task. One hypothesis is that this is a symptom of ADHD (not that a single indicator is positive proof of a disorder). Difficulties with retention of information needed to successfully execute a task—say, learning his multiplication tables—may predispose Jonah to tear up his math sheet and storm out of the room. However, another hypothesis is that he demonstrates a good dose of magical thinking. He believes mastering tasks should somehow be automatic—not the outcome of commitment, perseverance, and effort. Jonah's self-esteem may also be so tenuous that it fluctuates greatly. For instance, when Jonah anticipates success, he productively cruises through work, eager to receive the recognition that he expects from parents and teachers. He is on a high. He definitely feels good about himself. But in the face of challenging work, he completely shuts down, expects failure, outside criticism, and wants to just give up. He feels rotten about himself. His life sucks. Wild swings in productivity like this are sometimes evidence of nothing other than shaky self-esteem in kids. These are kids whose feeling about themselves is overly dependent on outside praise and criticism. When they experience success, they believe they are outstanding individuals, and when they experience failure, they believe they are worthless individuals.

Similarly, does Samantha exhibit the disorganization commonly seen in ADHD children or a sense of entitlement whereby she resists accommodating others, believing that others should accommodate her by giving her special dispensations?

And does Ernesto have impulse-control problems or are his emotional boundaries underdeveloped? Does he absorb the feelings of those he comes into contact with in ways that unhinge and frazzle him?

When we truly listen to parents and refrain from shoehorning their descriptions into nifty behavioral phrases, overlaps begin to emerge between what is often described as ADHD phenomena and normal childhood narcissism.

TURNING TO THE RESEARCH

I don't expect readers to be entirely satisfied with my informal proposals linking ADHD phenomena with childhood narcissism. These days, scientific findings have an exalted status—especially with ADHD. This disorder is widely considered to be neurological in nature, perhaps best left to the brain specialists to investigate with modern imaging technology. If I leave out scientific findings demonstrating linkages of the sort I am proposing, I run the risk of being perceived as just another naysayer who naively equates ADHD with childish behavior. As we shall see later in this chapter, I am not in the same camp as the pediatric neurologist Fred Baughman, who has gone on record with his rather brazen perspective: "ADHD is total, 100 percent fraud."[6] Therefore, off we go.

Let's return to Frank, introduced earlier. Frank thinks he's a good planner. According to his mother, that's plain hogwash. Frank also sees himself as focused and organized when it comes to his homework. Is he, as his mother suspects, a pathological liar? Could he be suffering from amnesia? Dr. Betsy Hoza of Purdue University would say that Frank is neither a pathological liar nor an amnesiac but given to engaging in "positive illusory bias." For years, Dr. Hoza and her colleagues have examined the peculiar habit ADHD children often have of trumping up their beliefs about themselves relative to their true abilities. Across a variety of research projects, she has discovered that ADHD children tend to believe that they are more socially and academically competent than they indeed are. They also believe their capacity for self-control is higher than what parents and teachers confirm. Dr. Hoza holds fast to the theory that ADHD kids inflate their self-images for protective reasons, because their ADHD confronts them with daily experiences of failure.[7]

But what if, in many cases, it is a child's inflated self-image that sets him or her up for failure, not ADHD per se? What if, rather than having ADHD, a child has unrealistic performance expectations that make him or her reluctant to persevere in the face of challenge or likely to abort a task at the first sign of failure? What if, instead of treating a child for ADHD, caregivers worked with the child to address his or her overconfidence? Curiously, Dr. Hoza hints at the need for "humility training" with ADHD kids to address their overly positive self-images. This same approach would be applied to problematic childhood narcissism.

In 2006, Dr. Mikaru Lasher and colleagues from Wayne State University in Michigan did what several ADHD investigators have done before and others have done since. They demonstrated to the scientific community that ADHD children tend to score very poorly on measures of empathy (showing concern for others and being aware of how one might make others feel).[8] They even took a page from the work of Dr. Hoza. It was substantiated that ADHD children's self-perceptions of empathy were inflated compared with what their parents were seeing. As cognitive psychologists, they chalked this up to the lack of cognitive flexibility shown by ADHD children. No doubt, if pushed, they would wax eloquently on ADHD children's brain deficiencies. Nonetheless, it is tempting to wonder if what they were really measuring were subtle narcissistic tendencies in children labeled ADHD. Lacking empathy and exaggerating one's skill set are, as we have seen, quintessential narcissistic traits.

ADHD kids are seldom perceived to be perfectionists. Don't perfectionists persevere until they get it right? Don't they relish looking for the devil in the details? Don't they scan their work for errors and revise, revise, revise? Such behaviors are hardly associated with ADHD. Therefore, I had to reflect thoughtfully when I uncovered a bit of scientific knowledge on ADHD kids put out by University of New Orleans psychologist Michelle Martel and her team: "We also found evidence of an unexpected rare group of youngsters with ADHD and obsessive or perfectionistic traits."[9] What are we to make of this? Actually, there is another way to think of perfectionistic traits. A kid who refuses help and persists in using an ineffective method over and over to no avail is a perfectionist. So too is a kid who avoids or fails to finish tasks that he or she cannot master easily and impeccably. Then again, there is the kid who is only motivated to perform in areas where he or she has a track record of excellence. It must be these forms of perfectionism that Dr. Martel and her colleagues found to be true of a subset of ADHD kids. But wouldn't that suggest that these particular "ADHD" kids fall on the outer edges of the continuum of normal childhood narcissism?

Let's return to the examples given in the previous section. Take Maria. She's the drama queen. Parents who think their kid has ADHD often describe scenarios at home where the kid reacts to minor setbacks with bloodcurdling screams or to modest successes with over-the-top exuberance. I can't tell you the number of times I've had parents in my office describe to me a homework scenario where their otherwise bright, thought-to-be-ADHD kid complains bitterly, writhes around on the floor, and tears up homework in a rage—all to make the homework torture stop. Of course, some of these kids truly have ADHD, and homework truly can represent a form of mental torture. But for others, dramatic displays of emotion are attempts to get out of tasks that warrant commitment, application, and effort. If their caregivers repeatedly succumb to the pressure, these kids often do not acquire the emotional self-control necessary to buckle down and do academic work independently. These emotionally dramatic kids appear on the surface as if they had ADHD. Dr. Linda Thede of the University of Colorado at Colorado Springs would probably concur. At an annual American Psychological Convention, her presentation on the thirty "ADHD" children she had rigorously studied revealed that they were more likely to have histrionic and narcissistic personality traits than non-ADHD children.[10] ("Histrionic" is a fancy clinical word referring to overly dramatic behavior intended to call attention to oneself.)

This brings us full circle. Is it possible that what appear to be ADHD symptoms are really normal narcissistic personality traits that, in high doses, can become problematic for kids? I would say this is certainly true in many, but not all, cases. Hard-to-manage narcissistic traits oftentimes overshadow and better explain what on the surface looks like can certainly lead to a diagnosis of ADHD, when it is the narcissistic traits with which educators and mental health professionals should concern themselves. As we shall see in the following pages, a diagnosis of ADHD can mask the formidable social and emotional challenges that childhood narcissism presents.

HYPERACTIVITY OR RECOGNITION- SEEKING BEHAVIOR?

Sam had a mop of curly hair and an adorable Cheshire cat smile when I met him for the first time. It was a hot June day and I remember being impressed by his little biceps bulging out from his T-shirt. His frame was large for a five-year-old. He swung the waiting-room door back and gleefully dashed down the hallway to my office. It was this impetuous behavior that had gotten him in hot water at preschool. In fact, his habit of wandering off without permission during circle time, blurting out answers before being called upon, and ignoring warnings and reprimands by the preschool director had caused concern at his school. By the time of my initial meeting with Sam, I had in my possession an Achenbach Behavior Checklist filled out by his teacher. I had computer-scored it. He'd placed in the clinically significant range for ADHD.

Within minutes, Sam insisted on having me witness karate moves that he had learned from his sensei. He kicked, twirled around, and chopped at thin air. I watched admiringly: "Sam, you are so fit and you move your body around so well!" He gobbled up my attentiveness. Noticing the handle of a rubber sword poking out of my office toy chest, he grabbed hold of it. Rather than hand me a rubber sword, he literally threw one at my feet. He motioned for me to fetch it and mock fight him. Most of Sam's verbalizations revolved around his skillfulness as a swordfighter. When I pretended to stab him, he was quick to assert that he had "infinity lives." I thought to myself, "Where does a five-year-old get an expression like that?" True to form, Sam disallowed me this same dispensation and delightedly told me that within seconds I'd be dead.

Sam is, of course, impulsive. But it wouldn't be entirely valid to conclude that Sam is merely emitting an overflow of unintentional behavioral output, as the word "impulsive" means. There is intentionality in his actions. He seems eager to display his physical prowess. He clearly needs an audience. He seems bent on eliciting recognition from me. Herein lies the dilemma with kids like Sam. When we closely scrutinize the social contexts in which hyperactive/impulsive behavior occurs, as well as the underlying intentions of the child, we frequently find that the behaviors are benign attempts to show off how physically effective one's body is and have this sensitively witnessed. When impulsive acts are in reality exhibitionistic acts, they are intended to be witnessed in some public, emotionally rewarding way. Adults often forget how much of young kids' egos, especially boys' egos, is wrapped up in what can be done with the body, no matter how goofy or obnoxious this might appear. For kids to be anchored in their bodies and feel decisive in their movements, they need outside recognition during these showy demonstrations. It's the approving gleam in the eyes of those watching that solidifies a kid's sense of personal effectiveness and self-worth.

The supposedly hyperactive kid who is caught goofing off, clowning around, acting silly, and generally drawing attention to him- or herself may be manifesting yearnings to be seen, heard, and noticed. It is probably this phenomenon that makes pundits remark how we should be talking about deficit in attention disorder (DAD), rather than attention deficit disorder (ADD)! It is ironic that the acronym for deficit in attention disorder is DAD. For kids, especially boys, it is from Dad that pride and recognition are really needed to fortify the body self.

The kid who seems especially needful of attention may be the kid whose enthusiastic displays of mastery have been regularly met with rejection, indifference, or overindulgence by caregivers. This leads to what Heinz Kohut, the originator of modern narcissism theory, called "narcissistic vulnerabilities." The developmental conditions are ripe for the kid to become more stubborn, cunning, demanding, and desperate in his or her attempts to elicit or extract recognition from others. The kid who has been deprived of needed recognition, or routinely meets with too little warmth and appreciation from key adults in her life, may acquire a habit of holding out emotionally. Last-ditch efforts are frequently made by a child in the belief that, finally, a parent, teacher, or big brother will pay attention. What appears on the surface like impulsive behavior—always waving a raised hand and making vocalizations in attempts to be called on by the teacher—might reflect how desperate she is to be thought of as special and important. On the other hand, the kid who is used to an overgenerous outpouring of praise by caregivers can resent it when others don't see him or her as brilliant.

Either way, these narcissistically vulnerable kids are the ones who can be misperceived as ADHD. These are the kids who have considerable difficulty being "one of the gang" in the average classroom, where rules and regulations are set up to maximize learning for groups of students. These are the kids who get emotionally triggered when forced to share the teacher's attention with others. At home, their ego needs might be front and center and they thus expect to be front and center in their teacher's eyes; or at home, their ego needs might be far from front and center and they desperately need to be front and center in their teacher's eyes.

ADHD-type behavior abounds in these kids. Blurting out answers before being called on can reflect their sense that they are special and should not have to wait to be recognized. This habit, unpopular with teachers, also can reflect a desperate need to be seen as knowledgeable.

Attention-seeking behaviors can also serve to elevate a child's social cachet among peers. A sideways glance or fleeting chuckle from a classmate, especially a popular one, in response to a kid's "taking the dare" or engaging in risk-taking behavior can be a huge ego boost—something narcissistically vulnerable kids are always seeking.

Back-talking, talking out of turn, talking over people, talking off-topic, or simply talking too much can speak to how much a kid needs, or expects, to be heard. I once had a cocky kid come to see me after getting in hot water due to making an offhanded comment during a classroom discussion in the aftermath of the World Trade Center attack: "9/11—isn't that a Porsche?" His teacher had reached her breaking point. She told me over the phone: "This boy is impulsive beyond belief." Strictly seeing this as evidence of hyperactivity or impulsivity misses the point entirely.

Expertly twirling a pencil instead of completing a math assignment or suddenly aborting a Lego construction project to perform cartwheels can be the emotionally vulnerable kid's way of grasping at a tried-and-true talent, no matter how inconsequential. Displaying talent in such moments readily elevates his or her feeling of self-worth in the face of a task carrying the potential for failure.

Problems waiting one's turn can be due largely to difficulties managing the potential euphoria or emotional deflation swirling around in situations where emotionally vulnerable kids are called upon to show their stuff. A kid who frequently cuts in line to shoot hoops on the playground (and thereby slowly becomes socially exiled by peers) might be a kid who, once again, either desperately needs the accolades or arrogantly expects them. These kids can get emotionally undone by the anticipatory elation or deflation associated with winning and losing. They can also get emotionally carried away by the intense pride they feel over outdoing rivals or the intense envy they feel over being outperformed by rivals.

Needless to say, as parents, educators, and mental health professionals, we have to get smarter at detecting when a kid's hyperactive behavior belies emotional vulnerabilities. If we reduce the latter to the former, we completely miss the boat. These kids are demanding not because they have ADHD. They are demanding because they need or expect to be seen as narcissistically vulnerable or extra special.

FAILING TO FINISH TASKS OR TROUBLE PERSISTING IN THE FACE OF OVERCONFIDENT EXPECTATIONS?

Malcolm Gladwell, the darling of hard workers everywhere, didn't know he was an antinarcissist when he coined the "10,000-Hour Rule." In his blockbuster book *Outliers: The Story of Success*, he dispelled the myth that success is due to pure genius or innate ability.[11] His alternative viewpoint was a humble one: put in somewhere in the region of ten thousand hours of practice at what you want to excel at and you have a shot at success. It also helps to be in the right place at the right time around people who are well positioned to make things go right for you. So much for simply willing success to happen, or feeling entitled to success without putting in the effort. Of course, there are a select group of people who will stop at nothing to achieve greatness. They zealously apply themselves year in and year out. It's as if they fear they will rapidly decompose into a nobody if they don't keep putting in the hours to become or remain a somebody. That too is a type of narcissism, but not the sort that I think gets wrongly labeled ADHD, as we shall see.

Let's go with Gladwell's logic. How many hours of concerted application would it take for the average kid to rise to the top in any academic subject or athletic pursuit? Assuming he or she enters kindergarten at age five and graduates high school at age eighteen, that would be 769 hours a year, 64 hours a month, or 2 hours a day, give or take. And that's for just one subject or pursuit!

By happenstance, the kid also would need to endear him- or herself to mentors who could further his or her ambitions. Any such mentors would have had to have put in their ten thousand hours to be in a position of genuine mentorship. And so the wheel turns. Granted, to take these numbers and propositions too literally would be bogus science. I am mostly trying to make a point, albeit in a roundabout way, that to be successful at anything requires some combination of grit, perseverance, hanging in during the boring spells, and endearing oneself to others who happen to have advanced themselves in your chosen pursuit. These are qualities with which ADHD kids struggle. They also are qualities that don't come easily for kids with narcissistic traits.

On his official website, the ADHD guru Dr. Russell Barkley defines one of the hallmark symptoms of ADHD as follows:

> Poor sustained attention or persistence of effort to tasks. This problem often arises when the individual is assigned boring, tedious, protracted, or repetitive activities that lack intrinsic appeal to the person. They often fail to show the same level of persistence, "stick-to-it-iveness," motivation and will power of others their age when uninteresting yet important tasks must be performed. They often report becoming easily bored with such tasks and consequently shift from one uncompleted activity to another without completing these activities. Loss of concentration during tedious, boring, or protracted tasks is commonplace, as is an

ability to return to their task on which they were working should they be unexpectedly interrupted. They may also have problems with completing routine assignments without direct supervision, being unable to stay on task during independent work.[12]

Buried in his book, *Taking Charge of ADHD: The Complete, Authoritative Guide for Parents*, Dr. Barkley locates the cause of this symptom, and others making up ADHD, in the brain, in particular "the orbital-frontal region, and its many connections through a pathway of nerve fibers into a structure called the caudate nucleus (which is part of the striatum), which itself connects further back into an area at the back part of the brain known as the cerebellum."[13] Who wouldn't be impressed and defer to the expert?

Yet when we widen the lens and reread his definition of this core symptom of ADHD, other causal hypotheses pop out. Viewed through another lens, Dr. Barkley has provided us with a marvelous description of kids whose sense of grandiosity and entitlement render them unproductive.

A propensity to suddenly end a difficult task simply reflects, at times, grandiosity on the part of a kid. These are the kids who abstain from and abort tasks that cannot be immediately mastered. These are the kids whose emotional life stance reflects the anthem "I will pull back from, or refuse to play, any game at which I cannot be an easy champion." They may have narrow domains in which they naturally excel and rely on to derive a sense of self-importance. But they always top out and reach a plateau because they resist the extra practice and effort required to go from being good at something to being great at it. Domains falling outside of their natural abilities, or that are not loaded for pleasure and easy ego boosts, are avoided or approached in a way that is rushed.

Kids with hard-edged grandiosity, who have a sense of conviction about their own specialness, expect to know things without having to learn them. They also cannot fully accept deep down inside how in order to be considered knowledgeable, they have to show what they know on tests, homework, and via classroom presentations. Having to "show their work" on math problems is a bummer. Teachers, they believe, should just plain accept that they're knowledgeable. Also, a trial-and-error approach to learning is anathema because the whole idea of failures and errors may not square with such kids' larger-than-life self-image.

Kids with soft-edged grandiosity, who fluctuate back and forth from feeling extra special to feeling unspecial, may be overreliant upon great achievements to buttress their feeble sense of self. One minute, the kids are whipping through math problems, swelling up with pride over how well-versed they are, emotionally fueled by a teacher's overt praise. The next minute, such kids' productive output comes to a grinding halt because they are stumped by one math problem: heck, that could mean the difference between an A and a B on an upcoming quiz. The whole enterprise of making errors and either shaking them off or learning from them is just too emotionally painful. A failed math quiz means that they are failures as individuals. Zoning out, being mentally preoccupied, drumming their fingers on the desk, in short, acting ADHD become a desperate means to cope with a failure experience.

DISORGANIZATION? OR MAGICAL THINKING?

Right before midsemester grades are released, my business booms. This is the time of reckoning for those kids who are amazingly adept at magical thinking. In a quasi delusional way, they wholeheartedly believe that they had been keeping pace with the work. They usually have their parents convinced. The midsemester report card becomes the ultimate reality check. When it is released, there's no fanfare. The kids express surprise or disbelief. The parents feel lied to. The kids resent being called liars. They were not consciously lying each time they swore the homework was done. They were just oddly emotionally detached from it all, mouthing words. That's when I get called.

Marco, a sixth grader, is one such kid. Handsome and articulate, he has definite swagger. When I met him for the first time, he addressed me with, "Whaaassupp, dude?" I rebutted: "What's up is you're in deep doo-doo." Piecing together what Marco and his parents told me, as well as the information his teachers e-mailed me, the story of what was up with Marco was an all-too-familiar one. He had started out the school year strong, acing some key assignments. For weeks thereafter, he had rested on his laurels, replaying these successes in his head anytime he had doubts about whether his grades might be slipping. Because he was a sixth grader, his teachers expected him to self-monitor his homework. Weeks would pass between Marco handing in incomplete or inadequate homework and him obtaining concrete feedback from teachers. With the long gaps between feedback, he simply detached more and more from any reality-based notions of how his grades were going. In class, he frequently appeared bored and distracted. At home, his parents were on him to read more.

On the surface, Marco looks like he has ADHD. But the real issue is his magical thinking, his capacity to maintain a state of mind where he thinks very highly of his own abilities, despite bountiful evidence to the contrary—in short, his capacity for "positive illusory bias."

Another intriguing pattern of Marco's was his penchant for doing well on tests, yet leaving homework undone, or failing to hand it in— even when it was completed. The latter is often seen as a red flag for ADHD. And sometimes it is. Nevertheless, I have learned over the years that the pattern of does-well-on-tests/does-poorly-on-homework often goes hand in hand with—surprise, surprise—childhood narcis- sism. There may be glory in studying hard for and acing a test, but there is no glory in the monotonous grind of churning out homework. It can be adventurous and quest-like to cram for a test and rush to class, heart thumping, ready to show what you know in such a public way. Whipping through a test or in-class assignment and being one of the first to finish—even though speed might have compromised quality— confidently strutting to the teacher's desk to turn in finished work, can be a high for kids. But planning and tracking what homework is due when, and trundling forth in a daze each morning to slot it away on the teacher's desk—where it will likely not be handed back for weeks—is ever so private and does not exactly inspire chest pounding.

The relatively small, private victories associated with doing well on menial homework assignments are not particularly important to kids like Marco, who derive little ego satisfaction from such efforts. They want the big payoff that comes with doing well on a midterm or final. That's something about which they can brag. That's something that can be floating around in the forefront of your consciousness allowing you to get a good night's sleep, when in the back of your mind you know the homework Ds are down the pike.

FORGETFULNESS? OR WHAT'S-THE-POINT-OF-PRACTICING SYNDROME?

ADHD terminology has crept so completely into common parlance that I fully expect baby boomers heading into their twilight years to talk about "ADD moments" rather than "senior moments" when they misplace their keys. But not all moments of forgetfulness are due to ADD or to age-related cognitive decline. Forgetfulness can also be the outcome of resisting immersion in and repetitive exposure to subject matter—particularly if that subject matter holds little personal interest for an individual. If a kid spaces out all the time in history class and fails to remember that during George Washington's presidency, for example, five states were added to the union—North Carolina, Rhode Island, Vermont, Kentucky, and Tennessee—it doesn't necessarily mean that he or she's in the ADHD red zone. It could mean that the kid is simply academically disaffected.

Reenter Marco, the sixth-grade client of mine with good looks and swagger. If only Marco's litany of complaints about school was new to me: "Why study all those dead guys?"; "I'm not planning on going to Cal Tech, so why do I have to memorize the periodic tables?"; "Where is knowing algebra going to get me in life?"; "I don't see why I have to show my work in math. Isn't it enough just to get the right answer?"; "My English teacher is boring. She won't let me read *Calvin and Hobbes* during sustained silent reading time."

Curiously, Marco has an encyclopedic knowledge of the weaponry in his favorite Xbox 360 game, *Call of Duty: Modern Warfare 2*, affectionately known to preteens around the world as COD. He is eminently able to rattle off facts about M4 carbines, SCAR-Hs, and TAR-21s. Not surprisingly, this was subject matter he had immersed himself in and to which he had repetitive exposure—so much so that he had nicknamed himself "the COD Father."

Dr. Daniel Willingham, a leading cognitive scientist and psychology professor at the University of Virginia, boldly states: "It is virtually impossible to become proficient at a mental task without extended practice."[14] In his thoroughly practical book, *Why Don't Students Like School?*, he persuasively argues that there is only so much room in children's working memory, the brain area responsible for deep thinking. For space to open up in working memory allowing for more creative and deeper thinking, basic ideas and mental functions have to become automatic. For them to become automatic, they have to be practiced over and over. Take the example of a girl learning to play tennis. If she is to master a good serve, she cannot be constantly reminding herself to bring the racket all the way behind her back. Practice makes this step automatic rather than something she consciously brings to mind when she serves; that way she can run other thoughts through her mind that improve her game, such as serving away from where her opponent is standing or imagining where she will best reposition herself once she has served.

As we have seen, it is often proposed that ADHD kids have deficits in working memory due to brain abnormalities. But we cannot overlook how deficits in working memory also are due to overconfident kids resisting the sort of practice that makes basic knowledge automatic, freeing up working memory to work more efficiently and complexly.

We often get romantic about education, saying kids need to find themselves at school. But maybe kids like Marco need to focus more on losing themselves in their education. What I mean here is overcoming their narcissism and connecting to people, places, and things outside their own narrow comfort zones. They need to get used to the idea that speed-reading is no substitute for actual studying. It hardly leads to consolidation of information. Information superficially grazed from a text will evaporate fast. Overconfidence leads to inadequate planning, studying, and preparing. It leads to a forgetful mind.

ARE RISING RATES OF ADHD AND NARCISSISM RELATED?

The story of Steven Slater, the JetBlue flight attendant who was dubbed a working-class hero back in August 2010 because of the dramatic fashion in which he quit his job, is proof positive of how accepting of narcissistic behavior Americans have become. Disgruntled because of a run-in with a passenger, Slater got on the plane's PA system upon landing at JFK Airport and, according to the *New York Daily News*, yelled: "To the f--king a--hole who told me to f--k off, it's been a good 28 years. I've had it. That's it." He then activated the emergency chute, helped himself to two beers from the beverage cart, and slid down the chute out onto the tarmac.[15] Within weeks, he had a Facebook fan page with over 210,000 members. A Steven Slater Legal Defense Fund raised thousands of dollars for his defense; after all, his gallant actions resulted in charges of criminal mischief, reckless endangerment, and trespassing.

The facts of the case did not dampen Mr. Slater's popularity. At thirty-eight years old, he could hardly have had a twenty-eight-year career run as a flight attendant. The *New York Daily News* reported that another passenger on the same flight had asked Mr. Slater for a towel to clean up some spilled coffee only to find him "roll his eyes in a rude manner," then grunt, "No, maybe when we get in the air. I need to take care of myself first, honey."[16] The danger to his fellow workers on the tarmac posed by activating the emergency chute may have been lost on Mr. Slater but not on JetBlue officials, who reminded the public that "slides deploy extremely quickly, with enough force to kill a person" and "slides can be as dangerous as a gun."[17]

Setting aside my armchair presuppositions about the Steven Slater incident, what do social scientists have to say about the rise in narcissism in America? It may go against the grain, but the current worry of parents, according to Drs. Jean Twenge and Keith Campbell, authors of *The Narcissism Epidemic: Living in the Age of Entitlement*, should not center on kids and teens having too little self-esteem but too much of it. They cite numerous studies conducted by themselves and other experts uncovering the steady increase in narcissism in the United States over the past several decades.[18] One poll they mention involves 93 percent of middle school students in 2000 scoring higher on measures of self-esteem than their same-aged peers did in 1980. Another indicates that one-third of current high schoolers are "completely satisfied with who they are" compared to one-quarter endorsing this same statement back in 1975. Yet another shows that 50 percent of recent high schoolers believe they are capable of attending medical, law, dental, or graduate school, twice the number of students who believed similarly in the 1970s.

Many college students now believe that good grades are more of an entitlement than something for which to strive. In a 2008 study mentioned by Drs. Twenge and Campbell, two-thirds of college students polled claimed they were deserving of leniency in a professor's grading policy just for trying hard. One-third thought that by simply attending class, they should procure a B grade. Remarkably, one-third were of the opinion that they should be able to reschedule a final exam if it conflicted with their vacation plans. Present-day teenagers apparently think very highly of themselves. Ninety-one percent view themselves as "responsible," 74 percent as "physically attractive," and 79 percent as "very intelligent."

This begs the question: Is too much self-esteem a bad thing? The straightforward answer is yes. The line between too much self-esteem and unhealthy narcissism is a thin one. This is when kids and teens stubbornly retain beliefs about their own abilities that are not backed up with successful accomplishments achieved through commitment and effort; feel entitled to special consideration and react negatively when they don't get it; feel entitled to easy successes and react negatively when held accountable for poor performance; are more intent on elevating their social status and reputations than building wholesome and loving relationships; and dismiss appropriate criticism from adults as being due to adults' faulty or outmoded thinking rather than a valid assessment of their shortcomings, thereby acknowledging mistakes and learning from them.

Curiously, the rise in narcissism since the 1970s parallels the upsurge in diagnosable cases of ADHD. If you recall from earlier in the chapter, only 1 percent of kids in the 1970s warranted an ADHD diagnosis. Present-day numbers range from 5 to 10 percent and even higher. What are we to make of this increase? It is tempting to speculate that at an underlying level, in many cases, ADHD and narcissism are really the same phenomenon.

BE STRAIGHT WITH US: DOES ADHD EXIST?

When my lithe, quick-acting ten-year-old client Paula rifles through my office cupboards without asking, I'm not terribly annoyed. She has ADHD. However, when my sparky, bumptious seven-year-old client Frank engages in the same behavior, I get somewhat irked. He has a narcissistic flavor to his budding personality. They both know my office rule: no going through my cupboards without asking. Yet they both perpetually violate it. Based on behavior checklists I had their parents and teachers complete, both fit the criteria for ADHD. Yet in my eyes, Paula has it and Frank doesn't.

So what is it about Paula that makes her a bona fide case of ADHD? Her actions *feel* undeniably impulsive to me. It often does not occur to me to reflect on her motives when she behaves impulsively. For instance, Paula has a problem with compulsive stealing. On many occasions, I have had to intervene with her because she has stolen something shiny or colorful at school or at a friend's house. Typically, it is an object that is out in the open and ready at hand, not something hidden away that requires sneakiness to procure. She seems to steal simply because an object has the potential to stimulate her senses and can be had with immediacy. When she steals it is as if she is utterly oblivious to the expected consequences. A look of genuine confusion crosses her face when I confront her with this unacceptable behavior. It takes me framing her stealing as a misdeed for her to actually experience it in any palpable way as a misdeed. She usually does not make excuses for her behavior, show outward signs of guilt or shame, or appear manifestly upset. She mostly wants to change the subject and talk about something else, not really appreciating what all the fuss is about.

Compare this to similar behavior on the part of Frank. At the end of our play-therapy sessions, Frank and I have a fun routine where I promise to give him two candies if he helps with cleanup. Most of the time, he pleads with me to give him three or four. I usually hold my ground, and he usually complies, though displaying more than a measure of frustration. On several occasions, I caught him taking four candies while my back was turned, slipping two into his pocket while watching me turn away to close the cupboard door where I keep my candy jar. We have a rule that if he takes more than two candies without permission, he is prohibited from having any candies that day. When I enforce this rule, he tends to erupt in anger, accusing me of being mean and refusing to leave the office until I give him at least one candy.

The difference between Paula and Frank is that Frank steals with apparent knowledge of the expected consequences, believing that if he puts up enough of a fracas the consequences will somehow not be enforced. When confronted with his misdeed, he does not look confused but mobilizes to make excuses for his behavior, offers a quick apology, and hopes to have the whole matter overlooked or anticipates how he might get around the consequences. In short, his actions feel to me to be motivated by a narcissistic agenda whereby I should surrender to his wishes because he desperately needs things to go his way.

Another example will help distinguish signs of true ADHD. Frank and Paula are both in the habit of ending the games we play in the office midstream and jumping around from activity to activity. However, what motivates their behavior feels qualitatively different to me. Frank hates to lose. If he is behind in goals at foosball, or cannot knock down cardboard targets easily with the Nerf guns in my office or win handily playing cards, he is prone to make sudden, unilateral decisions to end a game or activity and start up a new one. His behavior seems rich with motives to me. He is trying to keep alive the fantasy that he should be an automatic champion at whatever he pursues. Ending a game or activity suddenly because he is losing is his way of keeping himself from being flooded with feelings of shame and frustration. Switching over to a game or activity that elevates his self-esteem shows how radically his self-esteem can fluctuate based on winning and losing.

When Paula ends or flits between games and activities abruptly, the context is not one of her self-esteem being on the line. She may become restless because she is cognitively unable to follow the rules or has trouble keeping them in her short-term memory. The attraction of a different game in these moments is often based on her having played it a bunch of times and therefore being proficient at following its rules. Another game may simply appear more stimulating to her or may have caught her eye from across the room. Neither pride nor shame motivates her actions in any obvious way.

Even Frank and Paula's overactivity feels different to me. It seems important to Frank that I be an audience who witnesses his jumping skills, boxing abilities, or prowess at wielding a rubber sword. He seems to thrive on my emotional involvement during these behavioral demonstrations, wanting me to recognize his physical adeptness. My caring gaze in these moments matters to him. When Paula is overactive, she is moderately unaware of my presence in the room. She does not keep eye contact, appears mentally busy and physically overstimulated, needing to stay active to achieve some greater body-comfort level.

So, yes, like Russell Barkley, the leading ADHD expert, I do believe that "ADHD is real, a real disorder, a real problem, often a real obstacle."[19] ADHD can have lifelong, debilitating effects, and it is a diagnosis that should not be ascribed casually to kids. Medications are often necessary to afford the ADHD kid a more functional life. But, as we saw earlier in the book, medications frequently have unpleasant side effects. An ADHD diagnosis should be accurate to warrant a kid taking medication despite these unpleasant side effects.

That said, it is my contention that ADHD is definitely overdiagnosed. It is overdiagnosed because we are often not sophisticated enough in teasing apart what problem behavior in children is due to narcissistic struggles and what is evidence of ADHD, defaulting too much of the time to explanations favoring the latter. As parents, educators, and mental health professionals, we need to become far more *psychological* and far less *neurological* in our thinking when we encounter ADHD-like behavior in kids. As I have tried to show in this chapter, oftentimes ADHD symptoms stem from common narcissistic traits that all children possess to a greater or lesser degree. If we wrongly apply the label ADHD, legions of kids will be deprived of the educational, therapeutic, and parenting interventions necessary to assist them with building more realistic self-images and greater empathy skills, and with forming academic expectations based on effortful application.

CHAPTER SEVEN

Bipolar Disorder? Or Teenage Storm and Stress Twenty-First-Century Style?

"I've lost the son I knew," Martha stated. As she spoke, her thirteen-year-old son, Joseph, sat on the farthest edge of the couch in my office. The communication in their relationship had deteriorated. Ordinarily, Joseph was a talented student. He was now pulling Cs. Joseph showed all the unmistakable signs of early adolescence. His eyes peered at me through hair that covered most of his face, which was blotchy in places and peppered with acne. He had a full mouth of braces. His voice cracked when he spoke. Joseph exuded awkwardness and sullenness.

I asked Martha the usual questions: Is Joseph unmotivated in general or just when it comes to schoolwork? Does he have friends? Is he sociable? How does he get along with his father? His brothers? Martha painted a picture of Joseph as a boy with a split personality. At home, he complained endlessly of boredom and cloistered himself in his room playing video games and surfing the net. His curt answers to her questions guaranteed that conversations came to a grinding halt. The boy who had once been affectionate and chatty with her was now standoff-ish and close-lipped.

Yet when she observed him in public around his friends, Joseph was lively and talkative. Indeed, Martha worried about Joseph's immature behavior with his friends, as well as with his younger brothers. I pressed her for examples. Martha shared an incident in which Joseph had wildly chased two of his friends around a car in the parking lot at school, eventually pinning one of them down with his knees, then farting in his face. There were countless examples of Joseph "taking it too far" with his younger brothers in the swimming pool at home, ignoring their pleas to stop squirting them with water guns, scaring them by dunking their heads under water, or sneaking up on them and shoving them off the diving board.

School was a mixed bag. If he liked a teacher or the subject matter, Joseph did well. If he disliked a teacher or the subject matter, Joseph did poorly.

Joseph was an avid soccer player. He rarely missed his late-afternoon practices. Martha half chuckled when she referred to Joseph's soccer coach as a "tyrant." If only she could garner the respect and compliance from Joseph that he did. Joseph apparently listened better to the males in his life. This was as true of his soccer coach as it was with his father. Martha relied heavily on Joseph's father to "talk sense into him." Yet she confessed to feeling guilty about relying on Joseph's father in this way, since he was the designated breadwinner in the family and worked long hours. Martha believed that she should be able to handle Joseph all on her own since it was "her job" to raise the children.

According to Martha, Joseph could go from appearing super-confident to extra-insecure, depending on the hour or the day. Sometimes he would brag about his accomplishments, even stretching the truth. She referenced a time when he told his friends that he could easily get a scholarship to a top-flight university because of his skillfulness as a soccer player. Then the next day, he complained bitterly about being a lousy soccer player who was never going to step foot on a soccer field again.

Conflicts between Martha and Joseph were often volatile. Indeed, it was one such recent conflict that had convinced Martha that it was time to get help. On that particular night, Martha had insisted that Joseph show her a math homework assignment so that she could check it for errors. It was ten o'clock. She expected it to be done. Joseph brazenly reached into his backpack, extracted the unfinished assignment, crumpled it into a ball, and threw it at her feet. Martha admitted to then calling Joseph a "lazy little brat." What ensued left Martha thinking that her son surely needed to be hospitalized. Joseph began screaming at her, using a stream of profanity. He punched the wall and loudly proclaimed that he wished the wall was her face. With a mixture of tears and rage, he claimed that he hated his life but hated her more. He demanded that she leave the room. When she complied, Joseph slammed the door behind her. Thirty minutes later, Joseph came downstairs and blithely asked his mother to make him a grilled-cheese sandwich, seemingly oblivious to the whole eruption.

Therapy was quickly initiated. I began formulating an understanding of Joseph's problems. I conceived of the problems mostly in terms of a difficult adolescence, aggravated by a great deal of emotional reactivity between Joseph and his mother during conflicts. Clearly, Joseph was *pushing away* his mother more than *pulling away* from her. Perhaps this more extreme way of separating from her reflected how overly close they had been leading up to Joseph's teenage years. If I was to be of help, I would have to assist Joseph with being more assertive than aggressive in communicating his need to have a life away from his mother, face struggles on his own, be his own person, and emerge out of boyhood. I would have to actively coax Joseph to choose more sensitive words while in the throes of anger. He would have to realize that his use of profanity was not just disrespectful but lazy, in the sense that defaulting to the use of curse words when angry reveals little in the way of specific grievances that point to possible remedies. Saying your teacher is "an asshole" discloses no real information about what exactly bothers you about the teacher, or why or what, if anything, can be done about it. Investing the effort in verbalizing specifics about what upsets him and why, using a range of words, would be the tougher, more mature approach and the one most likely to provide him with remedies.

Other maturational steps I conceived of included challenging Joseph's early-adolescent, black-and-white, all-or-nothing mind-set about himself and others. Did he really hate his life? Were there happy times? Did he really hate his mother? Did he also have loving feelings for her as well? Did he really hate school?

During sessions with his parents, I explained Joseph's silly, impulsive, over-the-top behavior in the context of normal adolescence, describing it as indicative of the ambivalence young adolescents feel about growing up. Their overtly immature behavior is an attempt to cling to a childhood sensibility that is slipping away. They know how to act like a child, but they are clueless about how to act like a would-be adult. They regress because childish behavior is familiar and reassuring in the face of the anticipated anxieties of adulthood. Joseph, like all young adolescents, required hands-on socialization from his parents and teachers in order for him to concretely learn that roughhousing shouldn't be carried too far and that there's a time and a place to be silly and a time and a place to be serious. Of course, I also foresaw scheduling family sessions aimed at reducing the amount of emotional reactivity that flared up during conflicts between Joseph and his mother.

About two months into therapy, even though there was steady progress, Martha took Joseph to see a local child psychiatrist for a medication evaluation. She could not get the words Joseph used the night of the horrendous conflict out of her head: "I hate my life, but I hate you more." After a forty-five-minute meeting, the psychiatrist was adamant in his belief that Joseph had bipolar disorder. He used medical jargon like "mood swings," "irritability," "explosiveness," "grandiose thinking," and "impulsivity" to refer to Joseph. Despite her stated wish to hold off with any medication, the psychiatrist insisted on writing Joseph a prescription for Seroquel, which he described as a mood stabilizer that would "even Joseph out."

In consultation with me, Joseph's parents decided that the psychiatrist's assessment was inaccurate and that use of medication was unnecessary. After a year of a combination of individual and family therapy, Joseph's situation improved. The mother-son conflicts became fewer and less volatile. A skillful tutor was brought in to work with Joseph on improving his homework habits. Joseph's extracurricular activities resulted in his having less time to attend therapy sessions. We stopped meeting. I fell out of touch with Joseph and his parents. Several years later, I happened upon a write-up on Joseph in the sports section of a local newspaper. It delighted me to learn that he was a hot soccer prospect who had accepted a full scholarship to a nationally ranked university. His grandiose adolescent dream ended up being not so grandiose after all.

Joseph's case is one of several instances in which I have been alarmed by the laxness with which a mental health professional has diagnosed bipolar disorder in a kid or teen. Many veteran psychologists, including me, still view this disorder as a severe, debilitating, lifelong mental illness, the diagnosis of which should never be made lightly. How is it that clear signs of normal adolescent storm and stress can be medically construed as bipolar disorder? Have the criteria for diagnosing this condition become so loose that we've blurred the distinction between a difficult adolescent passage and mental illness? Are we particularly susceptible to such misdiagnoses in the twenty-first century because, as a society, we haven't fully grasped the impact of new technologies and multimedia exposure on teenagers' overall moods and expressive options? Let's turn our attention to these vexing questions.

THE EXPERTS ARE BIPOLAR ON WHAT JUVENILE BIPOLAR DISORDER IS

Most parents don't know that the mental health community is split on how to define bipolar disorder in kids and teens. Leading experts in the mental health field have varying understandings of what constitutes manic episodes in the young. There's less debate on what depression looks like in those of a tender age. Depression is thought to take its usual form: fatigue and decreased energy, despair and feelings of hopelessness, irritability, problems concentrating, drastically reduced desire to pursue proven sources of pleasure and enjoyment, and thoughts of self-harm. This is the cluster of symptoms one would see in a person who is severely depressed. But to have bipolar disorder, a person has to display extreme highs in their moods, as well as extreme lows. As we shall see, there is disagreement and confusion about the behaviors associated with manic highs in kids and teens.

In one camp, there's Barbara Geller and her research team at Washington University in St. Louis. Back in the mid-1990s, Dr. Geller and her colleagues began proposing that bipolar disorder in children was different from that in adults. They did retain classic definitions of mania in the childhood version of bipolar disorder: grandiose thinking or inflated self-worth, a reduced need for sleep, rapid and excessive speech, a mind that jumps from one disconnected thought to another, an overabundance of energy to pursue life goals, and a propensity for engaging in risky, pleasurable actions. However, they introduced a new line of thinking about the brevity and frequency of manic episodes. In adults, manic episodes needed to last at least a week to meet any clinical threshold. Geller's team proposed that bipolar children cycle in and out of manic episodes lasting anywhere from a few hours to less than four days. This was termed "ultrarapid cycling." They also coined the term "ultradian cycling" to identify manic episodes lasting from minutes to hours.[1]

During the same time period, another research team out of Massachusetts General Hospital in Boston, spearheaded by Joseph Biederman, arrived at its own definition of bipolar disorder in children. The hallmark sign of the disorder in their eyes was irritability. The Biederman team threw out classic definitions of mania and lengths of time a child needed to be manic to be considered ill. They were more interested in explaining mania in terms of explosive tantrums or tirades that were long lasting and triggered by seemingly minor life events.[2]

Geller's and Biederman's ideas caught on like wildfire in the mental health field during the mid-1990s and beyond. Bipolar disorder was newly applied to children having brief manic experiences lasting minutes or hours, as well as to those who were not classically manic at all but whose demeanor was sullen, aggressive, and explosive. Hypersexuality, or an excesss of sexual thoughts, feelings, and actions, was added to the mix of symptoms that made a kid or teen diagnosable with bipolar. So too was an inappropriate level of giddiness or silliness.

This new and expanded portrayal of childhood bipolar disorder became popularized with the publication of Demitri and Janice Papolos's best-selling book *The Bipolar Child* in 1999.[3] These authors documented the up-to-date thinking on childhood bipolar disorder using compelling stories and accessible language. Since then, the book has undergone three editions and spawned a website—BipolarChild .com—dedicated to disseminating information about childhood bipolar disorder. This website is only one of many that have cropped up to get the word out about the disorder. Granted, for parents with kids who truly have bipolar disorder, these websites are a lifeline. However, there's a downside to the way websites and organizations make the disorder understandable for a general audience. Symptoms tend to be characterized in folksy ways that blur the distinction between the ordinary developmental struggles all kids and teens face and evidence of mental illness. Even organizations as prestigious as the National Institute of Mental Health fall prey to this tendency. Take the following characterizations of childhood bipolar disorder, prominently displayed on the NIMH website:

> *Being in an overly silly or joyful mood that's unusual for your child. It is different from times when he or she might usually get silly and have fun.*
> *Having an extremely short temper. This is an irritable mood that is unusual.*
> *Behaving in risky ways more often, seeking pleasure a lot, and doing more activities than usual.*
> *Being in a sad mood that lasts a long time.*
> *Sleeping or oversleeping when these were not problems before.*[4]

A news bulletin out of Washington University in St. Louis, where Barbara Geller's research team operates, explains manic and depressive symptoms in ways that would place doubt in the mind of even the savviest of parents:

> *Being too happy or too silly or giddy*
> *Acting more irritable than other kids*
> *Believing they can do things better than anyone else*
> *Feelings of power, greatness or importance*

Becoming sad for no reason
Not wanting to play
Complaining of boredom[5]

And on BipolarChild.com, parents are told to be especially alert for hypersexual behavior, which takes the form of "a fascination with private parts and an increase in self-stimulatory behaviors, a precocious interest in things of a sexual nature, and language laced with highly sexual words or phrases."[6]

It should come as no surprise to the reader that the more broadly and simply the juvenile version of bipolar disorder has been defined, the more commonly it's been diagnosed. From the mid-1990s to the present, there has been a *4,000 percent* increase in the number of children diagnosed with it.[7] Yet with the passage of time, we are learning that an extraordinarily high number of these supposed bipolar kids and teens—30–40 percent, based on the University of Missouri study mentioned in chapter 5—no longer meet the criteria for the disorder as adults.[8] This flies in the face of the accepted wisdom that the disorder is a lifelong, impairing mental illness. A rising chorus of mental health experts are noticing that a substantial number of raging kids and teens do not go on to become manic adults and that the juvenile type of the disorder needs to be defined more carefully. But the issue that doesn't get addressed is how broad and folksy definitions of bipolarity make it complicated for parents to clarify for themselves whether their child has a normal developmental struggle or suffers from a mental illness. This is particularly difficult during the teenage years, when mood swings, tirades, fluctuations in self-esteem, and risky behavior go with the territory.

TWENTY-FIRST-CENTURY ADOLESCENCE
Self-Esteem Is Up

The self-esteem of contemporary teens is at an all-time high. That's the conclusion of Jean Twenge, a psychology professor at San Diego State University who has rigorously studied the topic. Compared with the previous generation, today's crop of teens rate themselves as more intelligent and state they are "completely satisfied" with themselves in higher numbers. Fifty-six percent of teens believe they'll make "very good" spouses, compared to 37 percent of those in 1975. Nearly two-thirds of teens believe they'll be exemplary workers. Only about half of teens thought that in 1975.[9]

To dispel any doubt about the unprecedented levels of high self-esteem in teens, one need look no further than the T-shirt slogans currently in circulation: "I'm Not a Snob. I'm Just Better Than You Are"; "As Seen in Your Dreams"; "Better Than Pretty"; "Stand Back. I Seem to Contain Unusually High Amounts of Awesome." Wearing a T-shirt with one of these slogans a generation ago may have resulted in being socially ostracized. Today, it evokes nothing more than a smirk. Song lyrics also give off messages that it's cool to be self-promotional. Jean Twenge and her colleagues recently sifted through and statistically analyzed the lyrics of *Billboard* top ten songs for the years 1980 through 2007.[10] They found dramatic rises in self-focused lyrics.

Isn't high self-esteem a blessing? That depends. It's more of a curse than a blessing if a youngster doesn't cultivate the talents and life skills that actually substantiate him or her having high self-esteem. Telling a kid over and over that he or she is a "talented athlete!" or "super intelligent!" can build false confidence in him if these claims are not backed up by real efforts and achievements. It can be a setup for an emotional breakdown when that kid is eventually held accountable in real-life ways. The psychologist Carol Dweck has made a career out of shedding light on how praising kids in unfounded ways can produce overconfidence and eventual setbacks. In her book *Self-Theories*, she pulls no punches in spelling out the trouble befalling overpraised, overindulged young adults: "It's a recipe for anger, bitterness, and self-doubt when the world doesn't fall over itself trying to make them feel good the way parents and teachers did, or when the world doesn't accept them quite as they are, or when the world makes harsh demands before it gives up its rewards."[11]

Often the emotional meltdowns we see in teens aren't indicative of bipolar disorder. They are expectable reactions to teens encountering conditions where they have to "show the goods," where they aren't automatically treated as great and lovable but have to earn status. Overpraised teens may feel duped and ill prepared for life situations that require them to prove their worth. Anger and frustration are understandable reactions. In addition, parents, educators, and mental health professionals have to be careful about assuming that casually uttered, grandiose self-beliefs by teens denote a clinical problem. As I've shown, there may be a generational trend in the direction of blasé self-promotion.

Rage Is All the Rage

Teens are influenced by what they ogle on TV and the Internet, and on these media, rage is all the rage. In the spring of 2011, Charlie Sheen went on a manic tirade after being fired from the sitcom *Two and a Half Men*. In a *20/20* interview with Andrea Canning, he proclaimed: "I'm on a drug. It's called Charlie Sheen. It's not available because if you try it once you will die. Your face will melt off and your children will weep over your exploded body."[12] He added, "I have this bitchin' rock star life and I'm going to completely embrace it, wrap both arms around it and love it violently. And defend it violently through violent hatred." Curiously, his antics led to his popularity soaring. That spring, Global Language Monitor pored over communications on Twitter, Facebook, and YouTube and determined that of the top twenty persons or topics being talked about, Charlie Sheen led the pack.[13]

Countless teens use the Internet as a platform to showcase themselves and others at their most regressed. A YouTube video titled *Greatest Freak Out Ever* involves a teen who has just received news that his mother has canceled his *World of Warcraft* video-game account.[14] He becomes completely emotionally undone. He tears his bed apart while screaming aloud how he plans to run away. He appears like he is having a seizure, flailing around on his bedroom floor. He whacks his head repeatedly with a sneaker while roaring about how he hates his life. At the time I am writing this, the video has had over fifty-five million hits. And this is only one video in the Greatest Freak Out Ever series. Videos like these model how to express anger and discontent for teens, even if they mock them. We should not be dumbfounded when the rebellious behavior and rants of teens with unfettered access to screens at home becomes more hard-edged and primal or if the language they resort to when angry is littered with hateful and morbid phrases.

Overt Sexuality

Teen culture has not only become more hyperbolic, it also has become more overtly sexual. A recent poll conducted over the Internet for the Associated Press and MTV found that nearly a quarter of fourteen to seventeen year olds had "sexted" via cell phone or the Internet.[15] While tracking 3.5 million Internet searches placed by youth age eighteen and under over an eighteen month period a few years ago, Symantec Corporation's computer safety service for families, Online-Family, discovered that the words "sex" and "porn" ranked fourth and sixth among the top searches.[16] In a bygone era, engaging in risqué behavior meant hiding away in the public library furtively glancing at the anatomical drawings on the pages of *Our Bodies, Ourselves* or stealing some moments with Dad's *Playboy* stash when he was away at work. Now such behavior involves sending or receiving nude photos of oneself or a love interest via cell phone or the Internet. Today, with basic computer skills, precocious teens can have the virtual sex lives of an Egyptian pharaoh or Roman emperor. Left unsupervised, they can satisfy their most base masturbatory sexual fantasies with tailored Internet searches. Accidental popups and inadvertent searches can leave less precocious teens shocked by vivid sexual images. Unless parents are prepared to constantly monitor teens' media exposure, things can get out of hand. One way or the other, sexualized culture seems to win out. My thirteen-year-old son, whom my wife and I carefully watch, recently asked me what "anal" meant. I played dumb. In my generation, this was a Freudian reference for someone who was perfectionistic, uptight, and detail-oriented. In his generation, this has a decidedly sexual meaning.

Teen girls are sexualized in the media like never before, increasingly valued for their sex appeal to the exclusion of other personal characteristics. That's the conclusion arrived at by the Parents Television Council, a Los Angeles–based media watchdog organization, after analyzing the sexual content of the top twenty-five TV programs viewed by twelve- to seventeen-year-olds. This study was quite sophisticated. It looked at "sexual innuendo," "erotic kissing," "erotic touching," "implied intercourse," and "implied nudity." Results showed that teen girls were depicted in sexual ways far more frequently than adults, and in only 5 percent of the cases did female teen characters convey dissatisfaction with being sexualized.[17]

Given this context, when we notice hypersexual behavior in teens, we shouldn't presume they're ill. Hypersexuality isn't only a symptom of bipolar disorder. It's a symptom of a lack of adequate monitoring of teens' multimedia use and of our society's reluctance to endorse any rigorous governmental media censorship to protect children.

Changes in Sleep Habits

The National Sleep Foundation estimates the normal time for an adolescent to fall asleep is around 11:00 p.m.[18] Sleep onset may be later for adolescents, but they still need a minimum of nine and a quarter hours of sleep. Do the arithmetic. The average teen's alarm clock would have to go off at 8:15 a.m. for him to have obtained a full night's rest. There's an obvious snag. In most high schools around the United States, the first school bell of the day sounds before 8:00 a.m.[19] As it turns out, there's an inherent conflict between teens' sleep needs and their school schedule. Most often, school schedules win out and teens wind up with sleep deprivation. Some sleep specialists claim teens, on average, sleep an hour less a night than they did thirty years ago.[20] A recent Mayo Clinic bulletin quotes a robust study demonstrating how over 90 percent of teens sleep less than the recommended nine and a quarter hours of sleep each night.[21] Sleep deprivation seems to be a defining feature of twenty-first-century adolescence, and the emotional lability it leads to can make any parents wonder about their teen's mental state. The less sleep they get, the more moody teens become. Ron Dahl, a sleep specialist at the University of Pittsburgh, knows this dynamic well: "While sleepy teenagers don't experience different emotions from others, they tend to have feelings that are less controlled and more exaggerated. It's not just that they get more negative moods, they are likely to be more silly too. If they're frustrated, they're more likely to show anger; if they are sad, they're more likely to cry. They're less able to rein in an emotion. The feelings are more raw."[22] Heeding Dahl's analysis, before reaching for the diagnostic manual and considering bipolar disorder when teens appear emotionally temperamental, we should first examine the amount and quality of their sleep.

Stress Is the Tie That Binds

Monitoring their teens to make sure they're not consistently watching raunchy TV or YouTube videos and that they're getting adequate sleep are only two roles expected of a good parent. To keep up, parents feel they have to be their teen's homework sergeant, event planner, and personal chauffeur. Nowadays, parents actually spend more time with their children than was true years ago. According to a study by two economists at the Wharton School of the University of Pennsylvania, college-educated mothers in 2007 spent over twenty hours a week in direct contact with their children.[23] In 1995, the figure was closer to twelve hours a week. Even dads are pitching in more than they did in the past. In 2007, college-educated fathers averaged almost ten hours a week parenting their children. This is double the amount of time put in by their counterparts around 1995. One reason parents and teens are physically together more is because teens are delaying obtaining a driver's license in record numbers. They're relying on Mom and Pop for rides. Federal data indicates that about 30 percent of sixteen-year-olds get their driver's licenses compared with about 44 percent in 1988.[24] Rushing out to get a driver's license isn't quite the adolescent rite of passage it once was. Neither is rushing out to find a part-time job to have a healthy cash flow. About 33 percent of sixteen- to nineteen-year-olds are in the workforce. Thirty years ago, about 60 percent of them were.[25]

Parents and teens are not only physically together more; they're also psychologically together more. What do I mean by this? Parents now feel a remarkable degree of emotional responsibility for their teen's well-being and life prospects. Teens, in turn, take for granted the active role their parents play in this area. Nowhere is this more evident than in the investment of time and mental energy parents put into their teen's academic life. Daily in my practice, I meet with battle-weary parents who are at their wit's end over how to help their kids do well in school. The battle they're weary over is homework. The stories are familiar ones:

> *I needed to get Jimmy to call his friend about the geometry assignment he forgot to jot down in class and he resisted all the way.*

> *I finally had a chance to go online and check Francesca's social studies grade and she's getting a C because of missed homework assignments. I'm livid. She lied to me. She said she was pulling an A in that class.*

> *I discovered last night that Bill has been playing* World of Warcraft *in his room all week instead of working on his English essay. When I found out, it destroyed me.*

Just a few missing or inferior key homework assignments can lead to a student's grade plummeting. Parents often appreciate this more than teens. They often appreciate it so much that they step in and do their kid's homework for them. An Internet survey of 778 parents by the homework-resource website Ask Kids shows that 43 percent of parents admit to completing their son's or daughter's homework.[26] It's not that parents are just being overinvolved or controlling when it comes to their kid's homework. It's that they know the lay of the land more than kids. They know college has become the new high school, as the pundits say. They know a college degree is a prerequisite for most well-paying jobs. They know that more than a reasonably good high school academic record is necessary in order to get into a reasonably good college and to eventually enter a career that pays reasonably well. When parents discover missing homework assignments, the dominoes start falling in their head and their anxiety skyrockets.

Present-day family life is more stressful than we might imagine. Running a household efficiently and raising children responsibly re-quires parents to be master planners and time managers. The tension and conflict this can cause is significant. One of the most revealing studies ever conducted about family life in America documents this. At the turn of the twenty-first century, the daily in-home activities of thirty-two families in the Los Angeles area were meticulously video-taped over a three-year period. The $9 million study by the University of California at Los Angeles generated thousands of hours of parent-offspring interaction. Benedict Carey, covering the study for the *Los Angeles Times*, summed up its findings: "For the new model family, stress is the tie that binds." The countless hours of videotape showed that family life in America is "a fire shower of stress, multi-tasking, and mutual nitpicking."[27] Suffice to say that when explosive conflict erupts between teens and their parents, it may speak less to mental illness on the part of any family member and more to the stress that everybody is under.

PERFECT EMOTIONAL STORMS
Brandon's Rages

Brandon is one of those boys with chiseled good looks, poise, and a melodic voice that makes you think of Harry Potter. When I started therapy with him, he was two months shy of his eighteenth birthday. Life with his mother had become, in his words, "a living hell." He was convinced that she looked for reasons to be angry with him. Innocuous acts like failing to use a coaster when he put a glass on a countertop or forgetting to pick up dog droppings in the backyard sparked endless knock-down, drag-out arguments between the two of them. He believed that he could do no right in her eyes. He was of the opinion that his father should summarily stop paying child support to his mother and funnel the money to him; that way, he could have his own apartment and finish out his senior year of high school in peace.

By his own admission, Brandon was struggling at the academically rigorous private school he attended, but he fully expected to graduate. In fact, the more his parents and teachers hinted that he might not graduate, the more Brandon's pride seemed to kick in. He told me once, "I'm really going to show them all up and make them eat their words by doing well in school." Brandon didn't seem too concerned that his relationship with his girlfriend was of the on-again, off-again variety. In his mind, they argued a lot, but mostly over mundane issues—like his driving too fast for her liking, his forgetting to bring money to "go Dutch" when they dined out, and her needing him to pick up the phone immediately when she called. Brandon confessed that he felt nagged by her. When the nagging got to him, he either passively withdrew from the relationship or angrily berated her.

When I met Brandon's mother, Jessica, for the first time, she was visibly distressed. Earlier in the year, she had returned to the workforce as an insurance sales rep after having spent most of her adult life as a stay-at-home mom. She was bracing herself for the sudden drop in income that was soon to result from termination of child-support payments. Her ex-husband, Mike, Brandon's father, was a successful banker, and the child support she received from him was substantial. The salary and commission earned from her job would never support the lifestyle to which she was accustomed. In addition, she was in chronic pain because of unsuccessful back surgery, as well as burdened with the care of an ailing aunt.

Jessica spoke in a flat, droning tone that was nonetheless full of conviction about Brandon's issues. It was as if she had a steel-trap mind for all of his irresponsible behaviors, which included the countless times he was issued parking tickets and failed to pay up, the number of cell phones she had to purchase to replace the ones Brandon heedlessly lost, the failure to complete homework and prepare for tests, his staying up at all hours talking on the phone with his girlfriend, and his playing video games instead of filling out college applications. On the face of it, Jessica had objective reasons to be frustrated with Brandon. He clearly had a blind spot for how his careless actions were a setup for others calling him to task. Even though he despised being the recipient of his mother's frustration, he sure seemed to act in ways that made it inevitable. However, it wasn't the *content* of Jessica's concerns that bothered me. These were rather commonplace parent-teen concerns. It was her *delivery*. The way she spoke in a monotonous, critical voice, with conviction about Brandon's irresponsibility, made it seem as though she perceived him as all bad, but she seemed to have no conscious awareness of her excessively negative tone.

Jessica mentioned a curious pattern. When their arguments were heated, Brandon was completely unruly, screaming at the top of his voice, slamming doors, and hurling insults at her. Everything was her fault. She was all bad. Then, within hours, he would be extremely remorseful, sobbing uncontrollably, saying he was the horrible one, and begging for forgiveness. In other words, he went from emotionally exploding to emotionally imploding. The emotional hangover from these fights was often of such a magnitude that Brandon stayed in bed and refused to go to school. These episodes were so alarming to Jessica that she secured a psychiatrist for Brandon. Brandon was put on a therapeutic dose of Seroquel.

Brandon's father, Mike, lived an hour away. Moving in with him was not logistically feasible. With the morning traffic, Brandon would have to wake up at 5:00 a.m. in order to commute to school in time. Besides, as Mike told me during a parent visit alone with me, Brandon had "burned his bridges" with him. Hell would freeze over before Mike would allow Brandon to live with him. His reaction had merit. While living at his dad's the previous summer, Brandon had freely invited friends over and staged raucous daytime parties. Messes were made, furniture was broken, and household items were stolen without any attempt by Brandon even to "cover his tracks." Mike also wanted to protect his own sobriety. He was a recovering alcoholic and did not want any substances in his house. The occasional pot smoking and binge drinking Brandon engaged in troubled Mike. But it didn't trouble him to the point where he believed Brandon needed drug and alcohol treatment.

Mike's position was clear: Brandon had to stay at his mother's house and make their relationship work. Curiously, Mike put the ball squarely in Brandon's court to remedy the situation with his mother, characterizing her as a feeble person: "Jessica is a piece of work. I should know. I was married to her for fifteen years. But Brandon has to suck it up and deal with her until he graduates." Mike's smoldering resentment of Jessica wasn't even thinly veiled.

Eager to help Brandon's relationship with Jessica, I scheduled a visit with the two of them. It was naïve of me. I was used to family wars in my office, but this looked like the war to end all wars. Within minutes, Jessica had enumerated all the problems that she had with Brandon. She used phrases like "You always just think of yourself" and "You never help out around the house." Brandon followed suit: "You're the one who's selfish. You never act like a good mother. Dad pays you a mint and the fridge is always empty." They fed off of each other's anger. They talked over each other. They shouted each other down.

During more plaintive moments, Brandon seemed desperate to receive acknowledgment from his mother about her part in the problems that existed between them. It seemed critically important to him that she say something to affirm his perceptions of her problems. He even softened a bit and left open opportunities for Jessica to become conciliatory: "OK, I admit it. I can be a screwup. I need to be more responsible. But, come on, Mom, you have trouble being positive, wouldn't you say?" Not feeling the conciliatory tone, not seeing the opening, Jessica went on the defensive: "You don't give me much to be positive about these days."

To add insult to injury, Jessica read into Brandon's motives for why he acted the way he did and came across as convinced that she was right: "You have no idea about the value of things. It's because your father has spoiled you and you know one day you're going to inherit a bunch of money." This was when the lid really came off for Brandon. He stood up and hurled profanity-laced insults at Jessica. He ridiculed her for her aging looks and bad health. As if to deliver a verbal death-blow, Brandon then roared that once he left for college he would cut her out of his life.

Never in my wildest imagination did I consider Brandon capable of this degree of agitation and ruthlessness. During individual sessions, Brandon was mostly even-tempered and reflective. Frustrations did emerge. But these were mostly frustrations that he had a fairly good handle on and could talk his way through. What ingredients of the interaction with his mother could explain Brandon's morphing into such a rageful person?

Shame and Rage

More often than not, shame lurks behind the rage that we see in explosive conflict. Shame is one of the primal emotions, like disgust and panic, which have flooding effects. When ashamed, we feel washed over with bad feelings. In a very visceral way, the shameful experience is felt to control us, versus us controlling it. When someone shames us, our mood can swing from upbeat to deflated. There is a sudden onset of feelings of low self-worth.

When ashamed, we are lost for words. Emotion overrides reason. It's hard for even the most psychologically fit person to hang in there and give voice to what he or she is experiencing in any nuanced way. That said, unless we can stop, regain composure, and somehow effectively communicate the hurt caused by someone else's insensitivity, we are in a danger zone. More specifically, we are in a rage-danger zone. We are at risk for going on the counterattack and shaming the shamer. We are at risk for dumping our bad, out-of-control feelings onto him or her. This is especially the case if the shamer doesn't acknowledge his or her harmful behavior and back off. What if the shamer actually defends his or her actions and appears oblivious to any wrongdoing? Those are the perfect conditions for rage storms— the perfect conditions that explain, in part, Brandon and Jessica's rage storms.

Feeling Trapped

Brandon and Jessica feel stuck with each other. There's no out. Dad's house isn't an option. Somehow they have to live under the same roof, interact, and get along. Yet in the family calculus of loving and liking, they love but dislike each other. This can be the case in difficult parent-teen relationships. A parent may find his or her offspring's teenage personality and lifestyle choices repugnant. But this same parent may still love that offspring dearly. Similarly, a teenager might find a parent's personality quirks and lifestyle choices very off-putting, while still loving that parent.

In any relationship, the parent-teen one being no exception, forcing two people who love, but dislike, each other to live in close contact breeds resentment. That's especially true if they feel overly responsible for each other, as in the case of Brandon and Jessica. Brandon's ridicule of his mother's looks and health belied his fear that she would not fare well once he moved off to college. Jessica's barrage of complaints regarding Brandon's irresponsible behavior belied her fear that he would not emerge into a competent, college-ready adult. The groundswell of resentment based on them feeling stuck with each other was another storm condition.

As controversial as it may sound, when a difficult parent-teen relationship crosses the line into an intolerable one, an alternative living arrangement for the teen may need to be considered. This can be temporary or semipermanent. Maybe it's an uncle's house across town or Grandma's house. Sometimes this is the best and quickest harm-reduction step parents can take. It may be necessary to stop the emotional bleeding. In Brandon's case, it was his best friend's house. Within days of turning eighteen, he got permission to move into the spare bedroom there. Brandon's relationship with his mother remained tense. But their arguments were less volatile and vicious. They chose to dine in public a few nights a week, which offered a built-in incentive for them to treat each other decently. They learned that they could love each other, and even like each other better from a distance. Brandon continued living at his friend's house until he moved out to attend college on the East Coast. He Skyped his mother regularly from there.

Poor Emotional Boundaries and Failures to Empathize

Brandon and Jessica were quick to become flooded with each other's emotions. Frustrated looks and gestures by Jessica triggered the same in Brandon. Rising levels of anger in Jessica automatically provoked rising levels of anger in Brandon. To say that they fed off of each other's emotions is an understatement.

In the heat of passion, neither of them demonstrated an ability to contain their feelings, pause, listen, and respond to the other's feelings. This is what empathy is all about. It requires pausing, taking a deep breath or a series of them, staying quiet, and holding back from emotionally reacting. It requires actively showing that you're listening, and that you're tuned in and curious about what the person across from you is saying. It involves the ability to show sensitivity to another person's feelings without being oversensitized or desensitized by them. If you feel compelled to react, you've become oversensitized to the other's feelings; if you tune out, withdraw, and go numb, you've become de-sensitized by them.

Empathic expressions during conflicts are essentially what lead to them getting resolved. They leave the other person feeling listened to. They inject a conciliatory tone into things. It would have made all the difference in the world had Jessica somehow been able to pause, listen, and mirror back Brandon's feelings to him at key moments: *I can tell you're really mad at me right now. I know I can be hard on you and cause you pain.* The same applies to Brandon: *You look all torn up inside. I know I don't make your life any easier by tearing into you.*

Without the empathy skills to resolve conflicts, each new conflict stirred up residue from the last one. The backlog of unresolved con-flicts in Brandon and Jessica's life meant any new conflict, with other storm conditions present, could be a barnburner.

Too Many Conflict-Negotiation No-No's

Mild conflicts between parents and teens can escalate into serious con-frontations based on simple word choices resorted to in the heat of argument. Rationally, most of us know it's better to use "I statements" than "you statements" during conflicts. We have a general sense that "you statements" tend to put people on the defensive. "I statements," on the other hand, might result in a more receptive audience. Those of us growing up in the '70s, when the humanistic psychology tradition was popular, were steeped in the idea that you can't argue with some-one's feelings. Feelings are just feelings. When communicating feel-ings with "I statements," the person is less likely to protest. An example will help. Let's say I'm frustrated with being interrupted by my wife. If I express this with a "you statement," as in *You're not listening to me* or *You're not giving me a chance to speak*, pushback is a distinct possibility. Nevertheless, if I use an "I statement," as in *I'm feeling unlistened to* or *I have something I really want you to hear*, I'm essentially communicating the same feelings and ideas, while lessening the possibility of pushback.

Use of absolutist language also has a high probability of putting someone on the defensive. We've all heard the adage "Never say never." Putting it into practice in the middle of a heated argument is never easy. Telling teens that they are never on time, never pick up after themselves, or never study is unlikely to make them receptive listeners. Vocalize it along with a "you statement" and the communication conditions are ripe for a heated exchange: *You never can be trusted to be on time. You never leave your room clean. You never adequately prepare for quizzes.* "Always" is another oft-repeated absolutist word choice that when uttered as a "you statement" stokes a conflict: *You always stick your nose in my business, Dad. You always take my little sister's side and believe her. You always make me late for basketball practice.* Conflicts are more likely to remain mild and resolvable when there is frequent use of "I statements" mixed with qualifiers: *I sometimes feel that you don't respect my privacy, Dad. In my opinion, you take my little sister's side and believe her more often than you do me. Sometimes I get really mad about being taken late for basketball practice.*

Perhaps the single most significant thing we can do to incite a conflict is to "mind read" someone else's motives—more specifically, to mind read their motives as malicious when there's no real basis for this. This pertains to when we talk as if we have special knowledge about what drives the other person to do the things he or she does, as if we know them better than they know themselves. Throw in the fact that we believe what drives them is something dishonorable, like greed or envy, and we're playing with fire. Refuse to listen to the more accurate, benign version of their own motives and the war is on.

All of these conflict negotiation no-no's were present in ample amounts when Brandon and Jessica disagreed. They played a role in the escalation of their stormy conflicts.

TEASING OUT WHAT'S NORMAL
Expectable Rage

It's in vogue these days to assume that teens who rage, like Brandon, have a form of bipolar illness. The focus of the inquiry then becomes the teen as an individual or the teen's brain. The discourse becomes a medical one. People's ears and eyes turn away from the possible contribution of the teen's everyday life situation. Obvious triggers of the rages get overlooked—like a volatile parent-teen relationship marked by loose boundaries, mutual shaming, feelings of entrapment, and poorly developed conflict-resolution skills. On the teen's end, there are the potential aggravating effects of chronic sleep deprivation, poor diet, alcohol or drug use, school pressure, and insufficient exercise. On the parent's end, there are the potential aggravating effects of the multitude of roles taken on—social planner, homework tutor, chauffeur, etc.—for an ungrateful teen. The mix, as we've seen, can be a volatile one.

By plucking the raging teen out of his life situation and viewing him as the sole problem, we do him and his relationships a disservice. Oftentimes, a teen rages only under certain conditions. Not uncommonly, these are relationship conditions. For true and lasting change to occur, we need to carefully attend to and remedy these relationship conditions. Lifestyle adjustments, empathy training, conflict-resolution skill building, and harm-reduction steps, become highly relevant considerations.

Healthy Depression

Around the dinner table, some family friends of ours recently told us of the difficulties their fourteen-year-old daughter, Clare, had experienced transitioning to the ninth grade at a new school. Up until that point, Clare had attended a small, private school. It was a school with under two hundred students from kindergarten through the eighth grade. It comprised a tight-knit community. For Clare, the school was a home away from home. The dress was casual. There were no uniforms. She knew all of her teachers. Her classmates were like siblings. It was a progressive school where students received narrative evaluations and not grades for coursework. The classrooms were designed with the look of a living room. There were couches, old wooden round tables, and comfortable workstations. The learning atmosphere had been a lively one, and Clare thrived there. However, by the end of the eighth grade, Clare felt, as she put it, "claustrophobic." She craved a change.

The high school she entered was a girls' Catholic school. Regimentation was in the air. Uniforms were required. The academic competition was cutthroat. Most of the girls were veterans at taking timed tests and dealing with grades. Clare was completely unaccustomed to tests, grades, and competitiveness being displayed so conspicuously. Compared with her old teachers, those in high school seemed remote and demanding. The girls seemed to be sizing each other up all the time. Cliques formed fast. Clare did not seem to be fitting in socially. Her best friend from her old school was not returning her text messages and e-mails. Three months into the fall, Clare received her midterm grades. She got a D in English. Given that Clare was an avid reader and lover of literature, this hit her hard.

Clare became depressed. At first, she was more irritable than sad. She blamed her parents for sending her to a "dumb school that didn't give grades," causing her to be ill prepared for high school. She was less social. Upon returning from school, most days she hid away in her room. She lost interest in playing club soccer. Although she kept attending practice, her enthusiasm for playing was minimal.

Within a few weeks, Clare had become more sad than irritable. She had crying spells where she openly expressed missing her old teachers and friends. It hurt going from being a big fish in a little pond to being a little fish in a big pond. Clare feared that she would never be as popular at her new school as she was at her old one. She felt guilt over not spending more time with her best friend during the summer before high school started. Clare wondered if her best friend was avoiding her because of this neglect.

As time passed, Clare became less depressed. She slowly realized that she couldn't be instantly popular or automatically successful at test taking. These were works in progress. At heart, Clare was a competitive person and gradually began throwing herself into her schoolwork, determined to earn good grades. She returned to playing soccer regularly, and with gusto. Her best friend had indeed felt neglected by her that summer. They made up and started socializing more regularly. Clare was back on track.

Clare's depression was expectable and productive. The unavoidable changes that she was forced to adapt to were drastic. After all, our brains are designed to enable us to adapt, not to be happy. When life changes are thrust upon us and loss is unavoidable, depression is a natural human reaction. At first, Clare was angry and irritable. This is usually true in the early stages of normal depressive reactions. Emotionally, we hold out, believing what was lost somehow magically can be retrieved. We want our old boyfriend back, when in reality he's gone for good. We want our old job back, when it has been permanently outsourced. It shouldn't be this way. We feel unjustly treated. We're angry and irritable.

With time, there's the realization that what has been lost cannot be regained. Grief and sadness predominate. Tears get shed. With the tears, we shed old ideas about ourselves and our lives. In Clare's case, she was shedding the idea that she would be popular no matter what and that she would be a good student no matter what. Her life circumstances had changed. Nobody at her new school knew of, or cared about, her old reputation. A new reputation had to be earned. She would have to accept her lower status for now. This was the sad fact of her life. Isolation allowed her to think more deeply about these issues. It allowed her a period of introspection to bring her self-perceptions of worth and attractiveness into alignment with her new life circumstances. It was a time to dust herself off, regain courage, and try again. It also was a time to arrive at a fuller awareness of the new rules with which the game of life should be played.

The guilt that Clare had experienced over neglecting her friend was healthy guilt. She genuinely felt bad about failing to act as a good friend. This showed that Clare had a social conscience. Her guilt feelings were appropriate to the situation. They motivated her to face up to the rejection she caused. Relief could be gained by making amends, which she did. Not all guilt is bad. Another type of "good guilt" is what humanistic psychologists call "existential guilt." This involves a nagging feeling inside that we are not living up to our potential, not bringing to fruition the gifts and talents that we possess. It's the voice inside our head that's telling us we're frittering away our life, have become too complacent, and set the bar too low. Heeding the call of existential guilt keeps us honest about abiding by our inner ideals and realizing our capabilities. "Bad guilt" is pathological guilt, which is found in clinically depressed people. This involves a global feeling of badness. It's as if the person has an overactive conscience so that he or she is preoccupied with having done something wrong or about to do something wrong. The tragic part is, in reality, the person is decent and well meaning.

Other aspects of clinical depression are worth noting to give the reader a sense of perspective about true depressive illness. The so-called "vegetative signs" of depressions are disturbances in sleep and appetite, a flat mood, and a depletion of energy. Disabling depression typically finds someone oversleeping or undersleeping a great deal. There is significant weight loss or gain. The person appears fatigued and sickly. There may be long delays before answers to questions are delivered. Isolation does not serve the purpose it served for Clare. It serves the purpose of escaping from a life that is unbearable and perceived to forever be that way. The person has little energy to be social in basic ways—to smile when smiled at or to wave back when waved to. Attention and concentration are impaired. That's because the person is so preoccupied with his or her own faults and feelings that he or she has little mental energy in reserve to concentrate on other things.

In kids and teens, clinical depression is typically accompanied by more irritability than you see with adults. But it's pervasive irritability, not fleeting irritability. This is the youngster who has a scowl on his face more often than not, the one who stubbornly holds onto grudges and is generally mopey, unresponsive, and rejecting. This is the youngster who hates his life and means it—not the youngster who says he hates his life for shock value or as a crude and transitory expression of unhappiness. This is the youngster who seriously thinks about dying, about ending a life that has become miserable. We are now in the realm of true illness.

Healthy Mania

Let me summarize for you a story told to me by the mother of a fourteen-year-old teen that she thought had gone off the deep end emotionally. It centered around an Airsoft pellet-gun battle her son, Billy, had planned for days in advance. It was all he could talk about morning, noon, and night. He hogged discussions and rattled on in minute detail about the types of guns and ammo he and his friends would use and how he was going to redesign the back yard into a warzone. His excitement was palpable. It irritated Billy when family members failed to share his excitement. Anyone in the family who hinted at his plans being overly ambitious was fair game for being yelled at.

In setting up the event, Billy refused help from anyone. He was a boy on a mission. His mother saw a disaster in the making. The morning of the event, Billy got up at 4:00 a.m. and was in the garage busily constructing and spray-painting props. Empty spray-paint cans and torn cardboard were strewn everywhere. At about 10:00 a.m., his mother poked her head into the garage and asked sheepishly if he needed help. Billy shouted at her to leave.

Yet somehow Billy was able to single-handedly pull the event off. The backyard was, indeed, converted into a warzone for the afternoon. The way Billy and his friends greeted each other when they arrived at the house embarrassed his mother. They screamed comments like, "Hey, asswipe, I'm gonna wipe your ass out there today" and "I'm going to own your ass."

There was a definite buzz in the air. Billy was exuberant with all the attention he received for his warzone design. He could hardly contain himself. In a frenzy, he chased one boy around the backyard and punched him on the arm so hard that Billy's mother thought the boy would pass out. Instead, the boy laughed hysterically.

Billy gave his mother strict orders not to bother them in the backyard during the battle. It went on for hours. She snuck peeks out the window. At times, there was utter calm and silence. The boys hunkered down in hiding spots, waiting for sniping opportunities. At other times, there was all-out pandemonium. The boys ran around wildly and screamed at the top of their lungs. One event in particular troubled his mother. Billy snuck up on a friend and shot him repeatedly with pellets. He then stood on his stomach with both feet, simulated masturbation, and roared, "I rule. Eat me, sucker!" The friend played dead and didn't even try to push him off.

Had Billy really gone off the emotional deep end, as speculated by his mother? Actually, in my estimation, Billy shows hallmark signs of what we might call healthy teen mania. The excitement and elation he feels is focused around a set of highly desirable teenage goals. The goals are to impress his friends, achieve social status, and demonstrate his daring and heroism. He also wants to declare his independence by showing that can do things on his own without parental input. Psychologically, there's a lot on the line. If the event is successful in every way, his friendship bonds are strengthened, and he's a hero for the day. He can say, "I told you so" to those in his family who questioned his ambitiousness and capacity for independence. If the event fails in every way, his friends think he's uncool, they thereafter avoid him, and he's a loser. Family members then get to say to him, "I told you so" and he feels childish and foolish.

Naturally, Billy is both excited and stressed. He can hardly contain himself. Talking up the event, even overtalking it, is Billy's way of trying to sustain the energy necessary to execute his plan. It puts fuel in his tank. Puffing out his chest and appearing overconfident are his way of convincing himself that he can actually stage this event.

Billy is taking some huge risks in planning the event. Would his friends show up? Would they think, as he thought, that his backyard warzone was awesome? Would they be better snipers than he was in battle? Would they dominate him or would he dominate them? With risk comes excitement and dread. On the one hand, there's the anticipated joy over wished-for success that has to be self-contained. On the other hand, there's the anticipated dread of defeat. Understandably, Billy is extremely tense.

What about Billy's obscene gesture standing atop his friend? Alas, that's nothing other than the age-old manic gesture that evolutionary psychologists say is part of a "winning subroutine"—at least a twenty-first-century version of it. He's demonstrating for all to see that he's truly won, that he's the victor, and that his friend is the vanquished. Doing it in a brash, cocksure way conveys that if there's any attempt at a comeback by the vanquished, he'll be even worse off. If the vanquished reopens the struggle, he'll get completely pummeled. Billy's manic gesture of conquest is successful. His friend yields, accepts defeat, and plays dead. Evolutionary psychologists say this "winning sub-routine" is hardwired in our brains. It's a script that maintained rank, status, and social order in human groups for millennia.

Mania exists on a continuum. There's the low end, which is highly adaptive, as in Billy's case. Then there's the clinical variety. For it to be of the clinical variety, you usually don't see a frenzy of feeling and action around a central project. The person flits from one project to another, starting new ones as quickly as old ones are dumped. There may be little rhyme or reason that connects old and new interests. An example of this would be a teen who, one week, out of the blue, an-nounces that she's bent on becoming a top-class swimmer. School is skipped and meals passed up as she spends every waking minute in the pool. She charges hundreds of dollars buying one swimsuit after another, none of which seem to please her. Attempts to reel her in by parents are experienced as them trying to kill her "one true dream in life." She rages at them for being so cruel as to get in the way of her dream. Within days or weeks, she's onto a new project. This time, it's painting. She's blasé when questioned by her parents about swimming or flies into a fury, berating them for not understanding that she's a creative person with a lot of dreams.

The grandiosity you see in clinical mania is different from overcon-fidence. It's not just someone stretching the truth about what they're capable of. In a manic state, the grandiose teen makes utterly incredu-lous self-assertions. The people hearing them immediately feel em-barrassed for him or her. Yet the teen seems to have no sense of the shame and embarrassment surrounding his or her self-assertions. This might be a teen who, in all seriousness, unabashedly announces that John Lennon had a lousy voice and, if the clock could be turned back, the teen could do a better job singing for the Beatles—a statement made despite the fact that the teen has little background as a singer. If he was truly manic, that same teen might be a flamboyant, colorful dresser who strutted around thinking he would be the next John Len-non, oblivious to how pathetic this made him look. He might be prone to talking a blue streak. He would see sleep as just a nuisance because it interferes with all that needs to be accomplished to realize his dreams.

He would generally come across as happier than happy. This is the core experience of real clinical mania. This is when psychiatric help is really called for and when medication can be a veritable lifesaver.

PARENTS, BE ON GUARD

With new technologies and the lifestyle changes they bring, adolescent culture is changing in ways we barely understand. This is a culture where casual self-promotion doesn't raise eyebrows, where "rage quits," "freak-outs," and "sexting" are familiar teen experiences. Easy access to the Internet, iPods, cell phones, game stations, and cable TV expose teens to expressive options that are loud, raunchy, violent, and over the top. And for parents, running a household is a stressful enterprise. In the words of Elinor Ochs, the anthropologist who headed up the $9 million UCLA study on family life discussed earlier: "The coordination it takes, it's more complicated than a theatre production. And there are no rehearsals."[28] As the pundits say, high school has become the new college, and the academic pressure that teens face is profound. Adolescent storm and stress has to be understood in this context.

When we toss around vague definitions of bipolar disorder in terms of fleeting mood swings, rage outbursts, sexual acting out, and overconfidence, lines get blurred. We run the risk of confusing a difficult adolescent passage with a mental illness. Parents need to keep this distinction in mind when they are in the medical doctor's office. That's because the vast majority of medical doctors aren't schooled to think about how adolescent culture or family events shape a teen's behavior or about how things like lifestyle adjustments, empathy building, enhanced communication, and conflict resolution hashed out in psychotherapy might help. They are schooled to think about disturbed brains and the cornucopia of medications at their disposal. Unless parents keep all of this in mind, an inaccurate diagnosis of bipolar disorder with inappropriate treatments might ensue, which would surely compound the stress that the family is already experiencing.

CHAPTER EIGHT

Autism Spectrum?
Or a Brainy, Willful, Introverted Boy?

I have followed William in my therapy practice for close to a decade. His story is a prime example of the type of brainy, mentally gifted, single-minded, willful boys who often are falsely diagnosed with autism spectrum disorder when they are assessed as young children. This unfortunate occurrence is partly due to defining autism as a "spectrum disorder," incorporating mild and severe cases of problematic social communication and interaction, as well as restricted interests and behavior. In its milder form, especially among preschool- and kindergarten-age boys, it is tough to distinguish between early signs of autism spectrum disorder and indications that we have on our hands a young boy who is a budding intellectual, is more interested in studying objects than hanging out with friends, overvalues logic, is socially awkward unless interacting with others who share identical interests or is in a leadership role, learns best when obsessed with a topic, and is overly businesslike and serious in how he socializes. The picture gets even more complicated during the toddler years, when normal, crude assertions of willfulness, tantrums, and lapses in verbal mastery when highly emotional are in full swing. As we shall see, boys like William, who embody a combination of emerging masculine braininess and a difficult toddlerhood, can be fair game for a mild diagnosis of autism spectrum disorder, when it does not apply.

Jacqueline, William's mother, realized that he was a quirky baby within weeks of his birth. When she held him in her arms, he seemed more fascinated by objects in his field of vision than by faces. The whir and motion of a fan, the tick-tock of a clock, or the drip-drip of a coffeemaker grabbed William's attention even more than smiling faces, melodic voices, or welcoming eyes. His odd body movements concerned Jacqueline. William often contorted his body and arched his back upwards. He appeared utterly beguiled by the sensory world around him. He labored to prop himself up, as if desperately needing to witness it firsthand.

Some normal developmental milestones did not apply to William. He bypassed a true crawling stage and walked upright by ten and a half months. He babbled as an infant and spoke his first words at twelve months; however, by age two, he was routinely using full sentences and speaking like a little adult.

When William encountered an interesting object or event as a toddler, he became so captivated by it that he completely ignored the people around him. During a music class, he once stood off to the side, staring at a ceiling fan while all of the other kids sat together singing. Then suddenly, William ran toward the teacher. He was mesmerized by the synchronous movement of the teacher's lips and fingering of guitar strings that together produced melodic sounds, to the point of losing all awareness that his face was just inches away from his teacher's. At his two-year birthday party, while the other kids were playing in the backyard, William methodically took some folding chairs, lined them up, and pushed them over one at a time—intrigued by the noises the falling chairs made. He repeated this series of events over and over throughout the afternoon, as if conducting a series of well-crafted experiments.

By age three, William began developing a passionate interest in a range of adult-like topics. After being read a book on Pompeii, he talked endlessly for months afterwards about what he had learned. He pressured Jacqueline to check books out of the library on Pompeii in order to satisfy his need for more detailed knowledge on what Roman life was like before Mount Vesuvius erupted and buried the ancient city in ashes. He strove to know more about aqueducts and amphitheaters. He insisted that Jacqueline design a toga for him, which she did. He strutted around the living room not just pretending to be, but believing that he was, a citizen of the Roman Empire, circa AD 79.

Steve, the lovable host of the children's TV program *Blue's Clues*, became an idol for William. He avidly watched reruns of the show and lobbied his parents hard for a green shirt, khaki pants, and brown shoes so that he could look just like Steve—no compromises.

Next he became fascinated with the *Titanic*, amassing a detailed knowledge of the design of the ship. Facts such as the exact length of the *Titanic* (882 feet, 9 inches) mattered to him. He also knew that its top speed was 23 knots. William insisted on having a uniform just like Captain Smith's, the officer who was in command of the *Titanic*. Getting the color and the arrangement of the stripes and buttons correct seemed essential to William when he and his mother designed it. Jacqueline also helped William amass an impressive collection of pictures of ships, ocean liners, and uniformed officers, which he studied on his own for hours on end.

At preschool, William was a veritable pied piper. During his "*Titanic* phase," he arrived at school sporting his Captain Smith blazer and cap. He orchestrated *Titanic* reenactment scenes, assigning roles and telling his classmates where to stand and what to do and say. This would usually go well at first. William's enthusiasm was intoxicating, and the play scenes he devised were too exciting for the other kids to pass up. However, more often than not, the other kids eventually lost interest and wandered off because of William's need for them to follow his script.

At home, William's tantrums were wild and uncontrollable even as he approached age five. When he was asked by his parents to turn the TV off and join the family for dinner, he might scream and yell in protest, writhe around on the floor, and even throw and break things. Invariably, the situation that caused William to fly into a rage involved setting aside what he was doing in the moment to comply with a routine request—such as to get ready for bed or dressed for preschool. He simply hated transitions. Unless his parents regularly planned activities that were in line with his interests, William inevitably became agitated, overactive, and unmanageable.

Mealtime was another "powder keg" situation. William was repulsed by vegetables. If carrots, broccoli, or any other vegetable was placed on his plate, he thought nothing of throwing the entire dish on the floor. All he could stomach was a short menu of items like pizza, hot dogs, or peanut butter sandwiches.

William's parents were sociable. They spent a great deal of time in the company of other parents and children. They knew William's tantrums, fussy eating habits, and social difficulties were outside the norm. Their friends' kids were maturing, while William seemed stuck. When William was five years old, they decided to have him evaluated. A highly respected doctor at a university-based institute was sought out to conduct the initial evaluation. During a twenty-minute observation, William mostly sat staring at the doctor's bookshelves—either ignoring or providing one-word answers to the questions he was asked. At the end of this brief observation, the doctor concluded that William was "on the spectrum" and had Asperger's syndrome. The doctor reassured Jacqueline that her son's difficulties were due to him having a brain disorder and that she should in no way hold herself responsible. He advised her to have further testing conducted through the institute to confirm the diagnosis and to approach her local regional center to obtain services for him—"Mostly as a precaution in case he can't take care of himself when he gets older."

Years later, when recounting this experience for me, Jacqueline said this news was like a "blow to the solar plexus." But she convinced herself that failing to trust the conclusions of a highly respected doctor from a prestigious university hospital was nothing short of staying in denial about William. She followed through with a recommendation to have William more thoroughly assessed by autism experts at this same hospital. Their assessment revealed that William had an IQ of 144—placing him squarely in the mentally gifted range. A formal speech and language assessment indicated that William was well over a year ahead in all areas. However, in the final report, it was noted that while William was alone with the examiner, he was unable to initiate or sustain conversations. He either stared off into the distance or interrupted the examiner to talk about off-topic subjects that were of interest to him—such as tornadoes, hurricanes, and earthquakes. When asked about friends, William made vague references to two girls who had moved away and was unable to recall any recent activities he had engaged in with them. Due mostly to his behavior in the room, the examiner assigned him a diagnosis of autism disorder because of his "communication and qualitative impairments in reciprocal social interaction." Jacqueline was confused by the report. She wondered if the examiner had taken any time to actively engage William. She knew that William could be quite animated and talkative when adults took a liking to him.

Nevertheless, William's parents went along with the diagnosis and so began their bewildering odyssey into the mental health field. At the behest of the specialist who assessed William, they secured a lawyer to sue the local regional center to obtain autism services. The regional center had unilaterally denied such services, claiming William needed to have been formally diagnosed as autistic prior to age three. It took $22,000 in legal fees to bring their case before a judge, who ordered William to be formally assessed by a medical doctor at the regional center. That doctor determined that William had full-blown autism and did indeed qualify for services. However, as the years unfolded, William's parents had lingering doubts. They approached me when he was age eight.

I agreed to meet with William and to offer my clinical judgment. Within minutes of playing with William, I knew, unequivocally, that he was not "on the spectrum." He was enthralled by the range of dart guns I had in my office and asked if we could play a World War II game. I heartily complied. William took turns being Hitler, then Stalin, mentioning how he was in command of millions of troops who followed his orders. When I playfully acted as one of his minions awaiting orders to shoot the enemy, William became delighted. He threw himself into the role of dictatorial commander and ordered me to shoot an imaginary enemy soldier. I did so, making loud machine-gun noises. William was emotionally beside himself. He quickly asked if he could be Stalin and I could be Hitler, and if I would shoot him. We reenacted this Hitler-shooting-Stalin scene over and over, with William pretending to be in the throes of death, each time using louder gurgling sounds and ever-so-dramatic, jerky body movements.

For me, William's imaginativeness, as well as the emotional give-and-take in our pretend play interactions, was proof positive that it was folly to consider him autistic in any way.

Fast-forward to the present. William is now a high school student who is very active in student government. He is quite at ease with other teenagers who share his level of intellect. He continues to demonstrate the same thirst for knowledge that he had as a toddler. When classroom subjects interest him, his academic performance is stellar. When they don't, William's grades suffer. His report cards often contain peaks and valleys of As and Fs, which is immensely frustrating for his parents. His interests are not highly obscure and detail oriented, characteristic of autism, such as memorizing the names of dinosaurs or the serial numbers on Ford trucks. He is an abstract thinker who labors to understand issues more deeply. For instance, he has a complex understanding of different forms of government, and he is able to articulate the arguments for and against democratic, fascist, and oligarchical arrangements. This conceptual, philosophical way of acquiring knowledge tends not to be autism-friendly.

Granted, William is far more comfortable isolating himself and studying political geography and rock-and-roll memorabilia than he is hanging out at the mall. In addition, he can still explode emotionally when he is forced to switch activities, such as applying himself to his homework rather than researching Fender guitars or the geography of Iceland on the Internet. Moreover, he'll only incorporate new food items into his diet when he has tried them at a fancy restaurant that doesn't have kiddie foods such as pizza, hot dogs, or peanut butter sandwiches on the menu. However, these traits and behaviors don't mean that he's autism spectrum disordered. They reveal William to be a brainy, somewhat introverted, individualistically minded boy whose overexcitement for ideas and need for control cause problems with parents and peers.

As we shall see, boys with these traits and behaviors are often falsely diagnosed with autism spectrum disorder, especially when they are assessed at younger ages.

THE EARLY-DIAGNOSIS TRAP

True autism is a potentially very disabling neurological condition. Roy Richard Grinker, in his acclaimed book *Unstrange Minds*, masterfully documents the challenges he faced raising Isabel, his autistic daughter.[1] At age two, she only made passing eye contact, rarely initiated interactions, and had trouble responding to her name in a consistent fashion. Her play often took the form of rote activities such as drawing the same picture repeatedly or rewinding a DVD to watch the same film clip over and over. Unless awakened each morning with the same utterance, "Get up! Get up!" Isabel became quite agitated. She tended to be very literal and concrete in her language comprehension. Expressions like "I'm so tired I could die" left her apprehensive about actual death. By age five, Isabel remained almost completely nonverbal.

When the signs of autism spectrum disorder are clear, as in Isabel's case, early detection and intervention are essential to bolster verbal communication and social skills. The brain is simply more malleable when children are young. Isabel's story in *Unstrange Minds* is a heroic testament to the strides a child can make when afforded the right interventions at the right time.

However, the earlier an evaluation is conducted, the greater the risk of a false diagnosis. Many toddlers can be autistic-like in their behavior when they are stressed. Sometimes the procedures used by experts to evaluate toddlers generate the sort of stress that leads a struggling, but otherwise normally developing, toddler to behavior that is autistic-like.

Nobody has made this point more clearly than the late Dr. Stanley Greenspan, the internationally recognized child psychiatrist who developed the popular Floortime approach to treating autism spectrum disordered kids. In his web-based radio show several years before his death in April 2010, he cited an alarming statistic. Of the two hundred autism assessment programs his team surveyed across the country, many of which were located in prestigious medical centers, only 10 percent emphasized the need to observe a child along with a parent or guardian for more than ten minutes as they spontaneously interacted together.[2] He tended to observe children playing with a parent for forty-five minutes or more, waiting for choice points to engage a child to determine if he or she was capable of more sustained eye contact, elaborate verbalizations, or shared emotional reactions. Dr. Greenspan believed that these conditions of safety and sensitive interaction were essential in order to obtain an accurate reading of a child's true verbal and social skills.

For a sizable percentage of toddlers who don't transition well to new surroundings, freeze up with strangers, or temporarily dread being apart from a parent, the formal nature of a structured autism assessment can lead to their becoming mute, hiding under a table, avoiding eye contact, hand flapping, or exhibiting any number of other self-soothing behaviors that get misinterpreted as autistic-like. Trained professionals are supposed to conduct autism assessments in a standardized way. This is clinical jargon for being fairly neutral in one's approach to the child. This might involve an examiner assuming a seating position that requires a child to turn his or her head ninety degrees to directly look at the examiner when his or her name is called. If the child fails to look up and make direct eye contact with the examiner after his or her name is called aloud several times, the child is considered to be exhibiting autism red-zone behavior. Yet many distressed or slow-to-warm toddlers will only respond to their name if an unfamiliar adult strives to be warm, engaging, and nonthreatening—not just neutral.

It is these autistic-like situational reactions of struggling toddlers during formal testing conditions that make a false diagnosis a real possibility. A 2007 University of North Carolina at Chapel Hill study found that over 30 percent of children diagnosed as autistic at age two no longer fit the diagnosis at age four.[3] Several years ago, data supplied by parents of over seventy-eight thousand three- to seventeen-year-olds, as part of a National Survey of Children's Health, discovered that nearly 40 percent had a previous, but not a current, diagnosis of autism spectrum disorder.[4]

There are other reasons why a sizable percentage of toddlers get erroneously diagnosed with autism spectrum disorder. Up to one in five two-year-olds are late talkers.[5] They fall below the fifty-word expressive-vocabulary threshold and appear incapable of stringing together two- and three-word phrases. This sort of irregular language development is one of the hallmarks of early autism. Yet it is notoriously difficult to distinguish between toddlers with autism spectrum disorder and those who are afflicted with delayed language development. The situation is further complicated by the fact that toddlers with delayed language development tend to share other features in common with autism spectrum children. Scientific findings at the famed Yale Child Study Center have shown that toddlers with delayed language development are almost identical to their autism spectrum disordered counterparts in their use of eye contact to gauge social interactions, the range of sounds and words they produce, and the emotional give-and-take they are capable of.[6] Consequently, many toddlers who simply don't meet standard benchmarks for how quickly language should be acquired and social interactions mastered are in the autism red zone.

Expanding autistic phenomena to include picky eating and tantrums only amounts to more confusion when applied to toddlers. The percentage of young children in the United States with poor appetites and picky eating habits is so high that experts writing in the journal *Pediatrics* in 2007 commented, "It could reasonably be said that eating-behavior problems are a normal feature of toddler life."[7] Tantrums also are surprisingly frequent and intense during the toddler years. Dr. Gina Mireault, a behavioral sciences professor at Johnson State College in Vermont, studied children from three separate local preschools. She discerned that toddlers had tantrums, on average, once every few days. Almost a third of the parents surveyed considered their child's tantrum behavior to be distressing or disturbing.[8]

With the push to screen for and detect autism spectrum disorder at progressively younger ages, the risk is greater that late-talking, picky-eating, tantrum-throwing, transition-resistant toddlers will be misperceived as potentially autistic—especially if an evaluation is conducted in which the child is not sensitively engaged and put at ease. The risk is more acute, as I will soon illustrate, if this toddler is likely to develop into an introverted, cognitively gifted boy who tends to be single-minded and willful in his approach to life learning. Even more basic than that, if we don't have a firm grasp of gender differences in how young children communicate and socialize, we can mistake traditional masculine behavior for high-functioning autism.

HOW BOYS COMMUNICATE AND SOCIALIZE

A book I return to every so often is Eleanor Maccoby's *The Two Sexes*.[9] Her descriptions of boys' and girls' different speech styles jive with what I see daily in my office. She maintains, and I agree, that boys' speech, on average, tends to be more *egoistic* than girls'. Boys are more apt to brag, interrupt, and talk over others, and ignore commands or suggestions. They are more inclined to grandstand and "hold court," trying to impress listeners with all that they know. They seem to be less socially attuned than girls. They are less likely to scan the faces and body language of others for cues on whether they should stop talking and start listening—for basic social sensitivity reasons.

Simon Baron-Cohen, the Cambridge University professor who popularized the extreme-male-brain theory of autism, would say that boys' speech is more egoistic because, overall, boys tend to be less empathic than girls.[10] He backs this up with abundant scientific evidence. Putting yourself in someone else's shoes to figure out what they might be feeling comes more naturally to girls. Girls are simply more inclined to read a person's facial expressions in order to make sure that they are coming across sensitively. Faces tend to be sources of social feedback for girls in ways that they are not for boys. Dr. Baron-Cohen's research team has discovered that even at birth, female infants will look longer at faces than male infants and prolong mutual eye gazing.[11]

Many boys just get perplexed when you try to empathize with them. As an example, I recently had the following interaction with Alan, an eight-year-old:

ALAN: *In my soccer game over the weekend, the other forwards on my team never passed to me. I was so mad.*

DR. GNAULATI: *You were mad because your teammates didn't pass to you, eh.*

ALAN: *Why are you repeating what I just said? Didn't you hear me?*

This interaction with Alan captures how for many boys, grasping the literal content of their verbalizations matters more than "feeling understood." Appearing attentive, asking probing questions, and reflecting back what someone is saying may be the empathic glue that cements a friendship for the average female. However, for the average male, following along with and responding to the literal content of what they are saying is what's deemed valuable. A friend is someone who shares your interests and with whom you can have detailed discussions about these interests.

Watch boys at a sleepover and you'll quickly realize that they need a joint activity to buttress social interaction and verbal dialogue. If that joint activity is a videogame like *Red Dead Redemption*, the discussion will be peppered with pragmatic exchanges of information about how best to tame horses, free someone who has been kidnapped, or locate animal pelts. Without a joint activity that taps into their preexisting knowledge about that activity, boys are often at a loss for discussion. There are long silences. Eye contact is avoided. Bodies become more wiggly.

Watch girls at a sleepover and any shared activity they engage in is often secondary to the pleasure they seem to derive from just hanging out and talking.

The stereotype of boys as logical, inflexible, and businesslike in their communication habits is more than just a stereotype. A recent massive study out of the University of Florida involving fifty-four hundred children in the United States ages eight to sixteen indicates that twice as many boys as girls fit this thinking-type temperament. Conversely, twice as many girls as boys fit the feeling-type temperament—tactful, friendly, compassionate, and preferring emotion over logic.[12]

Many boys feel compelled to be logical and exact in their use of language. They withdraw and shut down around people who use language more loosely. A glaring example of this was shown to me recently by a fourteen-year-old client named Jordan. His parents brought him in for therapy because he was racking up school detentions for being rude to teachers. Jordan secretly confessed to me that his English teacher must be dumb because she referred to certain assignments as "homework" when she allowed them to be completed in class. She should have re-named them "schoolwork," he said, because they were being completed at school. In twenty-five years of therapy practice, I've never known a girl to make such a comment.

As educated people, we don't want to believe in overarching differ-ences in communication styles between the sexes. When I was in col-lege in the 1980s and '90s, "essentialism" was a dirty word. To believe that males and females might be different in essential ways was akin to admitting that you were unenlightened. There's still a pervasive sense in our culture that to be educated is to be gender-blind, and there is something of a taboo against voicing aloud explanations for a child's behavior in terms of his or her gender. If you don't believe me, try uttering some version of the following statements at your son's next parent-teacher conference: *Jamal is so logical and brusque when he talks. I know he needs all our help to ease up. But these are traditional masculine behaviors, after all, and we might need to accept him more for who he is.* Or, *Billy overtalks and really needs an audience, especially when he has a new favorite hobby or interest. He needs to be a better listener. But he's not unlike a lot of boys I know.*

It's this public discomfort with discussing children's gendered be-havior that gets many traditionally masculine boys inappropriately labeled as high-functioning autistic. Poor eye contact, long-winded monologues about one's new favorite topic, being overly serious and businesslike, appearing uninterested in other's facial expressions, and restricting friendships to those who share one's interests, may all be signs of Asperger's syndrome or high-functioning autism. However, these same traits typify boys who are traditionally masculine in their behavior. Parents somehow have to ask the uncomfortable question in the doctor's office: *Is he high-functioning autistic or really a more masculine-identified boy?* If it's the latter, what a boy may need is some combination of acceptance and personal and professional help to finesse his social skills over time—not an incorrect diagnosis and unnecessary medical treatment.

BRAINY, INTROVERTED BOYS BEWARE

Let's return to William. With all respect to the good doctors at the university-based institute who evaluated him, they were not up on the literature on mental giftedness. We know this because William manifested certain brainy, mentally gifted traits that can look autistic-like to the untrained eye, but aren't. Take his tendency to burrow deep into a topic and crave more and more information on it. There was his Pompeii phase, then his *Titanic* phase. He just had to learn all that he possibly could about these topics. He talked the ear off of anybody who would listen to him about them. On the face of it, William's obsessions appeared autistic-like. However, it is the enthusiasm with which he shared his interests with others that distinguishes William as brainy and mentally gifted, rather than autistic in any way. Remember, at preschool, he was sometimes a regular pied piper, amassing a following. Other kids were initially drawn to him when he held court or orchestrated his *Titanic* play. William lit up emotionally when he commanded the attention of the preschoolers who gathered around him.

When highly restricted interests are shared with relatively little spontaneity and enthusiasm, in ways that fail to entice children to come hither to listen and play—this is when we should suspect autism spectrum disorder. The same is true when a kid talks without interruption about a very technical topic, such as dinosaur names or bus schedules, seemingly indifferent to whether the listener congratulates him for his encyclopedic knowledge or is peeved by the lecture.

Another characteristic of William's that is evidence of mental giftedness and not autism spectrum disorder is how fluid and changeable his areas of interest could be. As he got older, William became fascinated by subjects as diverse as world geography, ancient history, the lives of rock stars (especially the Beatles), and vintage guitars. He approached his new areas of interest with the same degree of mental engrossment that he had approached his old ones, regardless of how unrelated the new ones were to the old ones. Autism spectrum disordered children tend to hold steadfast to their odd topics of interest over time and not readily substitute one for another.

One of the drawbacks to early screening and detection of high-functioning autism is that small children's cognitive development isn't sufficiently mature enough to judge what their sense of humor is like. Often it is a sense of humor that separates true cases of mild autism from mental giftedness. Mildly autistic kids often don't really comprehend irony, sarcasm, and absurdity. Mentally gifted kids, on the other hand, often thrive on irony, sarcasm, and absurdity. This distinction was brought home to me recently in an interaction with an intellectual eleven-year-old boy named Michael. His lengthy, detailed discourses on planets and the solar system made his parents wonder whether he might have Asperger's syndrome. One day, after meeting with his mother briefly for a check-in, I went out to the waiting room and warmly greeted Michael: "Speak of the devil, we were just talking about you." Michael came back to the office and, as he picked up a rubber sword to engage me, jokingly warned, "I am the devil, and you will get burned." I knew right then and there that Asperger's was completely out of the question.

Highly intelligent boys who happen to be introverted by temperament are probably the subpopulation of kids who are most likely to be erroneously labeled autistic. In her provocatively titled *Psychology Today* article "Revenge of the Introvert," Laurie Helgoe, a self-described card-carrying introvert, captures a key personality characteristic of introverts: "[They] like to think before responding—many prefer to think out what they want to say in advance—and seek facts before expressing opinions."[13] Introverted, highly intelligent boys may appear vacant and nonresponsive when asked a question like "What is your favorite animal?" Yet in their minds, they may be deeply and actively processing copious amounts of information on types and defining features of animals and zeroing in on precise words to use to articulate their complex thoughts. Thirty seconds, a minute, or even more time may pass before an answer is supplied. In the meantime, the listener might wonder if the boy is deaf or completely self-absorbed.

According to Laurie Helgoe: "Introverts seek time alone because they want time alone."[14] Brainy, introverted boys may cherish and look forward to alone time, which allows them the opportunity to indulge their intellectual appetites full throttle, amassing knowledge through reading or Internet searches. Solitude creates the time and space they need to totally immerse themselves in their preferred interests. They may get more turned on by studying ideas, pursuing science projects, or by solving math problems than by conversing with people.

In our extroverted culture, where being a "team player" and a "people person" are seen as linchpins of normalcy, the notion that a brainy, introverted boy might legitimately prefer the world of ideas over the world of people is hard for most people to accept. Parents of such boys may feel terribly uneasy about their tendency to want to be alone and try to push their sons to be sociable and to make more friends. But if you get to know such boys, they would much rather be alone reading, writing, or pursuing projects that stimulate their intellect than be socializing with peers who are not their intellectual equals. However, once they come into contact with a kindred spirit, someone who is a true intellectual equal with whom they can share the fullness of their ideas, that person just might become a lifelong friend. Around such kindred spirits, brainy, introverted boys can perk up and appear more extroverted and outgoing, wanting to talk as well as to listen. With people who share their interests, especially people who possess equal or greater knowledge in these areas, brainy, introverted boys can display quite normal social skills.

MY WAY OR NO WAY:
AUTONOMY SEEKING, NOT AUTISM

I'd like to engage the reader in a thought-provoking exercise. I'm going to list a collection of behaviors. As you peruse them, ask yourself if these behaviors are indicative of typical willful male toddlers or of possible autism at this age. Remember, the toddler years are from approximately age one to three.

*Doesn't look when you call their name, even if they seem to hear
  other sounds*

Doesn't look you in the eye much or at all

Doesn't notice when you enter or leave a room

Seems to be in their own world

*Doesn't look where you do or follow your finger when you point
  to something*

Leads you by the hand to tell you what they want

Can't do simple things you ask them to do

Has a lot of tantrums

Prefers to play alone

Wants to always hold a certain object, such as a flashlight

Doesn't play with toys in the usual way

It may surprise the reader to learn that I obtained this list of behaviors from a *Consumer Reports* health-related article titled "What Are the Symptoms of Autism?"[15] If this exercise left you thinking that these behaviors might be characteristic of both willful male toddlers and autistic children, that's commendable. This means that you have more than a passing familiarity with early childhood development. It also means that you are keenly aware of how toddler issues can get misconstrued as autistic tendencies.

The glee on the faces of toddlers upon discovering that they can propel themselves away from caregivers and into the world beyond—with the power of their own limbs—says it all. During the first year of life, they were relatively helpless. They were at the complete mercy of caregivers to gauge what they needed. Now their fast-evolving fine- and gross-motor abilities are being put to full use in exploring their surroundings. There is fire in their bellies. They insist on having personal control over what they get to see, hear, touch, smell, and taste and for how long. This is what developmental psychologists call the "need for autonomy" that kicks in during toddlerhood. The word parents tend to use is "willfulness." There is a world of sensory delight out there for toddlers to discover and sample, and they want nothing to get in their way.

Male toddlers advance at a faster rate than the opposite sex in their gross-motor development and visual-spatial skills. The science is there. Generally speaking, boys are more physically capable of exploring their environments than girls. When they do, objects are likely to be the object of their exploration. Little boys, especially those with strong visual-spatial intelligence, can appear as though they've entered a trance when they stare at, squeeze, lick, toss and fetch, arrange, stack, and knock down blocks—only to do it all over again. We forget how immersion in an activity, and repetition of it, can lead to an experience of mastery. Lining up trains in identical order, making the same sounds, and pulling them with the same force can rekindle the same feeling of mastery that was felt the first time this activity went well. Not all repetitiveness and needs for sameness speak to autistic tendencies. When a toddler appears driven to use his body effectively in the accomplishment of a task and to further an experience of mastery, it's unlikely that he's on the spectrum no matter how repetitive the task becomes—particularly if that toddler shows self-pride and wants others to share in the excitement of it all, even in quiet and subdued ways.

Boys' level of engrossment in discovering and manipulating objects can lead them to be oblivious to their surroundings. They may not look up when their name is called. They may appear unconcerned whether you're in the room or not. Self-absorption while studying objects is expectable behavior for male toddlers, especially for those on the upper end of the bell curve on visual-spatial intelligence.

Parents and educators shouldn't assume the worst when male toddlers play alone. Research shows that boys are far more likely to engage in solitary play than girls at this age. Many little boys are satisfied playing alone or quietly alongside someone else, lining up toy trains, stacking blocks, or engaging in a range of sensorimotor play activities. It is not until about age four or five that boys are involved in associative play to the same extent as girls.[16] That's the kind of play where there's verbal interaction and give-and-take exchanges of toys and ideas.

The difference between a relatively typical male toddler immersed in solitary object play and one who shows early signs of autistic behavior can be subtle. Typically developing male toddlers are more apt to experience periodic separation anxiety. They suddenly wonder where Mommy is. Needing Mommy in these moments takes precedence over the activity in which they were absorbed. Sometimes visually checking in and receiving a reassuring glance back from Mommy is enough. Sometimes more is needed, like approaching her for a hug or a pat on the back. This inspires confidence that Mom will be available if and when needed. The toddler can then go across the room and pick up where he left off playing. This "emotional pit stop" behavior is less apparent with toddlers on the spectrum.

Mentally gifted boys are often perfectionists. Their projects need to be done just right, and they will continue to work on a project until it is exactly what they want. During toddlerhood, when early signs of perfectionism are mixed with regular needs for autonomy, the combination can make a child look very controlling. A cognitively advanced three-year-old boy who is also a perfectionist might spend hours arranging and rearranging, stacking and restacking blocks to construct a castle that he feels needs to be flawless if he's to be satisfied. Attempts to get his attention, have him come to the kitchen for a snack, or put the blocks aside to get ready for bed are ignored or resisted. When such demands are issued suddenly, without forewarning, and instant compliance is expected, this is the emotional equivalent, for the toddler, of someone purposely tripping and badly injuring a front-place marathon runner right at the finish line. A tantrum is a distinct possibility. The child is in emotional pain due to being unable to prolong and achieve an experience of mastery.

Tantrums during the toddler years are, of course, commonplace. Under normal family circumstances, when a toddler's maturation is right on schedule, parents can expect a tantrum from their three- to five-year-old once every few days. That was the conclusion of Dr. Gina Mireault's study, cited earlier. Her research also revealed that the reason top ranked by parents as triggering a toddler's tantrum is this: "Denial of a request/not getting his or her way."[17] Most tantrums are triggered by parents directly confronting kids' assertions of autonomy or by kids' need to have personal control over what they get to see, hear, touch, smell, and taste, and for how long. Tantrums can be exacerbated by fatigue and hunger. Toddlers have different temperaments, and this influences the frequency, intensity, and duration of tantrums. But in general, tantrums occur because a toddler is denied ice cream before dinner, for example, or is prevented from grabbing Grandma's expensive Moorcroft pottery dish or insists on watching one more show when it's bedtime—or any such expectable parental challenge to their need to prolong a pleasurable activity or independently exercise sensorimotor mastery.

The tantrums of autism spectrum kids are less likely to be of the autonomy-assertion or mastery-seeking variety. Their tantrums more often than not reflect sensory overload. They may scream and writhe around on the floor because they are in physical pain due to their nervous system being bombarded by an intolerable level of stimulation. The sights and sounds at the mall when their family is shopping for holiday gifts may put them over the top. The buzz from and brightness of overhead lights might be a trigger. Rituals and routines are relied on to keep sensory stimulation at manageable levels. Tantrums may signal a need to keep a ritual or routine exactly the way it was to protect the kid from sensory overload.

Sometimes what appears to be an autistic-like tantrum is really what Dr. Stanley Greenspan, the world-renowned child psychiatrist, calls "sensory craving." This applies to toddlers whose ability to self-regulate their feelings while they're in the act of exploring their environments is underdeveloped:

> Many children show a pattern we call "sensory craving," where they're running around the house trying to get more sensation into their system, whether it's staring at fans, or bumping into things or touching everything or just shifting from one toy to another in a seemingly aimless way, or just spinning around and jumping around or shaking their arms and legs in seemingly disjointed ways. These all look like terrible symptoms and they scare parents and they scare some professionals as well, understandably so. But they're often signs of sensory craving—a child wants more sensory input, but doesn't know how to do it in an organized social way.[18]

These are toddlers who Dr. Greenspan thinks need abundant "sensory meaningful" interactions with parents and care providers to help them become more self-composed over time. This could amount to matching the child's energy and activity level in a fun airplane-ride game. Scooping him up, asking him to point his fist in the direction in which he wants to be flown, with a thumbs-up for faster and a thumbs-down for slower, would be an example of a sensory-meaningful interaction that still honors his need for autonomy.

Temper outbursts and quirky behavior around food preferences are widespread among autism spectrum children. But the same can be said of toddlers in general. It's important to have a sense of perspective regarding the pervasiveness of toddlers' habit of latching onto preferred foods and rejecting new offerings. A survey of more than three thousand households with infants and toddlers conducted by nutrition experts at the University of Tennessee–Knoxville indicates that a whopping 50 percent of two-year-olds are considered picky eaters by their caregivers. These nutritionists believe the numbers are so high because mothers are not persistent enough in introducing new foods in ways that ensure they'll eventually be eaten: "When offering a new food, mothers need to provide many more repeated exposures (e.g., eight to 15 times) to enhance acceptance of that food than they currently do."[19]

Let's call this the "eight-to-fifteen-times rule." If a toddler reacts with revulsion, aggressively throwing dishes on the floor or refusing to eat each time a new food item is introduced after eight to fifteen separate attempts, chances are that he or she is a picky eater. This is particularly true if, in the process, the parent stayed calm and conveyed confidence that the new food item was good to eat—not being too insistent on the one hand, or tentative, on the other.

But certainly not all picky eaters are that way because they are on the spectrum. Autism spectrum children who are picky eaters often have odd food preferences, such as only eating foods that are yellow-colored. Their reactions after repeated exposure to new foods frequently remain acute or become even more blustery. It's not about power struggles and control. A new food item may literally assault their senses. The smell, look, and texture of that food may induce a type of sensory revulsion and disgust. They can't be around it. Either it goes or the kid does—perhaps agitatedly running off.

OFF THE SPECTRUM

The younger in age a kid is when professionals screen for milder forms of autism, the greater the risk a struggling kid will be misperceived as a disordered one. A vast number of toddlers present in the doctor's office with a hodgepodge of social and emotional difficulties, such as poor eye contact, overactivity and underactivity, tantrums, picky eating, quirky interests, or social awkwardness. These phenomena need not be seen as telltale signs of autism spectrum disorder. Sometimes they are merely evidence of a perfect storm of off-beat events in social and emotional development mixed with difficult personality traits—with the upshot that the kid, for the time being, is very out of sorts.

When we mistake a brainy, introverted boy for an autism spectrum disordered one, we devalue his mental gifts. We view his ability to become wholeheartedly engrossed in a topic as a symptom that needs to be stamped out, rather than a form of intellectualism that needs to be cultivated. Boys like William don't need to be channeled into unwanted and unnecessary social-skills classes to obtain formal instruction on how to start and sustain normal conversations. They don't need to be prodded to be more sociable with the neighborhood kid whose mind works completely differently from theirs. They need unique school programs that cater to the mentally gifted in which others will not be chagrined by their intense love for ideas and where they have a shot at making true friends and therefore have the opportunity to feel truly sociable.

CHAPTER NINE

Parenting with Authority

Over the past four decades, we have gone from blaming parents for kids' problem behaviors to blaming kids' brains. Somehow the debate has been limited to two choices: nurture or nature. When their child acts out, lacks self-control, becomes depressed, or is socially withdrawn, parents have been railroaded into accepting the cause to be either faulty child rearing or faulty brain chemistry. Yet rarely can a child's behavior be explained exclusively in terms of child rearing or brain chemistry. In most cases, it is *causes*—plural, not singular—that explain why a child behaves the way he or she does.

It is not surprising that parents would seek to understand their child's troubling or troublesome behavior in terms of a single, straightforward cause. Parents are typically distressed and confused by their child's actions and desperate for a solution. Thus they tend to be easily persuaded by simple explanations and proposed remedies that promise fast results. Medical explanations and treatments can be particularly seductive: "Jasmine has a dopamine deficiency in her brain, which causes her to be impulsive. It can be easily corrected with medication." However, if parents are to be truly effective in addressing the situation, they must take the time to scrutinize all the parts of the bio-psychosocial puzzle that might explain their child's behavior. Through a sober examination of this multifaceted puzzle, parents can start to zero in on where and how they may be able to effect change in positive ways. When Paul's aggressive behavior becomes a concern, a range of issues might be looked at. For instance, what part might the following factors play in his behavior?

His temperament or basic personality style

His genetic similarity to his high-strung uncle

The lack of a quality preschool program in the neighborhood that might have bolstered Paul's emotional self-control early on in his life

His poor sleep patterns, aggravated by an early school start-time

The influence of Paul's rabble-rouser friends and their lack of access to a community center staffed with adults who could mentor them

The cumulative frustration of being afflicted with delayed fine-motor abilities resulting in poor handwriting skills while attending a school that emphasizes paper-and-pencil output

His school's zero-tolerance of roughhousing, which prevents Paul from burning off aggressive energy during recess

Mounting resentment in Paul because he only sees his father on a limited basis, when his father's erratic work schedule allows it

Being chronically harassed by his older sister

His math teacher's tendency to give automatic Fs for work completed in pencil rather than pen

His mother's tendency to be emotionally reactive, especially when she feels unsupported at home

Paul's own underdeveloped verbal assertiveness skills, which tend to lead him to be bossy in order to get his way

The fact that Paul has a computer and a TV in his bedroom and watches unsavory videos and sitcoms late at night, unbeknownst to his parents

Paul's resistance to acknowledging his underlying hurt feelings when his pride is injured, instead defaulting to angrily lashing out

It can be empowering for parents to look at their child's behavioral difficulties with the knowledge that the causes are a blend of biological, social, and psychological factors. It absolves them of the inaccurate and unfair charge that their child's troubles are due solely to parental faults and failings. Knowing that they might be contributing to their child's troubles, but are certainly not the sole cause of them, enables parents to step forward and, with self-respect, commit to parenting differently. The vast majority of the hundreds of parents I've worked with over the years have been both eager to examine their habits and receptive to my recommendations regarding how they might parent more effectively. Parents are typically innately aware that there are few virtuous goals in life that rival raising emotionally healthy children. In the pages that follow I will provide practical guidance to parents to spur self-examination and thereby fine-tune their parenting to advance their struggling child's ability to be more self-disciplined, even-tempered, and socially fluent. Of course, parents' willingness to acknowledge their shortcomings and fine-tune their parenting skills is even more admirable when we take into account how formidable the task of raising a child has become in the twenty-first century. As we have seen in the preceding pages, the various roles now associated with being a diligent parent can create unexpected challenges.

BURDENSOME NEW PARENTAL ROLES

Parents have had to absorb several new roles in recent decades that can be a source of serious conflict in the parent-child relationship unless they are handled carefully: event planner, electronic media supervisor, homework sergeant, and sleep monitor. Although previous generations of parents have always felt responsible for structuring their children's time to some degree, as well as overseeing their media and homework habits, these roles now dominate family life.

Event Planner

Social scientists have documented the profound changes that have occurred over time in the basic nature of children's play experiences. In the 1960s and '70s, children's play was likely to be active and social, and to take place outdoors. Nowadays, children's play primarily is inactive, asocial, and more likely to happen indoors. In bygone years, children were exhorted by their parents to go play outside, where they readily found a handful of their neighborhood friends encouraged to do likewise by their own parents. Away from any adult purview, children negotiated among themselves whether the communal activity would be kickball, handball, stickball, street hockey, kick the can, or any number of other time-honored childhood games. As a child, it was inconceivable for me to think that my parents were largely responsible for how I spent my free time. Now, as a parent, it is inconceivable for me to think that I am not largely responsible for how my son spends his free time.

There is now significant social pressure on parents to be decent event planners. There is the risk of being perceived as irresponsible or even neglectful if as a parent you are not filling your child's schedule with extracurricular activities. Participation in the American Youth Soccer Organization or Little League carries with it the assumption that parent volunteer hours are a staple of middle-class family life. Finding time to transport kids to baseball and soccer practice, music lessons, karate class, after-school tutoring, and a myriad of other activities is a given. Researching, planning, and saving for quality summer camps for one's kids can feel like a part-time job in itself.

The upshot is that there can be mutual resentment between parents and children. Parents feel that unless they structure their offspring's time, their sons and daughters will default to staying home, playing video games, watching television, and not getting the exercise they need. Yet the time and energy it takes to support children's outside activities can sap opportunities for parents to have their own regenerating and life-enhancing pursuits. The latest studies show that almost 60 percent of married fathers report that they have too little time for themselves.[1] Of course, the picture is even bleaker for mothers. Seventy-one percent of married mothers and 78 percent of single mothers report the same.[2] This can lead to frustration, and frustration can erupt into anger when kids are less than appreciative of all the sacrifices parents have made to ensure that they have adequate enrichment experiences.

At the same time, kids can take it for granted that their parents' lives revolve around scheduling and maintaining their activities, and they might be baffled that parents expect them to acknowledge and be appreciative of their efforts. This is, after all, what parents do: all their friends' parents do the same. They may be no more inclined to appreciate their parents' efforts in planning and executing fun, stimulating activities than to appreciate the fact that there is oxygen in the air for them to breathe. Kids may also resent all the forced interaction associated with parents being event planners. The heated negotiations over which activities or sports will be signed up for, the long car rides across town, the constant planning for pickups and drop-offs, and parents automatically assuming that their presence is desired at a kid's every practice, sports event, and performance, can leave a child feeling smothered. Angry expressions may be the child's way of communicating that there's too much forced parent-child contact occurring.

Parenting Tips

- View carpooling and ride sharing as an essential component of planning kids' activities.
- Don't assume that you should attend all of your child's sports events, practices, and performances. Attend the key ones. Check in with your child about whether your attendance is desired.
- Talk to kids periodically in a sensitive, nonpreachy way about the efforts and sacrifices you as parents make in order to provide them with extracurricular activities. Realize that they may not automatically feel appreciative.
- Insist on time for kids to engage in free play where they are responsible for deciding what games will be played, when such games will start and stop, what the rules will be, and how disagreements will be handled. Limit adult intervention to preventing harm.
- Treat your need for alone time and the pursuit of fulfilling life activities as sacred.

Electronic Media Supervisor

The most recent data on media use by eight- to eighteen-year-olds in the United States put out by the Kaiser Family Foundation indicates that children are watching TV, listening to music, using cell phones, surfing the net, playing on video-game consoles, or some combination of all of these, an average of seven hours and thirty-eight minutes a day.[3] That's up from six hours and twenty-one minutes in 2004. In 1999, approximately 65 percent of children had a TV in their bedroom. Today that figure stands at 71 percent. Over a third of eight- to eighteen-year-olds have a computer in their bedroom, and 50 percent of them have a video-game console right alongside it. Kids are nothing short of wedded to screens. Since there is little government censorship of content across media devices regarding what is suitable viewing for kids, parents are responsible for being the chief watchdogs.

Battles ensue between parents and children over what is permissible to view on screens, when, and for how long. A frequent lament of children is that their friends are allowed to play video games rated mature, so why shouldn't they? It appears that kids aren't making this up. The same Kaiser Family Foundation study noted above found that nearly 60 percent of eleven- to fourteen-year-olds have played *Grand Theft Auto*, a video game rated suitable for those seventeen and older, which contains sexual themes, violence, profanity, and references to illicit drugs. There is tremendous pressure on parents to compromise their better judgment and passively acquiesce to their children's demands that they buy them video games with questionable content.

Parents don't often grasp one essential difference between video games and TV programs that are popular among kids. The average video game played on a game console tends to have no consistent time boundaries. TV programs begin and end at a certain time. But once a kid launches into a *Call of Duty: Modern Warfare* battle, the event can be endless. When it ends depends on so many factors—how successful a kid has been at mortally wounding enemy combatants and avoiding being mortally wounded by them; how stealthy he or she has been in destroying the supplies and equipment of enemy combatants; and when friends and favorite gaming buddies go on- and offline. Suddenly demanding that a child immediately end a video game without putting up a fuss is an unrealistic expectation and can create resentment. To do so means to wrench him or her midstream from a game he or she has expended much time and energy on. It would be the equivalent of a parent from a bygone era showing up at the pavement midway through a street-hockey game and insisting that a kid pick up the puck right as he or she was about to score and come home immediately—without any snarky pushback.

This is not to say that kids can and should be left to monitor how much time they spend playing video games. One of the hazards of video gaming is that kids lose track of the time and underestimate the amount of time they actually spend gaming. Sometimes the anger they show at parents when they are told to break away from gaming is misdirected. Sometimes they are actually mad at themselves for playing for so long and feel guilty that they have allowed video gaming to monopolize their time.

Parenting Tips

- Don't allow children to have TVs, computers, smartphones, or game consoles in their bedrooms, where it can be difficult to monitor what they are watching and for how long.
- Institute a "no screens one-hour before bedtime" rule so your child's sleep is not disrupted.
- Always frame access to media devices as a privilege that can be revoked at any time if agreed-upon time limits are not followed or if children resort to viewing inappropriate or forbidden content.
- If your child constantly defaults to accessing screens when bored or restless, pull the plug on all screens for a designated amount of time. Help your child generate a list of nonscreen hobbies and activities that he or she can alternately pursue. Agree to restore screen time only when your child has put time and effort into pursuing these hobbies and activities.
- Realize that a child will need multiple reminders of when his or her allotted gaming time is about to expire in order to allow him or her some flexibility in deciding the best end point.
- Sensitively reframe the anger your child directs at you after hours of video gaming as him or her possibly feeling mad and guilty for mismanaging his or her time.

- Eliminate or heavily limit screen time on school days.
- Set up summer-camp experiences, sleepovers, and family vacations that are screen-free.
- Coordinate with parents of your children's friends to limit screen time on play dates and sleepovers.
- Allow handheld devices to be brought to social events and family outings only on special occasions or long trips.
- Understand that the main gateway to mature video games and age-inappropriate TV viewing for kids is an older sibling's screen habits. Enforce different media rules for siblings depending on their age. Older siblings will need to be encouraged to adopt a stewardship role.

Homework Sergeant

In the twenty or so years that I have been providing psychological services to children and families from different walks of life, I have seen a skyrocketing increase in complaints by parents of intractable struggles around homework. Many parents dread the afternoon and evening when they have to coax and cajole their kids to settle down and apply themselves to completing homework. There can be a volatile mix of circumstances. Kids have been at school all day suppressing their feelings and overregulating their behavior to fit in and be good pupils. When they arrive home, with the comfort and security they associate with being home, they are susceptible to unraveling emotionally. Children are often aware of the real-life drawbacks of avoiding, resisting, or refusing to do work at school. The prospect of being required to go to the principal's office or suffer negative judgments by teachers and peers can make a child think twice about balking about doing work. However, once he or she is home, in the presence of loving parents, that same child may give full expression to his or her dissatisfaction at having to just settle down and do work. Most kids would rather have an argument with a parent than do their math homework. They typically feel there is less emotional risk in giving a parent grief for enforcing schoolwork obligations than in giving a teacher grief.

The upshot is that children often are at their most volatile and regressed at home during that time period in the afternoon and evening when parents need them to be composed and productive. After all, many parents are coming off their own workday with its own stresses and strains. They naturally desire that their parental duties around homework, dinnertime, and bedtime be executed harmoniously and without undue friction.

Schools and teachers seem to underestimate the disruption to family life caused by assigning too much homework during the elementary and middle-school years before children have reached the maturity level to organize and focus their work habits and manage their time well. The buzz around high-stakes testing—making schools more accountable for the academic progress of students as reflected in test scores—has led to an increase in homework for the average student at a younger and younger age. Several years ago, a study out of the University of Michigan discovered that the amount of time six- to seventeen-year-olds dedicate to homework has jumped from two hours and thirty-eight minutes in 1981 to three hours and fifty-eight minutes today.[4] Yet a rising chorus of experts agree that there's no real correlation between the amount of homework assigned to elementary school children and their subsequent academic achievement. The "ten-minute rule" endorsed by the National Education Association is catching on.[5] This is the recommendation that ten minutes of homework time be added at each grade level, beginning in the first grade. Second graders should have no more than twenty minutes of homework, third graders no more than thirty minutes of homework, and so forth. The maximum recommended amount of homework in high school is considered to be two hours. The consensus is that homework should reinforce what a student has already learned in the classroom and should not introduce new material.

Parenting Tips

- Allocate a homework desk for your child to routinely use that is free from as many audio, tactile, and visual distractions as possible. It should be kept reasonably neat.

- When financially and logistically possible, take yourself out of the "homework mix" by hiring a tutor. Otherwise, enlist the help of a child's uncle, aunt, grandparent, or older cousin to step in and oversee the homework situation.
- Don't hover around your child and show outward frustration as he or she is doing homework. This can lead to a child baiting you into an argument that is preferred over having to actually do homework. Calmly redirect him or her back to what needs to be completed and remove yourself from the situation.
- Provide descriptive praise targeted at your child's good work habits: "Look at you sitting at your desk doing your spelling words without getting up and wandering around. That's true perseverance!" and "My, my I like what my eyes are seeing. You turned off your iPod and have been reading quietly on your own for over half an hour. What concentration!"
- Lobby teachers, school officials, and parent-teacher associations to implement the "ten-minute rule" homework guidelines recommended by the National Education Association.

Sleep Monitor

Because of the various roles parents are now playing in their children's lives and all that needs to be crammed into a day, parents often overlook the importance of setting the conditions that are conducive for kids getting a good night's sleep. Yet this is an especially important role parents must play. Ensuring that kids get a good night's sleep is one of the most important steps that parents can take to strengthen their children's attention and concentration, and to keep their moods stable.

Parenting Tips

- Maintain a consistent bedtime for your child, with soothing rituals. Consider activities like having your child take a hot bath or shower, listen to comforting music or books-on-tape, or reading a calming book.
- Remind yourself that children ages three to five need eleven to thirteen hours of sleep each night; those ages five to twelve need ten to eleven hours; and preteens and teens need at least nine hours.

- Carefully monitor caffeine intake. Remember, caffeine has an eight-hour half-life, which means that half the caffeine consumed is chemically active in your kid's body eight hours after it was consumed.
- Forbid screen time for at least an hour before bedtime.
- Remove all electronic devices from the child's bedroom, including cell phones.
- Keep the bedroom dark, cool (below seventy-five degrees), and quiet.
- Consider the use of earplugs if noise cannot be sufficiently controlled.
- Monitor the length of preteen and teen afternoon naps. More than twenty to twenty-five minutes can put them at risk of falling into deeper sleep states and interfere with nighttime sleep patterns.

FOSTERING SELF-DISCIPLINE

Young children are naturally impulsive, distractible, disorganized, forgetful, and prone to taking the easy way out. Their self-discipline is a perpetual work-in-progress. If they are to mature into older children with adequate ability to show self-restraint, focused attention, conscientiousness, and grit and perseverance, they need home environments where there is structure and predictable routines. They need parents to hold the maturational bar higher than they are inclined to hold it for themselves. This can be as simple as expecting an eight-year-old to clear the dishes off the dinner table, scrape the leftovers into the garbage, and correctly place plates and silverware in the dishwasher before watching his or her favorite TV show. We forget how much the building blocks of self-discipline are embedded in the ordinary aspects of family life. There are abundant, ready-at-hand ways that are available for parents to strengthen their kid's ability to take on and follow through with commitments, tolerate frustration along the way, finish what is started in a timely manner, and delay gratification.

Parents need to have one eye on their kid's long-term development. Teachers, professors, and bosses are not in the habit of dishing out easy praise. They define success in terms of actual performance. They tend to see through false overconfidence and be suspect of dramatically

expressed excuses for inferior work. To ensure that these future experiences will not psychologically derail our kids as they enter the adult
world, we as parents need to be active stewards of their more mature,
independent self. Fortunately, there are practical steps parents can take
to foster self-discipline in their kids.

*Gauge the Right Amount of Assistance
to Bolster a Child's Self-Mastery*

A good rule-of-thumb for parents to keep in mind is that the right
amount of support, given at the right time in the right way, can make
or break whether a kid perseveres in independently finishing a challenging task or gives up in frustration. Psychologists call this "scaffold-
ing" a task to ensure that a child strengthens his or her independent
mastery of it. For example, upon witnessing his five-year-old daughter
about to emotionally implode as she struggles to build a Lego house,
a father might say something soothing and reassuring like, "You did
such a good job building the walls of your house, but I can see that you
need help with building the roof. How about if I try to help you find
good roof parts?" Locating Lego parts within reach of his daughter
that have a high likelihood of fitting together to make a roof fuels a
successful experience and furthers her independent mastery. Similarly,
a mother might position a stepstool close to the toilet after her three-
year-old son protests over being too tired to move his body onto the
toilet by himself. In response to his eight-year-old kid crumpling up
a math worksheet after being unable to solve a long-division problem, a
father might calmly and assertively pick the worksheet up and smooth
and flatten it out while saying, "Wow, that long-division problem must
have been really hard for you to get that mad. Show me what part of it
you had trouble with."

Caregivers can undermine a children's emerging capacity for independent mastery by rescuing them during moments of frustration and
completing the task for them or allowing them to abandon it outright.
The high-water mark is to strive to calmly and assertively redirect the
child back to the task and restructure it so that it is achievable with
some outside support and encouragement.

Connect Success to Effort and Perseverance

Children often naively assume that success or failure at what they pursue is mostly due to innate ability or the lack thereof. If they ace a spelling test, it's because they're good spellers. If they score from far away on the soccer field, it's because they have a hard kick. This way of thinking can set them up for overconfident self-judgments and unproductive failure experiences. If they believe that ability alone can carry them, why practice, why study, or why prepare? When they fail because they underpracticed or underprepared, believing instead that it was due to a lack of ability, they can become demoralized and convinced that it's not worth trying again. Believing that success and failure pivot on ability doesn't give them much control over improving their performance. Believing that they turn on how much effort and perseverance they can muster does. There is much to be gained by parents making explicit linkages for children regarding their successes and failures being due to the amount of effort and perseverance that they put in:

> *Francesca, I bet you are so proud of yourself. You put so much time and effort into memorizing your lines and rehearsing them, and it really bore fruit. You were so confident in your school play tonight!*

> *I'm not surprised that your baseball coach sat you out today, Charlie. I watched you during practice this week and you seemed to be traveling at half speed and were goofing off with your friends. You didn't practice hard like the kids did that got the most game time today. If you want game time next week, you probably have to be more focused and committed at practice.*

Use Praise and Incentives Effectively

The use of praise and incentives with kids has gotten bad press of late. The person in the public spotlight who is most critical of praise as a socializing tool is Alfie Kohn, a prolific author of books that cater to parents and educators. He claims that praising and rewarding kids lessens their intrinsic motivation to pursue their interests and erodes their skill at self-judging their performance.[6] But not all types of praising and rewarding kids are created equal. Some do indeed lead to the effects mentioned by Kohn. However, others are an essential means to instilling greater motivation and mastery in kids.

The Columbia University psychologist Dr. Carol Dweck provides scientific backing for praise that highlights kids' effort and the approach or strategy taken to succeed.[7] Overall, the type of praise that bolsters kids' motivation and self-determination is that which is sincere, descriptive, and targets kids' effort and strategies:

> *I could see how you were huffing and puffing to make it to the other side of the monkey bars, sometimes taking one bar at a time, sometimes two when you felt strong. You were trying so hard!*

> *Wow, I'm impressed by your courage. You came all the way upstairs, looked me straight in the eyes, and with a strong voice asked me for help with your homework. I know how hard it is for you to ask for help, but you did it anyway.*

> *Great job on getting all your spelling words right today. I saw you in the car this morning right before school memorizing them. I guess you figured out that memorizing them right before the test gives you a better shot at doing well! That's the way I used to do it when I was your age!*

> *Was that dribbling move you used before you scored in the game the one you tried over and over at soccer practice this week? The one where you fake to the left and go around the right side of the player with the ball? That was real sweet!*

The type of praise that is ill advised is that which is insincere, global, and directed at a kid's presumed personality traits and attributes:

> *You're such a great, likable kid! You will succeed at whatever you try!*

> *You've got such musical talent. I could see you on Broadway.*

> *I don't know another kid who's as good looking as you. You're gonna have so many opportunities in life.*

Praise that is global and insincere like this, among other things, can lessen our credibility as parents. It results in kids questioning the accuracy, value, and genuineness of our perceptions of them: *You're just saying that because I'm your kid and you love me. Yeah, yeah, yeah, whatever.* They may then tune us out and ignore us when we have real wisdom to impart and real-life messages we want them to heed.

Rewards and incentives are best used when attempting to help kids achieve very specific goals where the steps involved are unpleasant and when we want to help them push the limits of what they are capable of in a pursuit that they otherwise essentially enjoy. Examples of this are:

> *You have a daughter who is an avid tennis player, whose game could be more competitive if she improved her serve. However, she loathes hitting serves over and over during practice in order to become a more proficient server. You promise her twenty dollars if she keeps at it during practice until she successfully hits twenty serves in a row.*

> *Your son spends hours in his room taking delight in playing the guitar. He wishes he could be in the school jazz band, yet he resists learning to read sheet music, which would make his goal realizable. You make a deal with him to buy him a new guitar once he has completed a class at the local music center on reading sheet music.*

Remember, a Rule Is Not a Rule until It Is Tested, Then Enforced

Most parents want to believe that the mere utterance of a rule should be enough to produce compliance in their children. They want to believe that just telling a kid not to hit his sister, to brush his teeth before bedtime, or not to yell inside the house should be enough to elicit compliance. When these directions are not followed, parents repeat themselves, retelling the kid what not to do—with mounting frustration each time. This is when warnings and threats get made: *What part of "Stop hitting your sister" did you not hear? If I have to warn you again, you'll be in big trouble.* A surefire sign that parents haven't acquired an effective disciplinary system is when they frequently find themselves nagging their kids, repeating themselves, overtalking an issue, and reissuing threats in an exasperated tone.

Kids need the concrete experience of testing a rule and having it be enforced by parents in order for the rule to feel legitimate. It's a form of experiential learning about the effects of their behavior in the real world. When six-year-old Hillary slips into bed without brushing her teeth, after her mother has made it clear that teeth brushing needs to occur before bedtime, it may be that Hillary doesn't quite grasp the seriousness of the rule. It has to be made serious by her mother with the enforcement of a consequence: *Hillary, sweetheart, I made it clear that if you don't brush your teeth before bedtime, there will be no candy treat the next day. So, tomorrow it's no candy treat.* Family life can be much more harmonious when parents get good at making rules and expectations clear in advance, putting kids on notice as to the likely consequences if they are not followed, and coolheadedly enforcing these consequences when called for.

George, you know the rule, no using your cell phone in bed after lights out. Please hand it over. I will keep it over the weekend and give it back to you on Monday morning.

Elaine, I need you to stop yelling at your brother. I'm going to count to five. If your voice isn't lowered by the time I count to five, there will be no TV for you after dinner. One . . . two . . . three . . . four . . . five. Whoops, you were unable to find your quiet voice. I need you to go to your room. The TV won't be going on for you tonight.

Shaneka, I mean it when I say that you have to pick up all the clothes on the floor, put the dirty ones in the clothes hamper, and fold the clean ones neatly and put them in your dresser. I'll be back in thirty minutes. If the job's not done, I'm not letting you go to the mall this afternoon with your friends. [With the job incomplete after thirty minutes] *Shaneka, I made myself quite clear, I think. There are dirty clothes in your dresser and clean ones in your hamper, and others stuffed under your bed. You can't go to the mall this afternoon.*

Be Careful about Automatically
Taking Kids' Protests Literally

All children at some point lobby hard to avoid having to switch from a desirable activity they are pleasurably immersed in to an undesirable one life requires of them:

> *Just give me thirty more minutes of Xbox time and I promise you, I really do, that I'll stay up late and do the best job I've ever done on my history homework.*
>
> *I know dinnertime is right now, but I'm in the middle of watching* Family Guy. *I'm not really hungry anyway. I'll be hungry later on. How about I just eat later while I'm doing my homework?*
>
> *That's right. I did agree to get a haircut today. But I can get my hair cut any old time. All my friends are online playing* Red Dead Redemption. *I don't feel like leaving the house. I've had a busy week at school. Don't I deserve some downtime?*

Parents need to guard against automatically getting caught taking a kid's utterances literally in these moments and giving in to their wishes. It's important to be flexible and to give kids a break here and there. However, if kids are to develop a capacity to do things out of a sense of duty and commitment, and not just because it's pleasurable and stimulating, parents need to hang tough.

> *I get it. You'd rather play Xbox than do history homework, especially with all the reading you have to do tonight. You've already used up all your Xbox time. I'll give you five to ten minutes to finish up, then it's time to hit the books.*
>
> *You can tape and watch* Family Guy *later; that is, if you eat a decent amount of your dinner. In two minutes, I need you at the dinner table.*
>
> *Yes, downtime is important. But you've had a good bit of it today already. Tell your friends you can go online later, after you get back from the hairdressers.*

Being held accountable to follow through with commitments and bring arduous projects to completion are also occasions for children to pull out all the stops in order to convince parents that terminating is the only compassionate course of action.

> *I'm bored out of my mind in karate. The sensei is so full of himself. He talks on and on about all the competitions he has won and never lets us use any of the new equipment. I'm totally done with karate.*
>
> *I don't see why I have to write out all my times tables without using a calculator. You're being so uptight right now. Dad gets it. He lets me use a calculator.*

In these moments, parents need to act as amateur psychologists, listening with their "third ear" to decipher what is really being communicated. Sometimes kids have good reasons for ending a commitment or discontinuing a project. There may be intolerable shame and anxiety involved. The costs of following through with a commitment might drastically outweigh any benefit the kid derives from it. Parents need to step back, acknowledge how the kid is feeling, and review the evidence to see if the kid's arguments are credible. However, more often than not, the child is experiencing transitory frustration and demoralization and, if he or she is to develop grit and determination, parents do the right thing by upholding a commitment.

> *I can tell you are mad at your sensei and wish he didn't talk so much about his achievements. However, your mom and I paid for karate until the summer and I know how badly you want to get your brown belt. I need you to at least follow through with this goal, then we can discuss whether you should continue with karate.*
>
> *Doing math in your head is hard, I know. I'm going to get dinner ready. I need you to start where you finished off doing your times tables without a calculator.*

Honor and Support Kids' Needs for Mentors and Role Models
Mentors and role models are important sources of inspiration as kids
grow older and become young adults. An older teenager might grow
very attached to a teacher the teen views as an ideal version of the type
of person he or she wants to become. It's as if this attachment is a lifeline to realizing goals, ambitions, and aspirations. The older teenager
might suddenly find traction in his or her life to give full expression to
a dormant talent, to pursue it full guns, confident that a mentor is there
to witness and support this endeavor. Maybe it's a basketball coach who
is a credible evaluator of athletic ability because he played college ball.
He sees his younger self in your son, as much as your son sees his future self in him. Maybe it's a literature teacher who's a published author
who recognizes your daughter's clever use of language and urges her
to take up writing seriously. The risk is when parents feel threatened
by or become suspect of a mentoring relationship that has become immensely important to a young adult son or daughter. However, parents
need to remind themselves that these relationships can be highly significant and greatly energize a young adult's work ethic.

FOSTERING EVEN-TEMPEREDNESS

One of the greatest developmental lessons that all kids need to learn is
that they cannot regularly control parents with their moods. If a parent frequently appears provoked when his or her son or daughter acts
provocatively, it can reinforce that child's sense that he or she has the
power to get under a parent's skin. When a parent gets triggered by
his or her kid's bad temper, "fight or flight" reactions usually occur.
Either the parent launches into a counterattack by criticizing, yelling
at, threatening, or lecturing the child, or the parent freezes up and appears intimidated, capitulating to his or her kid's demands to keep the
peace. We have all been there as parents. However, when these dynamics are present too much of the time, kids learn that they can be irate,
bossy, or agitated and affect parents in big ways.

The goal for parents (which, of course, is not always realizable)
should be to try to take the higher ground and to reach inward for the
most mature response under the circumstances. Temper outbursts can

bring a parent down to the child's level. Back-and-forth arguments or fighting fire with fire place parents in a sibling-type relationship with their kids, not a parent-child one. Remember, when your kid starts to lawyer up, you're not another lawyer; you're the judge!

Frequent explosive conflicts can signal the fact that there is too much emotional closeness or distance in the parent-child relationship. When twelve-year-old Frank screams, "I hate you!" at his mother, storms upstairs to his room, and slams the door shut, it can be his primitive way of communicating that he needs physical and emotional space from his mother. She is too emotionally wrapped up in him. She feeds off his feelings, becoming anxious when he's anxious, angry when he's angry, and excited when he's excited. The emotional boundaries have become too loose. His mother *sympathetically reacts* too much of the time, rather than *empathetically responds*. In other words, she gets flooded with his feelings and reacts, instead of being sensitized by his feelings and verbally acknowledging them for him. Frank can't just have his feelings without his mother being affected. Raging at his mother is his desperate attempt to push her away in order to get some emotional breathing space.

On the other hand, explosive conflict can indicate that a parent is too physically and emotionally absent. When thirteen-year-old Pauline rants at her father, "You are so selfish. For once, can't you just think of someone other than yourself? I wish I had a different dad. Just get out of my life!" it may be her primitive way of communicating that she feels too alone and vulnerable, and needs more predictable contact with him. Naturally, it goes against the grain to think that a kid's rage somehow conveys aloneness, vulnerability, and a need for more parental involvement.

In the case of Pauline, it would not be surprising if her father launched into his own tirade: "Selfish? Let me tell you about selfish. You, young lady, live in your own damn world!" Pauline would then have gotten negative attention. However, there is wisdom in the old adage, "negative attention is better than no attention at all." Kids would rather have an angry parent than no parent at all—a parent who is angrily involved, as opposed to icily uninvolved. The opposite of love is not hate; it's indifference. Sometimes kids would rather have a parent acting hatefully toward them, than indifferently. At least that way, there is emotional heat in the relationship and they have a sense that they matter to the parent.

It is helpful to think of a tantrum, or state of agitation, as a type of emotional seizure. In the throes of it, kids are under the influence of their brain's limbic system, an ancient brain structure associated with fight-and-flight reactions. When a child is emotionally worked up, it's because a switch in his or her brain has been flipped and the child is now at his or her most primal. Parents are dealing with an altered personality. It is not the time to assume that kids can see reason, respond to long conversations, or be commanded to emotionally pull themselves together. Kids' tantrums and states of agitation, as well as the explosive conflicts in the parent-child relationship that they potentially create, have to be weathered and skillfully handled by parents in order for kids to learn to be even-tempered.

Strive for Calm Assertiveness and Acknowledge Feelings

There are a variety of steps parents can take in response to their kid's mounting frustration to minimize the chances that a full-blown tantrum will occur. Calm assertiveness is the posture to strive for in these moments. Breathing deeply, stepping back, telling yourself quietly that you're the parent, and mobilizing your emotional resources in order to sharpen your ability to respond are all helpful ways of handling the situation. Often the first step is to actively listen to your child, hear him or her out, not interrupt, and extract and acknowledge the overriding feeling being communicated:

You're screaming at your brother. Maybe you're sick and tired of him teasing you and wish he would stop.

I'm going to ignore the names you called me and try to understand why you are mad. You seem so annoyed with me. Do you know why?

Sounds like you really wish I would quit checking your homework and leave you to be in charge of it, and that I'm being too intrusive.

It makes sense to me that you're grumpy. It's been a tough school week.

Sometimes compassionate recognition of what a kid might be feeling is enough to turn the tides of an interaction, to shift it in the direction of the child being open to toning down his or her reactions.

Challenge the Intensity of a Child's Feelings, Not the Legitimacy of Them

More often than not, children have good reasons for feeling the way they do. It is the intensity of their outward expression that gets children in trouble. Acknowledging the acceptable reasons for their feelings, while at the same challenging the immature and unrefined ways they go about expressing them, socializes them to more competently deal with strong emotions. In these moments, parents can prompt and cue children with more toned down, diplomatic expressive options.

> *Billy, I know you are really upset. I can tell. Your brother squirted water on your drawing, and there's good reason for you to be mad.* [In a firm tone] *But please get off of him right now and sit in the chair next to me. You know the rule; it's not OK to hit. Tell me without yelling what happened.*

Discourage the Use of Absolutist Language and Offer Softer Word Choices

When you carefully listen to kids whose frustration is mounting, you realize that the absolutist language they resort to makes them more self-righteous about being justifiably enraged. This can get them even more emotionally worked up. Sensitively challenging their all-or-nothing, black-and-white statements and offering softer language can keep a conflict from turning volatile:

> *You honestly think that I never take your side and that I always take your brother's side, and because of this I'm a lousy dad? I know you're mad at me right now, but "never" take your side? Maybe it's more like you're mad because I'm taking his side right now, not yours?*

I hear you say you hate me and that I'm always trying to control you.

Is this your way of telling me you're upset at me because I picked a terrible time to tell you to clean up your room since you're online with your boyfriend?

Model the Use of Language That Captures
the Transitory Nature of Feelings

During heated conflicts with children, parents can unwittingly verbalize their anger in ways that make it seem that they will be angry always and forever:

You're always so rough with your sister. Go to your room. I can't deal with you!

Another detention at school. What's gotten into you? Once again, I'm very disappointed.

To children, this can convey that a parent has stopped caring, that he or she is, and will stay, mad. Under these conditions, many children feel that they have nothing to lose if they take the lid off their own anger. They can go for broke, since their parent is angry anyway.

When parents use word choices that capture the transitory nature of their anger, it can convey to children that they still care, and that restoration of positive feelings is a future possibility. This can prevent the child from then taking his or her anger to the next level.

Right now, I'm angry with you because you hit your sister. I know I won't stay angry at you, but that's how I'm feeling right this minute.

I'm sad hearing about your getting a detention at school. I'll need some time to get over it. You've had such a good week and I've been so pleased.

Sensitively Put the Child in Conflict

Children are sometimes prone to pick a fight with a parent when the underlying reasons for them being distressed have little to do with what a parent has or has not done. If a parent is unaware of this and takes the bait, a parent can then react in ways that make him or her a legitimate target of the child's anger, when this was not true in the first place. It's a classic dynamic, especially during the preteen and teen years. The goal for parents is to not take the bait. It is to look for ways to sensitively put the conflict back where it belongs—inside the child— or to put the child in conflict about his or her own behavior.

> TEENAGER: *Duh, of course I'm hungry. Let me look at my watch. What do you know, it's dinner time.*
>
> PARENT: *Wow, you sure seem grumpy. I was actually making you curry chicken, your favorite. Is it me you are really upset at or did something happen at school today that you feel bad about?*
>
> TEENAGER: *. . . Actually, Sally broke up with me.*
>
> PARENT: *That must hurt.*

As the tail end of this interaction reflects, there is a human tendency, especially among males, to convert hurt feelings into angry ones. Having a grievance to get angry about can leave a person feeling revved up and strong. Contrastingly, admitting to being hurt can leave a person feeling deflated and vulnerable. Children, particularly boys, need to be actively cued by parents that they might be feeling more hurt about a situation than angry. Heated conflicts can be averted this way.

Think in Terms of Harm Reduction
The level of distress a parent feels during a heated exchange with a kid may be so great, and the kid's behavior so seemingly unmanageable, that the best a parent can do is to try to keep things from getting worse, rather than help things get better. There are key missteps to avoid.

Overtalking
Encountering a frustrated kid, many parents fall prey to the assumption that if they just verbalize their point of view differently, clarify themselves, talk the issue out more, the kid will come around. It is as if a child is truly capable of accepting the error of his or her ways through

being talked at and lectured. These are typically the emotional conditions for a child to tune a parent out or go on the counteroffensive. Sometimes the best course of action is to simply stop talking and walk away from the situation in order to regain emotional composure while explaining why to the child:

> *I can see that no good is coming from me talking on and on. This doesn't seem to be getting us anywhere. I need to walk away right now to calm myself down.*

Believing with Conviction That You Know Your Kid's True Feelings and Motives

Some of the most rageful reactions by teenagers are fueled by parents smugly communicating and stubbornly defending that they know the real reasons why a kid feels and acts the way he or she does.

> PARENT: *You are being so moody. It's because you failed your math test and you're taking it out on everybody else.*
>
> TEENAGER: *That's not true. I'm mad because you are never on time to pick me up after school.*
>
> PARENT: *If only that were true. Admit it, you failed your math test and you're taking it out on everybody else in the family.*
>
> TEENAGER [Screaming, yelling, and acting threateningly]: *You're such a retard. No wonder Dad left you.*

Pessimistic Forecasting

A child is likely to experience a parent as acting ruthlessly when he or she makes dreadful predictions about the child's life prospects because of some misdeed in the present. Such ruthlessness on the parent's part can simply stoke the child to behave ruthlessly him- or herself.

> PARENT: *Keep this academic record up and the only college you'll be going to is McDonald's college.*
>
> CHILD: *Like you've done a whole lot with your life.*

"You Statements" and Absolutist Language

Using phrases that are littered with absolutist language and "you state-ments" can light up a kid's limbic system, resulting in him or her react-ing in an inflammatory manner.

You never listen!

You're always yelling. Can't you ever be quiet!

You are such a selfish kid with absolutely no manners!

You are so lazy! All you ever want to do is play video games. Will you ever learn to manage your time better?

By contrast, when parents labor to use nonabsolutist language and "I statements," kids are often more receptive and conciliatory.

I'm finding myself getting frustrated because you don't seem to be listen-ing right now.

I am able to listen better and not get frustrated with you when you use a calmer voice.

I'm much kinder and more generous when you ask first before just taking things.

I'm upset at this very moment catching you playing video games again. I'm starting to think that I need to help you find some balance in your life and to help you manage your time better.

Recovery and Reparation

Regardless of how explosive a conflict was or how fiery tempers were, there is always recourse for parents seeking inroads with a child to make things right. Unless there is adequate resolution after an injuri-ous conflict, it can fester and negatively color any future parent-child conflicts. If a parent lost control, even if he or she was not the insti-gator, the onus is on that parent to take reparative action. Acknowl-edging harmful actions and appearing remorseful can be the crucial ingredients that create a face-saving opening for a child to do like-wise. Parents can take ownership for the part they played in mak-ing the interaction turn inflammatory. They can also carefully and caringly prompt and cue a child to take ownership for the part they played.

Children are prone to making a quick apology, just to be done with the whole affair. Parents may need to draw the child's attention on particular transgressive behaviors and expressions so that the child can register them as unacceptable. Parents may also need to think out loud with the child about possible ways the child can make amends. "If we could turn back the clock" type discussions are also useful to enable parent and child to highlight reactions that should have been avoided and, therefore, could be avoided next time.

PARENT: *Is now a good time to talk over what happened? I'm feeling bad about it. There's something I did that I wish I hadn't done. I yelled at you and called you lazy. I hate it when my feelings get the better of me and I name call like that.*

CHILD: *Yeah, I'm sorry too.*

PARENT: *Is there anything in particular you're sorry about?*

CHILD: *I called you a stupid retard. I guess I was name calling too.*

PARENT: *If I could turn back the clock, I would have ignored that silly comment you made about me being a horrible mother because there was no food in the refrigerator. What about you? If you could turn back the clock, is there anything you would have done differently?*

CHILD: *I would have just gone upstairs and taken a nap because I'm soooooo tired.*

PARENT: *So you were in a foul mood partly because you were tired?*

CHILD: *I guess so.*

PARENT: *Maybe next time you can clue me in and just take that nap rather than give me grief!*

FOSTERING SOCIAL KNOW-HOW

For better or for worse, American culture favors gregariousness. We live in a meet-and-greet world. If children are to emerge into young adults who are equipped to get ahead educationally and economically, they need to have a high comfort level with respect to interacting socially. This can be tough on traditionally masculine boys. They are innately predisposed to express themselves kinetically, through movement and gesture, instead of through verbal communication. When they do talk, they are prone to limit communication to practical and mechanical topics, like weather conditions or all the nifty features on their new laptop. They can embody a cut-to-the-chase communication style in which they expect verbal exchanges to contain only the basic information necessary to make a point. Comments like "Yuck, this soup tastes like it has mouthwash in it" may seem to them simply honest, not insensitive. They tend not to scan the facial expressions and body language of their listeners for cues as to when they need to stop talking and start listening. When they are silent, it may be because they don't really know what to say or how, not because they are being guarded or rude. They may be oblivious to the fact that standing too close or too far from a listener makes them seem odd.

Not that all boys behave this way, or that girls don't, for that matter. I am outlining aspects of a traditional masculine communication style that the average boy embodies, to a greater or lesser degree, and that many girls also embody. It is a communication style that poses special challenges for parents.

Parenting Tips

- Encourage perspective-taking: *What do you think George felt like when you told him that because the paint on his toy train was chipped, he would never be able to sell it on eBay?*
- Play word games: *Let's take turns seeing how many words we can come up with for "beautiful."*
- Reiterate phrases in longer forms: *So you felt jealous . . . maybe because John got invited to Frank's birthday party and you didn't, even though you were a good friend to Frank by inviting him to your birthday party earlier this year?*
- Emphasize faces and what they communicate: *Hillary is biting her lip and looking at the ground. What is she trying to tell you? I'm thinking she's letting you know it's her turn to speak.*
- Ask specific questions rather than global ones: *Was Mrs. Donahue, your English teacher, out sick again today or was she there to hand*

back your essay? How did you do on the essay conclusion that I helped you to write?

- Don't be satisfied with, or annoyed by, one-word answers: *Yes, you had a good day. What made it good?*
- Give prompts about appropriate personal space: *I think Monica would feel more comfortable if you stepped back one whole step to give her more personal space.*
- Frame working on social skills as being "brave" and "a good friend": *You looked Rudy straight in the eyes and with a kind voice asked him over for a play date. Now that's being brave. That's being a good friend.*
- Rehearse and role-play sensitive ways of answering the phone at home. Have your child then answer most calls that come in.
- View a trip to a restaurant as a socialization opportunity. Have your child place his or her own order. Sensitively cue your child to make eye contact and talk. Playfully rehearse and role-play at home.
- Know your child's special skills and interests well. Set up extracurricular activities where he or she will come into contact with like-minded souls.
- Buy tickets to events that you know your child's friends, or potential friends, will like.
- Playfully rehearse and role-play things your child could text or say over the phone. Have your child then text or call these children in your presence.
- Don't push your child to be popular. Be satisfied if your child is relatively satisfied with a few close friends.
- Model what it's like to have an active social life. Have friends over to the house.

WHEN PROFESSIONAL HELP IS CALLED FOR

In some respects, making the decision about whether it is time to reach out to a professional for help is far easier than the decision about whether the type of help that professional has to offer is desirable and effective. Most parents know when their child's behavior has become too problematic. It may be that because of a child's behavior, family life has become unbearably stressful and the parents' marriage is suffering. Key indicators are when a variety of adults in your child's life independently raise the same concerns you have about your child, and when there is indisputable evidence that the problem behavior you are seeing at home is occurring in other arenas. Compared with his or her same-age friends, you might notice that your child's emotional self-control, moodiness, or social awkwardness is too far off the charts. It may be that despite all of your best efforts, and a steady consumption of parenting self-help books, you keep getting triggered by your child with the same amount of excessive intensity over identical issues. As a parent, you might find yourself secretly ashamed to admit that although you love your child, you are growing to dislike him or her as a person.

If these criteria are met, it's probably time to consider outside consultation with a therapist who specializes in working with children and families. The term "therapist" is a generic term for a professional with a doctoral degree (PhD or PsyD) or master's degree (MA, MS, or MEd) in clinical or counseling psychology, or a master's degree in social work (MSW). Psychiatrists are medical doctors with MDs who nowadays mostly prescribe medications and tend to have limited education and experience engaging in talk or play therapy.

It is important to find a therapist who is a good fit for both you and your child. Therapists may be professionals, but they are people too, and you should use your regular social instincts to ascertain if they possess the attentiveness, genuineness, and confidence needed for there to be trust and a good rapport. A reputable therapist should also embody basic professionalism: return calls in a timely fashion; not take calls or texts during sessions; not personalize the therapy and share about themselves and their own lives; agree to keep information you or your child discloses confidential; and so forth. Other factors to consider include the following:

Does the therapist relate well to children? An effective child and family therapist will have a sparkle around children. He or she will be at ease acting playfully with your child, moving the interaction into pretend play, or talking using child-friendly language and themes that free your child up to talk and play more liberally.

Is the office child-friendly? A child therapist's office should appear like it's set up for children. There should be toys and play objects out in the open or ready at hand in a chest or cupboard. Ideally, there should be a range of toys that offer a variety of expressive options. For example, puppets can be used to talk through issues in pretend ways, balls can be tossed while a difficult conversation is ongoing, toy soldiers or dart guns can be used to work out aggression, and/or board games can be played with teenagers as ice-breakers and side-line activities during talk-therapy sessions.

Is the therapist receptive to questions? It is perfectly appropriate to want to know about a therapist's educational background and therapeutic experience working with children, and if the therapist has previously encountered and worked effectively with the type of problems your child is exhibiting. A conscientious therapist does not balk at keeping you up to date about your child's progress but is eager to do so. Granted, the therapist will want to keep sensitive facts and information from individual sessions with your child confidential. But this should not rule out more general discussions about your child's progress.

What is the therapist's philosophy about diagnosing children? Children don't need a diagnosis to qualify for help from a therapist. Diagnoses usually are salient when there are clear indications that a medication evaluation is worth pursuing or in order for insurance companies to pay for services. If a diagnosis is to be issued for medication or payment reasons, discuss with the therapist the pros and cons of one being used that is of greater or lesser severity. Is the therapist using a more severe diagnosis to ensure that treatment will be paid for by an insurance company? How might this help or hurt your child over the long run once it enters a databank system?

Does the therapist have background education and training in child development? It's important that your therapist has a concrete understanding of the developmental struggles of children across all age groups. As I've tried to show in this book, many childhood tendencies that are on the outer edges of normal can get misperceived as abnormal. Besides an aca-demic knowledge of child development, has the therapist been around many types of children in different life contexts sufficiently to have direct experiential knowledge of what's normal and not so normal?

Are the therapist's methods effectively defined? A skilled child therapist will have a rationale for performing the types of interventions he or she does with your child and for what purposes. The methods should seem plausible, from a child's point of view, and link up with your child's difficulties. Maybe it's puppet play around pretend conflicts where the child indirectly learns an array of verbal expressions that will help him or her to handle angry disagreements better, or maybe it's the use of competitive games to help a child cope better with feelings around winning and losing, turn taking, and following rules without cheating.

Is the therapist open to collaborating with teachers? More often than not, for therapy to be effective there has to be close contact between the therapist and a child's teacher. This way, the therapist can obtain a clearer picture of the child's functioning at school, so as to raise relevant issues with the child during therapy.

You will also want a therapist who honors your authority as a parent and one who has bedrock respect for how difficult it is to raise a child well in the twenty-first century. You will want one who is determined to work collaboratively with you during parenting sessions to draw out and build upon the skills you have as a parent to more effectively help your child. The wise therapist understands that only so much can be accomplished one-on-one in the therapy office with a child.

If there's one overarching idea I want the reader to walk away with it's the importance of thinking meaningfully about children's difficult behavior in commonsense, humanistic terms. Larger forces in the mental health field, ironically, tend to deemphasize this. The impetus is for children's problematic behavior to be diagnostically scrutinized and categorized, rather than seen as communicating basic psychological needs, intentions, and purposes. The more parents and those who work closely with children are able to *psychologize* the behavior of our youngsters—ask why and under what circumstances they act the way they do—the greater the chance of effective remedial action occurring. There is a preoccupation in our society with medicalizing childhood behavior and diagnostically pigeonholing children. My hope is that this book shifts this unfortunate trend in the direction of empowering parents, teachers, pediatricians, and child mental health professionals alike to decipher the ordinary purposes, intentions, and developmental needs that often underlie the difficult behavior of children under their charge.

Acknowledgments

In stubborn fashion, I completed most of this book before I even approached an editor, agent, or publisher. I was determined to be accountable, first and foremost, to my vision of the kind of book I sensed was calling out to be written, fearful that outside influence might dissuade me from this. There may be integrity to this approach, but there is also loneliness.

The journey was made less lonely by dialoguing with colleagues and friends along the way. John Broughton used his sharp wit and brilliant mind to keep me on task. Art Hansen, a history professor by trade, made the necessary paradigm shift and thought like a psychologist about my ideas. Steen Halling's voice was always there in my head, anchoring me to the humanistic thinking of my mid-1980s graduate school years in the Existential/Phenomenological Psychology program at Seattle University. Without the generosity of spirit shown by these three mentors-turned-friends at key moments in my life, I would not have acquired enough of a belief in myself as an intellectual to ever have considered writing a book like this. The same credit is due my longtime friend Steven Williams, who was a "Renaissance man" for me before I knew what the Renaissance was.

Tom Peters, Sam Alibrando, Jeanette Davis, Alan Karbelnig, and Josh Brody kindly indulged me across the dinner table on umpteen occasions as I ranted about the current state of affairs in the field of children's mental health. Greg Griffith and Susan Minado put me back on the horse when I was convinced my publishing options were bleak. My psychological assistants, David Lorentzen and Thomas Duke, conveyed their appreciation for the utility of the ideas contained in the book for early-career child psychologists. I benefited greatly from the meticulous editorial expertise of Janice Pieroni at Story Arts Management. Susie North, my cowriter on a previous project and true wordsmith, came through when I needed yet another opinion on phraseology. Wendy Mogel and her literary agent, Betsy Amster, opened my eyes to the ins and outs of the publishing industry and the crucial steps necessary to bring a manuscript to publication. Mary Jane Horton selflessly gave of her time to read over the original book proposal and, as fate would have it, supplied me with the relevant information that allowed me to make direct contact with the folks at Beacon Press.

My editor at Beacon Press, Amy Caldwell, deserves special praise. From day one she acquainted herself with my book and before long knew it better than I did. She pored over every line, making sure my ideas and expressions achieved their true aim. Better yet, as quaint as it sounds, she almost always picked up her office phone when I called and somehow had the time to lend an ear and offer a pep talk. I could not have asked for a more sagacious, kindhearted editor. She and the staff at Beacon Press are to be commended for both appreciating and preserving the dual focus of my book—a social critique pertaining to the medicalization of children's behavior and a self-help-style resource for parents and professionals working with children.

My father, Rodolfo Gnaulati, passed away before the book was finished. That is not to say he had any inkling of what the book was about or planned on reading it. He had a fifth-grade education and a spartan work ethic. The mere fact that I was muscling through five years to finish a book, any book, was enough to make him proud and me thankful. My mother, Carmen Gnaulati, also taught me that nothing of value can be brought to fruition without devotion, self-sacrifice, and hard work.

She does know what the book is about and has read it. My father-in-law, Donald Chunn, in the know because he's a retired psychotherapist, frequently offered words of encouragement, tacitly conveying that the project I was undertaking was a socially meaningful one. Stephen and Donna Wickersham, my dear in-laws, have been a veritable pep squad every step of the way.

The utmost gratitude goes to Janet, my loved and loving wife and avid coparent. Being more widely read and worldly than I, she kept abreast of relevant news reports and research findings and passed them my way. As my prose ventured into the snarky and polemical, she nudged me to soften my language without compromising my essential point of view. Not once did she question my need for extended periods of solitude to hammer out the book. My son, Marcello, just by being his ebullient self, was a stalwart reminder of all that is normal about children and childhood.

Notes

INTRODUCTION

1. Centers for Disease Control and Prevention, CDC Features, "Rates of Parent-Reported ADHD Increasing," http://www.cdc.gov.
2. "Autism Rates Up; Screening, Better Diagnosis Cited," *Los Angeles Times*, March 19, 2012. For the original Centers for Disease Control and Prevention study, see Jon Baio et al., "Prevalence of Autism Spectrum Disorders— Autism and Developmental Disabilities Monitoring Network, 14 Sites, United States 2008," *Surveillance Summaries* (CDC) 61 (2012): 1–19.
3. Alix Spiegel, "Children Labeled 'Bipolar' May Get a New Diagnosis," National Public Radio, February 10, 2010, http://www.npr.org.

CHAPTER ONE: MAD SCIENCE AND MAD MEDICINE

1. Gary L. Freed et al., "Recently Trained General Pediatricians: Perspectives on Residency Training and Scope of Practice," *Pediatrics* 123 (2010): 538–43.
2. Ibid.
3. Ruth E. K. Stein et al., "Attention-Deficit/Hyperactivity Disorder: How Much Responsibility Are Pediatricians Taking?" *Pediatrics* 123, no. 1 (2009): 248–55.
4. Alicia Merline, Lynn Olson, and William Cull, "Length of Pediatric Visits Actually Increasing," paper, Pediatric Academic Societies Annual Meeting, Baltimore, May 2009.
5. Ramin Mojtabai and Mark Olfson, "National Trends in Psychotherapy by

Office-Based Psychiatrists," *Archives of General Psychiatry* 65, no. 8 (2008): 962–70.

6. Khurshid A. Khurshid et al., "Residency Programs and Psychotherapy Competencies: A Survey of Chief Residents," *Academic Psychiatry* 29 (2005): 452–58.

7. Daniel J. Carlat, *Unhinged: The Trouble with Psychiatry—A Doctor's Revelations about a Profession in Crisis* (New York: Free Press, 2010), 15.

8. Catherine M. Lee, "From Clinical Trials to Professional Training: A Graduate Course in Evidence-Based Interventions for Children, Youth, and Families," *Training and Education in Professional Psychology* 1, no. 3 (2007): 215–23.

9. Anne E. Pidano, Eileen C. Kurowski, and Kathleen M. McEvoy, "The Next Generation: How are Clinical Child Psychologists Being Trained?" *Training and Education in Professional Psychology* 4, no. 2 (2010): 121–27.

10. Effie M. Mitsis et al., "Parent-Teacher Concordance for DSM-IV Attention-Deficit/Hyperactivity in a Clinic-Referred Sample," *Journal of the American Academy of Child and Adolescent Psychiatry* 39, no. 3 (2000): 308–13.

11. Desiree W. Murray et al., "Parent Versus Teacher Ratings of Attention-Deficit/Hyperactivity Disorder Symptoms in the Preschoolers with Attention-Deficit/Hyperactivity Disorder Treatment Study," *Journal of Child and Adolescent Psychopharmacology* 17, no. 5 (2007): 605–19.

12. Lydia Mary Furman, "Attention-Deficit Hyperactivity Disorder (ADHD): Does New Research Support Old Concepts?" *Journal of Child Neurology* 23, no. 7 (2008): 775–84.

13. Jodi Polaha et al., "The Assessment of Attention-Deficit/Hyperactivity Disorder in Rural Primary Care: The Portability of the American Academy of Pediatrics Guidelines to the 'Real World,'" *Pediatrics* 115, no. 2 (2005): 120–26.

14. Assegedetch Hailemariam, Sharon Bradley-Johnson, and C. Merle Johnson, "Pediatricians' Preferences for ADHD Information from Schools," *School Psychology Review* 31, no. 1 (2002): 94–105.

15. Tracy P. Alloway et al., "The Diagnostic Utility of Behavioral Checklists in Identifying Children with ADHD and Children with Working Memory Deficits," *Child Psychiatry and Human Development* 40, no. 3 (2009): 353–66.

16. Laszlo Erdodi, Renee Lajiness-O'Neill, and Karen K. Saules, "Order of Conners' CPT-II Administration within a Cognitive Test Battery Influences ADHD Indices," *Journal of Attention Disorders* 14, no. 1 (2010): 43–51.

17. Evelyn Pringle, "US Kids Represent Psychiatric Drug Goldmine," December 12, 2009, Truthout.org.

18. David Armstrong, "Children's Use of Psychiatric Drugs Begins to Decelerate," *Wall Street Journal*, May 18, 2009, http://online.wsj.com.

19. James P. Morris and George Stone, "Children and Psychotropic Medication: A Cautionary Note," *Journal of Marital and Family Therapy* 37, no. 3 (2011): 299–306.

20. Quoted in Gianna Kali, "Drugging Our Children to Death," *Health News Digest*, June 29, 2009, www.healthnewsdigest.com.

21. Duff Wilson, "Side Effects May Include Lawsuits," *New York Times*, October 3, 2010.

22. Jim Edwards, "Pfizer Paid for Doc's Helicopter in Off-Label Geodon Push, Suit Claims," CBS News, September 17, 2009, http://www.cbsnews.com.

23. Joseph Krueger, "Fans of Fanapt Are on to Something," TapeBeat.com, June 19, 2010.

24. Carl Elliott, "The Drug Pushers," *Atlantic*, April 2006.

25. Ibid.

26. Daniella A. Zipkin and Michael A. Steinman, "Interactions between Pharmaceutical Representatives and Doctors in Training," *Journal of General Internal Medicine* 20, no. 8 (2005): 777–86.

27. Michael A. Steinman, Michael Shliplak, and Stephen J. McPhee, "Of Principles and Pens: Attitudes and Practices of Medicine Housestaff Towards Pharmaceutical Industry Promotions," *American Journal of Medicine* 110, no. 7 (2001): 551–57.

28. National Survey of Physicians, Kaiser Family Foundation, March 2002.

29. Benedict Carey, "Bipolar Illness Soars as a Diagnosis for the Young," *New York Times*, September 4, 2007.

30. Wilson, "Side Effects May Include Lawsuits."

31. Hans Melander et al., "Evidence B(i)ased Medicine—Selective Reporting from Studies Sponsored by Pharmaceutical Industry: Review of Studies in New Drug Applications," *British Medical Journal* 326 (2003): 1171–73.

32. Irving Kirsch, *The Emperor's New Drugs: Exploding the Antidepressant Myth* (New York: Basic Books, 2010), 11.

33. Daniel J. Carlat, "Do Antidepressants Work for Kids?" *Carlat Psychiatry Report* 1, no. 11 (2003): 1–6.

34. Michael Price, "Placebos Produce Effect Even When Patients Know It's Just Sugar," *Monitor on Psychology*, March 2011.

35. Duff Wilson, "AstraZeneca Pays Millions to Settle Seroquel Cases," *New York Times*, October 29, 2009.

36. Heidi W. Ashih, "Atypicals for Non-Psychotic Disorders," *Carlat Psychiatry Report* 7, no. 3 (2009): 1–8.

37. Caroline Fisher, "Management of Antipsychotic Induced Weight Gain," *Carlat Child Psychiatry Report* 1, no. 5 (2010): 1–5.

38. Wilson, "Side Effects May Include Lawsuits."

39. Quoted in Michael W. Firmin and Annie Phillips, "A Qualitative Study of

Families and Children Possessing Diagnoses of ADHD," *Journal of Family Issues* 30, no. 9 (2009): 1155–74.

40. "A High-Fat Diet Alters Crucial Aspects of Brain Dopamine Signaling," *Science Daily*, July 19, 2010, http://www.sciencedaily.com.

41. Amber L. Howard et al., "ADHD Is Associated with a 'Western' Dietary Pattern in Adolescents," *Journal of Attention Disorders* 15, no. 5 (2011): 403–11.

42. Jules Lavalaye et al., "Effect of Age and Gender on Dopamine Transporter Imaging with [123I]FP-CIT SPET in Healthy Volunteers," *European Journal of Nuclear Medicine and Molecular Imaging* 27, no. 7 (2000): 867–69.

43. Quoted in Robert Whitaker, "The Successful Creation of a Societal Delusion . . . and the Increase in Stigma It Has Spawned," *Psychology Today*, November 4, 2010.

44. John Horgan, *The Undiscovered Mind* (New York: Free Press, 1999), 37.

45. Quoted in Colin Meek, "SSRI Ads Questioned," *Canadian Medical Association Journal* 174, no. 6 (2006): 754.

46. Forest Laboratories, "Forest Laboratories, Inc. Announces Positive Results of Lexapro Phase III Study in Adolescents with Major Depression," press release, November 29, 2007, http://www.frx.com.

47. Torkel Klingberg, "Training and Plasticity of Working Memory," *Trends in Cognitive Science* 14, no. 7 (2010): 317–24.

48. Laura Chaddock et al., "A Neuroimaging Investigation of the Association between Aerobic Fitness, Hippocampal Volume and Memory Performance in Preadolescent Children," *Brain Research* 1358 (2010): 172–83.

49. Britta K. Holzel et al., "Mindfulness Practice Leads to Increases in Regional Brain Gray Matter Density," *Psychiatry Research: Neuroimaging* 191, no. 1 (2011): 36–43.

50. Walter Goldschmidt, *The Bridge to Humanity* (New York: Oxford University Press, 2006), 11.

51. National Institute of Mental Health, *Bipolar Disorder* (Washington, DC: NIMH, 2009), http://www.nimh.nih.gov.

52. "What Is Autism?" Autism Speaks, http://autismspeaks.org.

CHAPTER TWO: THE RUSH TO DIAGNOSE

1. Todd Elder, "The Importance of Relative Standards in ADHD Diagnoses: Evidence Based on a Child's Date of Birth," *Journal of Health Economics* 29, no. 5 (2010): 641–56.

2. Quoted in Andy Henion, "Nearly 1 Million Children Potentially Misdiagnosed with ADHD," *Michigan State University News*, August 17, 2010, http://news.msu.edu.

3. Linda Jacobson, "Preschoolers Expelled from School at Rates Exceeding That of K–12," *Education Week*, May 18, 2005.
4. "Aggression in the Kindergarten Classroom," white paper, Mayor's Commission for Children, Springfield, MO, August 10, 2005, http://www.springfieldmo/gov.
5. Ibid., 7.
6. Deborah Brauser, "High Rate of Psychiatric Disorders in Preschoolers during Transition to Kindergarten," *Medscape Medical News*, July 14, 2010.
7. Ibid., 1.
8. Bellevue School District, Bellevue, WA, http://www.bsd405.org.
9. Lynbrook Public Schools, Lynbrook, NY, http://www.lynbrook.k12.ny.us.
10. Fort Zumwalt School District, O'Fallon, MO, http://www.fz.k12.mo.us.
11. Quoted in Jay Mathews, "Extra Credit: Damaging Changes in Kindergarten?" *Washington Post*, March 19, 2009.
12. Amy Dickinson, "Kinder Grind," *Time*, November 8, 1999.
13. Edward Miller and Joan Almon, *Crisis in the Kindergarten: Why Children Need to Play in School* (College Park, MD: Alliance for Childhood, 2009), 1–72.
14. Ibid.
15. Quoted in Claudia Wallis, "Does Kindergarten Need Cops?" *Time*, December 7, 2003.
16. Quoted in Jennifer Lin Russell, "Defining Kindergarten Education in an Era of Accountability" (Roseville, CA: California Kindergarten Association, 2008), 2.
17. Leonard Sax and Kathleen J. Kautz, "Who First Suggests the Diagnosis of Attention-Deficit/Hyperactivity Disorder?" *Annals of Family Medicine* 1, no. 3 (2003): 171–74.
18. Jerry L. Rushton, Kathryn E. Fant, and Sarah J. Clark, "Use of Practice Guidelines in the Primary Care of Children with Attention-Deficit/Hyperactivity Disorder," *Pediatrics* 114, no. 1 (2004): 22–28.
19. Miller and Almon, *Crisis in the Kindergarten*, 27.
20. J. Michael Havey et al., "Teachers' Perceptions of the Incidence and Management of Attention-Deficit Hyperactivity Disorder," *Applied Neuropsychology* 12, no. 2 (2005): 120–27.
21. National Association of Special Education Teachers, "ADHD Topic Categories, Characteristics, Clinical Characteristics," http://www.naset.org.
22. Kathleen L. Lane, Joseph H. Wehby, and Cristy Cooley, "Teacher Expectations of Students' Classroom Behavior across the Grade Span: Which Social Skills are Necessary for Success?" *Exceptional Children* 72, no. 2 (2006): 153–67.

23. "The Amount of Homework to Be Given to a Student," *Homework Help*, October 13, 2009, http://www.homework-help.net.

24. National Center for Education Statistics, "Fast Facts: Students with Disabilities," n.d., http://www.nces.ed.gov.

25. Helen Schneider and Daniel Eisenberg, "Who Receives a Diagnosis of Attention-Deficit/Hyperactivity Disorder in the United States Elementary School Population?" *Pediatrics* 117, no. 4 (2006): 601–9.

26. Jay P. Greene, "The National Review: Special Education Needs Help," National Public Radio, September 15, 2009, http://www.npr.org.

27. Ibid.

28. La Vonne Cornell-Swanson et al., "Psychiatric Diagnosis and Concomitant Medical Treatment for 1st and 2nd Grade Children," *International Journal of Special Education* 22, no. 2 (2007): 46–55.

29. National Education Association, *Truth in Labeling: Disproportionality in Special Education* (Washington, DC: NEA, 2007), 6, http://www.nea.org.

30. James T. Webb et al., *Misdiagnosis and Dual Diagnoses of Gifted Children and Adults* (Scottsdale, AZ: Great Potential Press, 2005).

31. Anne N. Rinn and Jason M. Nelson, "Preservice Teachers' Perceptions of Behaviors Characteristic of ADHD and Giftedness," *Roeper Review* 31, no. 1 (2008): 18–26.

32. Quoted in John M. Grohol, PsyD, "Congress Passes Historic Mental Health Parity Bill," *PsychCentral*, September 24, 2008, http://psychcentral.com.

33. Marcia C. Peck and Richard M. Scheffler, "An Analysis of the Definitions of Mental Illness Used in State Parity Laws," *Psychiatric Services* 53, no. 9 (2002): 1089–95.

34. Margo L. Rosenbach et al., "Implementation of Mental Health Parity: Lessons from California," *Psychiatric Services* 60, no. 12 (2009): 1589–94.

35. Stephen C. Phillips, "The Dilemma of Diagnosis in Clinical Practice: Over Diagnosis, Under Diagnosis and Insurance Fraud," *California Psychologist* (November–December 2010).

36. Joseph C. Blader and Gabrielle A. Carlson, "Increased Rates of Bipolar Disorder Diagnoses among US Child, Adolescent, and Adult Inpatients, 1996–2004," *Biological Psychiatry* 62, no. 2 (2007): 107–14.

37. Quoted in Alix Spiegel, "What's a Mental Health Diagnosis? Even Experts Can't Agree," National Public Radio, December 29, 2010, http://www.npr.org.

38. Karla C. Van Meter et al., "Geographic Distribution of Autism in California: A Retrospective Birth Cohort Analysis," *Autism Research* 3, no. 1 (2010): 19–29.

39. Adrian Angold et al., "Stimulant Treatment for Children: A Community Perspective," *Journal of the American Academy of Child and Adolescent Psychiatry* 39, no. 8 (2000): 975–84.

CHAPTER THREE: CASUALTIES
OF CASUAL DIAGNOSING

1. Captain Cynic Psychology Forum, "Eminem Schizophrenic or Bipolar or Both," http://www.captaincynic.com.

2. "The Different Types of Attention Deficit Hyperactivity Disorder," ADHD Information Library, http://www.newideas.net.

3. Quoted in Stephanie Whyche, "Mentally Ill Youth Face Fear, Stigma From Adults," *Psychiatric News* 42, no. 11 (2007): 9.

4. Tally Moses, "Being Treated Differently: Stigma Experiences with Family, Peers, and School Staff among Adolescents with Mental Health Disorders," *Social Sciences & Medicine* 70, no. 7 (2010): 985–93.

5. Susan dosReis et al., "Stigmatizing Experiences of Parents of Children with a New Diagnosis of ADHD," *Psychiatric Services* 61, no. 8 (2010): 811–16.

6. City of Los Angeles Personnel Department, Medical Services Division, Medical and Psychological Assessment, http://per.lacity.org/.

7. State of Kansas, Office of the Secretary of State, 2010 General Election Official Vote Totals, http://www.kssos.org.

8. Robert McMillan, "Misdirected Spyware Infects Ohio Hospital," *PCWorld*, September 17, 2009, http://www.pcworld.com.

9. Matthew Sturdevant, "Health Net Sued By Blumenthal Over Lost Data," *Hartford Courant*, January 13, 2010.

10. Jenna Wortham, "More Employers Use Social Networks to Check Out Applicants," *New York Times*, August 20, 2009.

11. Peter Breggin, "The Hazards of Psychiatric Diagnosis," *Huffington Post*, June 21, 2010, http://www.huffingtonpost.com.

12. Ethan Watters, "The Americanization of Mental Illness," *New York Times Magazine*, January 8, 2010.

13. Christina S. Batzle et al., "Potential Impact of ADHD with Stimulant Medication Label on Teacher Expectations," *Journal of Attention Disorders* 14, no. 2 (2010): 157–66.

14. Allen J. Frances, "Psychiatric Diagnosis Gone Wild: The 'Epidemic' of Childhood Bipolar Disorder," *Psychology Today*, April 7, 2010.

15. L. Alan Sroufe, "Ritalin Gone Wrong," *New York Times*, January 29, 2012.

16. Katy Abel, "Ritalin Alert: As Abuse Rates Climb, Schools Are Scrutinized," Family Education, September 2, 2012, http://school.familyeducation.com.

17. Irving Kirsch, *The Emperor's New Drugs* (New York: Basic Books, 2010), 4.

18. Elisa Cascade, Amir H. Kalali, and Sharon B. Wigal, "Real-World Data on Attention Deficit Hyperactivity Disorder Medication Side Effects," *Psychiatry* 7, no. 4 (2010): 13–15.

19. Lydia Mary Furman, "Attention-Deficit Hyperactivity Disorder (ADHD):

Does New Research Support Old Concepts?" *Journal of Child Neurology* 23, no. 7 (2008): 775–84.

20. "When Preschool Children Have ADHD," *Journal Watch*, http://pediatrics .jwatch.org.

21. Barbara C. Galland, E. Gail Trip, and Barry J. Taylor, "The Sleep of Children with Attention Deficit Hyperactivity Disorder On and Off Methylphenidate: A Matched-Case Control Study," *Journal of Sleep Research* 19, no. 2 (2010): 366–73.

22. Robert L. Findling et al., "Changes in Emotions Related to Medications Used to Treat ADHD. Part II: Clinical Approaches," *Journal of Attention Disorders* 15, no. 2 (2011): 113–21.

23. Daniel J. Carlat, "Psychostimulants and ADHD: An Update," *Carlat Psychiatry Report* 4, no. 9 (2006): 1–6.

24. Nancy Shute, "Study Finds Scant Evidence of Heart Risks from ADHD Drugs for Kids," National Public Radio, November 1, 2011, http://www .npr.org.

25. Christopher J. Kratochvil, "ADHD Pharmacology: Rates of Stimulant Use and Cardiovascular Risk," *American Journal of Psychiatry* 169, no. 2 (2012): 112–14.

26. Almut G. Winterstein et al., "Safety of Central Nervous System Stimulants in Children and Adolescents with Attention-Deficit/Hyperactivity Disorder," *Pediatrics* 120, no. 6 (2007): 1494–1501.

27. Laurel K. Leslie et al., "Cardiac Screening Prior to Stimulant Treatment of ADHD: A Survey of US-Based Pediatricians," *Pediatrics* 129, no. 2 (2012): 222–30.

28. Stephanie L. Doherty et al., "Children's Self-Reported Effects of Stimulant Medication," *International Journal of Disability, Development and Education* 47, no. 1 (2000): 39–54.

29. Mina K. Dulcan and R. Scott Benson, "Summary of the Practice Parameters for the Assessment and Treatment of Children, Adolescents, and Adults with Attention Deficit Hyperactivity Disorder," *Journal of the American Academy of Child and Adolescent Psychiatry* 36 (1997): 1311–17.

30. "Concerta ADHD Ad," *Depression Introspection*, February 19, 2009, http:// depressionintrospection.wordpress.com.

31. Daniel J. Carlat, "Do Medications Boost Academic Achievement in Children with ADHD?" *Carlat Child Psychiatry Report* 3, no. 2 (2012): 1–8.

32. National Institute of Mental Health, "Short-Term Intensive Treatment Not Likely to Improve Long-Term Outcomes for Children with ADHD," March 26, 2009, http://www.nimh.nih.gov.

33. "More Kids Taking Antipsychotics for ADHD: Study," *Medline Plus*, August 7, 2012, http://www.nlm.nih.gov.

34. "Use of Antipsychotic Medications by Children and Adolescents Associated with Significant Weight Gain," *Science Daily*, October 29, 2009, http://www.sciencedaily.com.

35. "Risks and Benefits of Antipsychotics in Children and Adolescents," *Science Daily*, September 3, 2008.

36. Elisa Cascade et al., "Real-World Data on Atypical Antipsychotic Medication Side Effects," *Psychiatry* 7, no. 7 (2010): 9–12.

37. Ibid., 9–12, 13–15.

38. "Attitudes about Children's Mental Health," *Parents*, May 2012, http://www.parents.com.

39. Jonathan S. Comer, Mark Olfson, and Ramin Mojtabai, "National Trends in Child and Adolescent Psychotropic Polypharmacy in Office-Based Practice 1996–2007," *Journal of the American Academy of Child and Adolescent Psychiatry* 49, no. 10 (2010): 1001–10.

40. Joanna Moncrieff, *The Myth of the Chemical Cure* (London: Palgrave Macmillan, 2009), 228.

CHAPTER FOUR: ABNORMALIZING BOYS

1. "Autism Rates Up; Screening, Better Diagnosis Cited," *Los Angeles Times*, March 19, 2012. For the original Centers for Disease Control and Prevention study, see Jon Baio et al., "Prevalence of Autism Spectrum Disorders—Autism and Developmental Disabilities Monitoring Network, 14 Sites, United States 2008," *Surveillance Summaries* (CDC) 61 (2012): 1–19.

2. National Education Association, *Truth in Labeling: Disproportionality in Special Education* (Washington, DC: NEA, 2007), http://www.nea.org.

3. Steven P. Cuffe, Charity G. Moore, and Robert E. McKeown, "Prevalence and Correlates of ADHD Symptoms in the National Health Interview Survey," *Journal of Attention Disorders* 9 , no. 2 (2005): 392–401.

4. La Vonne Cornell-Swanson et al., "Psychiatric Diagnosis and Concomitant Medical Treatment for 1st and 2nd Grade Children," *International Journal of Special Education* 22, no. 2 (2007): 46–55.

5. Tamar Lewin, "Research Finds a High Rate of Expulsions in Preschool," *New York Times*, May 17, 2005, http://www.nytimes.com.

6. J.S. Matthews, Claire Cameron Ponitz, and Frederick J. Morrison, "Early Gender Differences in Self-Regulation and Academic Achievement," *Journal of Educational Psychology* 101, no. 3 (2009): 689–704.

7. Joyce F. Benenson, Hassina P. Carder, and Sarah J. Geib-Cole, "The Development of Boys' Preferential Pleasure in Physical Aggression," *Aggressive Behavior* 34, no 2 (2008): 154–66.

8. Thomas L. Reed and Mac H. Brown, "The Expression of Care in the Rough

and Tumble Play of Boys," *Journal of Research in Childhood Education* 15, no. 1 (2000): 104–16.

9. Mary Ellin Logue and Hattie Harvey, "Preschool Teachers' Views of Active Play," *Journal of Research in Childhood Education* 24, no. 1 (2010): 32–49.

10. Quoted in Kara Jesella, "Five-Minute Time Out: The Boy Crisis," Babble .com, October 10, 2008.

11. Brian McVicar, "Ionia Kindergartner Suspended for Making Gun with Hand," *Grand Rapids (MI) Press*, March 4, 2010, http://mlive.com.

12. Matthews et al., "Early Gender Differences in Self-Regulation and Academic Achievement."

13. Angela Lee Duckworth and Martin E. P. Seligman, "Self-Discipline Gives Girls the Edge: Gender in Self-Discipline, Grades, and Achievement Test Scores," *Journal of Educational Psychology* 98, no. 1 (2006): 198–208.

14. Gwen A. Kenney-Benson et al., "Sex Differences in Math Performance: The Role of Children's Approach to Schoolwork," *Developmental Psychology* 42, no. 1 (2006): 11–26.

15. National Education Association, *Rankings & Estimates: Rankings of the States 2009 and Estimates of School Statistics 2010* (Washington, DC: NEA Research, December 2009), http://nea.org.

16. Ibid.

17. Roberta G. Williams, "Preserving Gender Balance in Pediatrics," *California Pediatrician* (Summer 2010): 4–6.

18. Amy Cynkar, "The Changing Gender Composition of Psychology," *Monitor on Psychology* 38, no. 6 (2007): 46.

19. Ibid.

20. Center for Health Workforce Studies, "Licensed Social Workers in the United States, 2004," School of Public Health, University at Albany, Rensselaer, NY.

21. Peg Tyre, "No More A's for Good Behavior," *New York Times*, November 28, 2010.

CHAPTER FIVE: THE NORMALCY
OF PROBLEM BEHAVIOR

1. David C. Cicero, Amee J. Epler, and Kenneth J. Sher, "Are There Developmentally Limited Forms of Bipolar Disorder?" *Journal of Abnormal Psychology* 118, no. 3 (2009): 431–47.

2. National Institute of Mental Health, "Brain Matures a Few Years Late in ADHD, but Follows Normal Patterns," press release, November 12, 2007, http://www.nimh.nih.gov.

3. Quoted in Denise Gellene, "ADHD May Be Temporary, Study Suggests," *Los Angeles Times*, November 13, 2007.

4. Quoted in "ADHD Brain Delay," *Science Central*, May 23, 2010, http://www .sciencecentral.com.

5. Ibid.

6. Russell A. Barkley et al., "The Persistence of Attention-Deficit/Hyperactivity Disorder Into Young Adulthood as a Function of Reporting Source and Definition of Disorder," *Journal of Abnormal Psychology* 111, no. 2 (2002): 279–89.

7. Ibid., 287.

8. Laurence Steinberg, "Are Adolescents Less Mature Than Adults?" *American Psychologist* 64, no. 7 (2009): 583–94.

9. Brent W. Roberts, Kate E. Walton, and Wolfgang Viechtbauer, "Patterns of Mean-Level Change in Personality Traits Across the Life Course: A Meta-Analysis of Longitudinal Studies," *Psychological Bulletin* 132, no. 1 (2006): 1–25.

10. Elizabeth A. Harvey et al., "Predicting Attention-Deficit/Hyperactivity Disorder and Oppositional Defiant Disorder from Preschool Diagnostic Assessments," *Journal of Consulting and Clinical Psychology* 77, no. 2 (2009): 353.

11. Jamie M. Kleinman et. al., "Diagnostic Stability in Very Young Children with Autism Spectrum Disorders," *Journal of Autism and Developmental Disorders* 38, no. 4 (2008): 606–15.

12. John Axelsson et al., "Beauty Sleep: Experimental Study on the Perceived Health and Attractiveness of Sleep Deprived People," *British Medical Journal* 341 (2010): c6614.

13. Mary A. Carskadon et al., "Sleep in America Poll," National Sleep Foundation (2006): 1-77, http://sleepfoundation.org.

14. Reut Gruber et al., "Sleep Disturbances in Prepubertal Children with Attention Deficit Hyperactivity Disorder: A Home Polysomnography Study," *Sleep* 32, no. 3 (2009): 343–50.

15. Quoted in Seema Adhami, "Normal and Disordered Sleep in Kids," *Carlat Child Psychiatry Report* 2, no. 2 (March 2011): 4.

16. Quoted in John Naish, "Does Labeling Children with Behavioural Problems Such as ADHD Help?" *Times* (London), February 16, 2009.

17. "High School Seniors with Excessive Daytime Sleepiness Have an Increased Risk of Depression," *Science Daily*, June 11, 2010, http://sciencedaily .com.

18. Annys Shin, Ylan Q. Mui, and Nancy Trejos, "Drug Ads: Taking Medicine Never Looked So Good," *The Checkout*, *Washington Post*, January 1, 2007.

19. "Our Children Aren't Sleeping and We're Medicating Them, Survey Finds," *Science Daily*, July 26, 2010, http://www.sciencedaily.com.

20. Genevieve Belleville, "Mortality Hazard Associated with Anxiolytic and

Hypnotic Drug Use in the National Population Health Survey," *Canadian Journal of Psychiatry* 55, no. 9 (2010): 558–67.

21. William J. Warzak et al., "Caffeine Consumption in Young Children," *Journal of Pediatrics* 158, no. 3 (2011): 508–9.

22. Amanda Chan, "Chuck the Sodas If You Want Kids to Sleep," December 16, 2010, MSNBC.com.

23. Jennifer Cowher Williams, "Annual Sleep in America Poll Exploring Connections with Communications Technology Use and Sleep," National Sleep Foundation, press release, March 7, 2011, http://www.sleepfoundation .org.

24. Quoted in ibid.

25. Ibid.

26. Robert Vorona et al., "Dissimilar Teen Crash Rates in Two Neighboring Southeastern Virginia Cities with Different High School Start Times," *Journal of Clinical Sleep Medicine* 7, no. 2 (2011): 145–51.

27. Judith A. Owens, Katherine Belon, and Patricia Moss, "Impact of Delaying School Start Time on Adolescent Sleep, Mood, and Behavior," *Archives of Pediatrics and Adolescent Medicine* 164, no. 7 (2010): 608–14.

28. Thom Hartmann, "Hunters in Our Schools and Offices: The Origin of ADHD," *Thom Hartmann Program*, January 1, 1994, http://www .thomhartmann.com.

29. Dan T. A. Eisenberg et al., "Dopamine Receptor Genetic Polymorphisms and Body Composition in Undernourished Pastoralists: An Exploration of Nutrition Indices Among Nomadic and Recently Settled Ariaal Men of Northern Kenya," *BMC Evolutionary Biology* 8 (2008): 173.

30. Andrea Faber Taylor, Frances Kuo, and William C. Sullivan, "Coping with ADD: The Surprising Connection to Green Play Settings," *Environment and Behavior* 33, no. 1 (2001): 54–77.

31. Barbara A. Hanawalt, *Growing Up in Medieval London: The Experience of Childhood in History* (New York: Oxford University Press, 1995), 56.

32. Ibid.

33. Suzanne A. Alchon, *A Pest in the Land: New World Epidemics in a Global Perspective* (Albuquerque: University of New Mexico Press, 2003), 21.

34. Niall P. A. S. Johnson and Juergen Mueller, "Updating the Accounts: Global Mortality of the 1918–1920 'Spanish' Influenza Pandemic," *Bulletin of the History of Medicine* 76, no. 1 (2002): 105–15.

35. October 12, 2005, Minerva Center for Economic Growth, Paper No. 02-05, Social Science Research Network, http://ssrn.com.

36. *Encyclopedia Britannica Online*, s.v. "Mortality," http://www.britannica .com.

CHAPTER SIX: ADHD? OR CHILDHOOD
NARCISSISM AT THE OUTER EDGES?

1. "One in Ten Children Using Cough Syrup," *Science Daily*, August 4, 2008, http://www.sciencedaily.com.

2. Centers for Disease Control and Prevention, "Rates of Parent-Reported ADHD Increasing," CDC Features, http://www.cdc.gov.

3. Gretchen B. Le Fever, Ardythe Leslie Dawson, and Keila V. Dawson, "The Extent of Drug Therapy for Attention-Deficit Hyperactivity Disorder among Children in Public Schools," *American Journal of Public Health* 89, no. 9 (1999): 1359–64.

4. David F. Bjorklund, *Why Youth Is Not Wasted on the Young: Immaturity in Human Development* (Malden, MA: Blackwell Publishing, 2007), 115.

5. Deborah Stipek, "Children's Perceptions of Their Own and Their Classmates' Ability," *Journal of Experimental Child Psychology* 73, no. 3 (1981): 404–10.

6. Fred A. Baughman Jr., *The ADHD Fraud: How Psychiatry Makes 'Patients' of Normal Children* (Bloomington, IN: Trafford Publishing, 2006).

7. Betsy Hoza et al., "Do Boys with Attention-Deficit/Hyperactivity Disorder Have Positive Illusory Self-Concepts?" *Journal of Abnormal Psychology* 111, no. 2 (2002): 268–78.

8. Mikaru S. Lasher et al., "Cognitive Flexibility and Empathy in Children with ADHD," presentation, American Psychological Association Convention, August 12, 2006.

9. Michelle M. Martel et al., "A Person-Centered Personality Approach to Heterogeneity in Attention-Deficit/Hyperactivity Disorder," *Journal of Abnormal Psychology* 119, no. 1 (2010): 193.

10. Linda L. Thede, "Personality and Mood Differences in ADHD, Asperger's Disorder, and Autism," presentation, American Psychological Association Convention, August 7, 2003, Toronto.

11. Malcolm Gladwell, *Outliers: The Story of Success* (New York: Little, Brown, 2008).

12. "Fact Sheet: Attention Deficit Hyperactivity Disorder (ADHD) Topics," Russell A. Barkley website, http://www.russellbarkley.org.

13. Russell A. Barkley, *Taking Charge of ADHD: The Complete, Authoritative Guide for Parents* (New York: Guilford Press, 2005), 71.

14. Daniel T. Willingham, *Why Don't Students Like School? A Cognitive Scientist Answers Questions about How the Mind Works and What It Means for the Classroom* (San Francisco: Jossey-Bass, 2009), 107.

15. Alison Gendar, Oren Yaniv, and Dave Goldiner, "JetBlue Flight Attendant

Who Went Nuts Was in Bed with Boyfriend When Found by Cops," *New York Daily News*, September 3, 2010.

16. "JetBlue Flight Attendant: Hero or Heel?" CBS News, August 12, 2010, http://www.cbsnews.com.

17. Courtney Comstock, "JetBlue Doesn't Want Steven Slater to Be a Hero Anymore Because 'He Could Have Killed Someone,'" *BusinessInsider*, August 13, 2010, http://www.businessinsider.com.

18. Jean M. Twenge and W. Keith Campbell, *The Narcissism Epidemic: Living in the Age of Entitlement* (New York: Free Press, 2009).

19. Quoted in Elizabeth Carpenter-Song, "Caught in the Psychiatric Net: Meanings and Experiences of ADHD, Pediatric Bipolar Disorder and Mental Health Treatment among a Diverse Group of Families in the United States," *Culture, Medicine and Psychiatry* 33, no. 1 (2009): 69.

CHAPTER SEVEN: BIPOLAR DISORDER? OR TEENAGE STORM AND STRESS TWENTY-FIRST-CENTURY STYLE?

1. Sharna Olfman, ed., *Bipolar Children: Cutting-Edge Controversy, Insights, and Research* (Westport, CT: Praeger, 2007), 4–5.

2. Ibid., 5.

3. Demitri Papolos and Janice Papolos, *The Bipolar Child: The Definitive and Reassuring Guide to Childhood's Most Misunderstood Disorder* (New York: Broadway Books, 1999).

4. National Institute of Mental Health, *Bipolar Disorder in Children and Teens* http://www.nimh.nih.gov.

5. "Bipolar Disorder in Kids Often Confused with ADHD," Washington University in St. Louis, Newsroom, March 21, 2005, http://news.wustl .edu.

6. Janice Papolos and Demitri Papolos, "Hypersexuality: A Symptom of Early-Onset Bipolar Disorder," *Newsletter* 11 (June 1, 2002), http://www .bipolarchild.com.

7. Alix Spiegel, "Children Labeled 'Bipolar' May Get a New Diagnosis," National Public Radio, February 10, 2010, http://www.npr.org.

8. David C. Cicero, Amee J. Epler, and Kenneth J. Sher, "Are There Developmentally Limited Forms of Bipolar Disorder?," *Journal of Abnormal Psychology* 118, no. 3 (2009): 431–47.

9. Jean M. Twenge and W. Keith Campbell, *The Narcissism Epidemic: Living in the Age of Entitlement* (New York: Free Press, 2009).

10. C. Nathan De Wall et al., "Tuning In to Psychological Change: Linguistic Markers of Psychological Traits and Emotions Over Time in Popular US Song Lyrics," *Psychology of Aesthetics, Creativity, and the Arts* 5, no. 3 (March 2011): 1–8.

11. Carol S. Dweck, *Self-Theories: Their Role in Motivation, Personality, and Development* (Philadelphia: Psychology Press, 2000), 128.

12. Andrea Canning interview with Charlie Sheen, *20/20*, March 1, 2011, http://abcnews.go.com.

13. Damien Scott, "Charlie Sheen Is the Most Popular Person on the Internet," March 9, 2011, Complex, http://www.complex.com.

14. *Greatest Freak Out Ever*, YouTube, http://www.youtube.com.

15. Jan Hoffman, "A Girl's Nude Photo, and Altered Lives," *New York Times*, March 27, 2011.

16. Symantec, "School's Out and Your Kids Are Online: Do You Know What They've Been Searching for This Summer?" press release, August 10, 2009, http://www.symantec.com.

17. Joe Flint, "TV's Portrayal of Teen Girls Decried," *Los Angeles Times*, December 16, 2010.

18. National Sleep Foundation, "Backgrounder: Later School Start Times," http://www.sleepfoundation.org.

19. Amy R. Wolfson and Mary A. Carskadon, "A Survey of Factors Influencing High School Start Times," *NASSP Bulletin* 89 (2005): 47–66.

20. Po Bronson and Ashley Merryman, "Why Children Need More Sleep," *Guardian* (UK), January 22, 2010, http://www.guardian.co.uk.

21. Mayo Clinic, "Teen Sleep: Why Is Your Teen So Tired?" August 8, 2009, http://www.mayoclinic.com.

22. Quoted in Barbara Strauch, *The Primal Teen: What the New Discoveries about the Teenage Brain Tell Us about Our Kids* (New York: Anchor Books, 2003), 161–62.

23. Tara Parker-Pope, "Surprisingly, Family Time Has Grown," *New York Times*, April 5, 2010.

24. Donna St. George, "More Teens Are Choosing to Wait to Get Driver's Licenses," *Washington Post*, January 24, 2010.

25. "Teen Employment Rate at Historic Low as More Parents Encourage Education, Activities," NJ.com, June 21, 2010.

26. Sara Bennett, "New Survey: 43 Percent of Parents Have Done Their Kids' Homework," Stophomework.com, September 17, 2008.

27. Benedict Carey, "Families' Every Hug and Fuss, Taped, Analyzed and Archived," *Los Angeles Times*, May 23, 2010.

28. Ibid.

CHAPTER EIGHT: AUTISM SPECTRUM?
OR A BRAINY, WILLFUL, INTROVERTED BOY?

1. Roy Richard Grinker, *Unstrange Minds: Remapping the World of Autism* (New York: Basic Books, 2007).

2. Stanley I. Greenspan, "The Misdiagnosis of Autistic Spectrum Disorders: The Most Important Signs of Progress," February 26, 2004, Interdisciplinary Council on Developmental and Learning Disorders, http://www.icdl.com.

3. Lauren M. Turner and Wendy L. Stone, "Variability in Outcome for Children with an ASD Diagnosis at Age 2," *Journal of Child Psychology and Psychiatry* 48, no. 8 (2007): 793–802.

4. Michael D. Kogan et al., "Prevalence of Parent-Reported Diagnosis of Autism Spectrum Disorder Among Children in the US, 2007," *Pediatrics* 124, no. 5 (2009): 1395–403.

5. Linda Carroll, "Toddler of Few Words? Late-Talkers Can Catch Up," *Today*, July 4, 2011, http://today.msnbc.com.

6. Rhea Paul, Katyrzyna Chawarska, and Fred Volkmar, "Differentiating ASD from DLD in Toddlers," *Perspectives on Language Learning and Education* 15, no. 3 (2008): 101–11.

7. Charlotte M. Wright et al., "How Do Toddler Eating Problems Relate to Their Eating Behavior, Food Preferences, and Growth?" *Pediatrics* 120, no. 4 (2007): 1069–75.

8. Gina Mireault and Jessica Trahan, "Tantrums and Anxiety in Early Childhood: A Pilot Study," *Early Childhood Research and Practice* 9, no. 2 (2007): 10–19.

9. Eleanor E. Maccoby, *The Two Sexes: Growing Up Apart, Coming Together* (Cambridge, MA: Harvard University Press, 1998).

10. Simon Baron-Cohen, *The Essential Difference: The Truth about the Male and Female Brain* (New York: Basic Books, 2003).

11. Ibid., 5.

12. Thomas Oakland and Chryse Hatzichristou, "Temperament Styles of Greek and US Children," *School Psychology International* 31, no. 4 (2010): 422–37.

13. Laurie Helgoe, "Revenge of the Introvert," *Psychology Today*, September 1, 2010, 4, http://www.psychologytoday.com.

14. Ibid., 3.

15. "What Are the Symptoms of Autism?" *Consumer Reports*, March 16, 2011, http://www.consumerreports.org.

16. Stephanie Barbu, Guénaël Cabanes, and Gaïd Le Maner-Idrissi, "Boys and Girls on the Playground: Sex Differences Are Not Stable across Early Childhood," *PlosONE* 6, no. 1 (2011): e16407.

17. Mireault and Trahan, "Tantrums and Anxiety in Early Childhood."

18. Stanley I. Greenspan, "The Do's and Don'ts of Early Identification and Early Intervention," December 16, 2004, Interdisciplinary Council on Developmental and Learning Disorders, http://www.icdl.com.

19. Betty R. Carruth et al., "Prevalence of Picky Eaters among Infants and Toddlers and Their Caregivers' Decisions about Offering a New Food," *Journal of the American Dietetic Association* 104, 1 Supp. 1 (2004): 57–64.

CHAPTER NINE: PARENTING WITH AUTHORITY

1. Suzanne M. Bianchi, John P. Robinson, and Melissa A. Milkie, *Changing Rhythms of American Family Life* (New York: Russell Sage Foundation, 2006), 136.

2. Ibid.

3. Victoria J. Rideout, Ulla G. Foehr, and Donald F. Roberts, *Generation M2: Media in the Lives of 8- to 18-Year-Olds* (Menlo Park, CA: Henry J. Kaiser Family Foundation, 2010).

4. See LynNell Hancock, "Do Kids Have Too Much Homework?," *Smithsonian*, August 22, 2011, http://www.smithsonianmag.com.

5. Mary Ellen Flannery, "Do They Have Science Fairs in Tibet?" *National Education Association Today*, November 11, 2009, http://www.nea.org.

6. Alfie Kohn, *Punished by Rewards: The Trouble with Gold Stars, Incentive Plans, A's, Praise, and Other Bribes* (New York: Houghton Mifflin, 1993).

7. Carol S. Dweck, *Self-Theories: Their Role in Motivation, Personality, and Development* (Philadelphia: Psychology Press, 2000).

Index

AAP (American Academy of Pediatrics), 5, 10

Abilify, 63

academic disaffection, 117–18

academic stress, 26–28, 30–32, 72–73

accountability standards, school, 35–36

Achenbach Behavior Checklist, 109

action-orientated behavior, ancestral advantage of, xiii, 93–97

Adderall, 13, 58, 60

Adhami, Seema, 90

ADHD: academic disaffection and, 117–18; aggressiveness in, 67–70; ancestral adaptations and, xiii, 93–97; behavior rating forms/checklists and, 9, 10, 109; brain-based explanations for, 18–19, 80–84, 114, 118, 123; brain-imaging and, 24–25; CDC statistics on, x, 98; childhood narcissism as mimic of, xiii, 104–9, 113–15, 120; classroom rigidity and, 24–28; consequence anticipation and, 121–22; continuous-performance tests and, 11–12; core symptoms of, x, 98–99, 121–23; descriptions of, 34, 96–97; developmental explanation for, xiii, 80–84, 104–9, 113–15, 120; diagnosis numbers by gender, 19, 66–67, 98; diet and, 19; disappearing diagnosis of, xiv; DRD$_4$ gene and, 95; emotional self-control and, 108; empathy maturation and, 105–7; environmental changes and, 97; evidence of, x; exercise and, 95; gifted children misdiagnosed as, 37–38, 41–43; histrionic personality traits in, 108; medications, 13, 37–38, 48, 58–64, 59–64; memory training and, 20; parental perceptions of, 52, 99; pediatric diagnosis of, 4–5, 99; personality traits in, 106–12; self-esteem issues and, 106–7, 122; sleep deprivation and, 60, 89–90; stigma of, 56–57; teachers as front-line diagnosers of, 24–25, 32–35, 38–39; teachers' assumptions about, 56–57

adolescents: all-or-nothing mind-set of, 126–27, 196–97; developmental explanation for behavior of, 80–84, 127–28; overt sexuality in culture of,

existential guilt, 148
expectable rage, 145–46
extrapyramidal side effects, 64
extreme-male-brain theory of autism
 spectrum disorder, 163

familial stress, 136–38
family social status and autism
 diagnosis rates, 47–48
fathers, 84–87, 125, 136, 178. *See also*
 mothers; parents
FDA medication approval process,
 13, 16
females. *See* girls
Floortime approach to autism spectrum
 treatment, 160–61
food/eating behavior problems, 162,
 173–74
forgetfulness and overconfidence,
 xiii–xiv
Fox, Robin, 94
Frances, Allen, 57
Frankenberger, William, 61–62
Freed, Gary L., 4–5
Frontalot, MC (hip-hop artist), 50
Fuligni, Allison, 31–32

Gellene, Denise, 81
Geller, Barbara, 129, 130–31
gender, 19, 66–67, 74–75, 98
gender essentialism, 165. *See also* boys;
 girls
Generation Z, 92
genetic risk of mental health disorder,
 21, 95
Geodon, 14, 63
gifted children: ADHD misdiagnosis
 of, 37–38; classroom mindset of,
 41–43; humor appreciation and, 167;
 misdiagnosed as autism spectrum
 disorder, 154–60, 174; personality
 characteristics of, 40–41, 171; rebel-
 lion in, 41, 43–44; stereotypes, 40,
 44; teachers' assumptions about,
 39–40
girls: ADHD diagnosis in, 66–67;

behavior expectations of, xii, 68,
 70–75; dopamine production in, 19;
 gross-motor development of, 170;
 overt sexualization of teen girls,
 134–35; school performance of, 72;
 solitary play in, 170; speech styles of,
 163, 164; visual-spatial skill development of, 170
Gladwell, Malcolm, 112–13
Global Language Monitor, 133
goal-directedness, 82
Goldschmidt, Walter, 21
Goodman, Wayne, 20
Graham, Scott, 54
grandiosity: hard-edged, 114–15;
 soft-edged, 115
Greatest Freak Out Ever series
 (YouTube), 133
Greene, Jay P., 36–37
gregariousness, 201–3
Grinker, Roy Richard, 160
gross-motor development, 169–70
growth rate and stimulant use, 59
Gruber, Reut, 89
guilt, 148–49

Hale, Lauren, 92
harm reduction, 198–200
Hartmann, Thom, 94–95
Havey, Michael, 34
Head-Toes-Knees-Shoulders Task,
 71–72
health-insurance plans, 6, 45–48
healthy depression, xiii, 146–49
healthy guilt, 148
healthy mania, xiii, 149–53
heart irregularities risk of stimulant
 use, 59, 61
Helgoe, Laurie, 167–68
high productivity, 82
high school start times, 92–93, 135
Hinshaw, Stephen, 32
HIPAA violations and mental health
 diagnosis stigma, 54
histrionic personality traits, 108
Holloway, Molly, 31